A to Z Guide to Your Child's Behavior

A PARENT'S EASY AND AUTHORITATIVE
REFERENCE TO HUNDREDS OF EVERYDAY PROBLEMS
AND CONCERNS FROM BIRTH TO 12 YEARS

Compiled by the Faculty of the
Children's National Medical Center
under the Direction of

David Mrazek, M.D.,
and William Garrison, Ph.D.,

with Laura Elliott

A Perigee Book

Perigee Books
are published by
The Putnam Publishing Group
200 Madison Avenue
New York, NY 10016

Quote on page 15 reprinted by permission from *Night Lights* by Phyllis Theroux. Copyright © 1987 by Phyllis Theroux. Used by permission of Viking Penguin, a division of Penguin Books USA

Library of Congress Cataloging-in-Publication Data

A to Z guide to your child's behavior:
a parent's easy and authoritative reference to hundreds of everyday problems and concerns from birth to 12 years / compiled by the faculty of the Children's National Medical Center under the direction of David Mrazek and William Garrison, with Laura Elliott.
    p.   cm.
"A Perigee Book."
ISBN 0-399-51796-0 (alk. paper)
1. Behavior disorders in children. 2. Parenting. I. Mrazek, David. II. Garrison, William T. III. Elliott, Laura. IV. Children's National Medical Center (Washington, D.C.)
RJ506.B44C48   1993   92-40260 CIP
618.92'89—dc20

Cover design by Mike McIver
Cover photo © by Arthur Tilley/FPG
Printed in the United States of America
5 6 7 8 9 10

This book is dedicated to all the children and families
who receive medical and psychological care
at the Children's National Medical Center in Washington, D.C.

Acknowledgments

Darlene Atkins, Ph.D., Staff Psychologist, Departments of Psychology and Adolescent Medicine; Director of the Eating Disorders Clinic, Children's National Medical Center

Irene Chatoor, M.D., Director of Infant Psychiatry and Eating Disorders Programs, Children's National Medical Center

Kathy Connell, M.S.W., Clinical Social Worker, Department of Psychiatry, Children's National Medical Center

Penny Glass, Ph.D., Developmental Psychologist, Department of Psychology, and Director of the Child Development Center, Department of General Pediatrics, Children's National Medical Center

Sharon Lockwood, Ph.D., CCC-SSP, Director, Speech-Language Pathology, Department of Hearing and Speech, Children's National Medical Center

Lorraine Lougee, M.S.W., Clinical Social Worker for Inpatient Unit, Department of Psychiatry, Children's National Medical Center

Irene Pafitis, M.A., CCC-A, Coordinator of Audiology, Department of Hearing and Speech, Children's National Medical Center

Patricia Papero, Ph.D., Director, Neuropsychology Service, Department of Psychology, Children's National Medical Center

Tommie L. Robinson, Jr., Ph.D., CCC-SLP, Director, Scottish Rite Center, Department of Hearing and Speech, Children's National Medical Center

Susan Theut, M.D., Medical Director, Satellite Centers, Department of Psychiatry, Children's National Medical Center

W. Douglas Tynan, Ph.D., Director of Psychology Training, Department of Psychology, Children's National Medical Center

Felicia Valdez, Ed.D., Director, Early Intervention Institute, Department of Hearing and Speech, Children's National Medical Center

Thomas Walsh, M.D., Director of Consultation/Liaison Service, Department of Psychiatry, Children's National Medical Center

Acknowledgments

Jill Weissberg-Benchell, Ph.D., Staff Psychologist, Departments of Psychology and Endocrinology, Children's National Medical Center
Marilyn Benoit, M.D., Susan Besharov, M.S.W., Dana Czapanskiy, M.S.W., Ralph Gemelli, M.D., and Barbara H. Herman, Ph.D., also contributed to this volume.

Contents

Contents

8

Contents

Preface

This book is the product of a close collaboration between mental-health and child-development professionals who work at the Children's National Medical Center in Washington, D.C., and Ms. Laura Elliott, an experienced journalist with special interests in family and children's issues. The idea to create this book arose from a perceived need for a handy, authoritative reference book on the subject of child behavior that was also easily accessed by parents of young children from all walks of life.

Our role in this book—as expert child psychologists, psychiatrists, and clinical social workers working at a premier metropolitan medical center—was to provide essential information about the many types of behaviors, both normal and atypical, that children can show. Ms. Elliott's role was to render what can often be rather dry clinical and theoretical material more readable for curious and inquiring parents, with a sensitivity to the complex issues that child behavior problems can sometimes create for mothers and fathers.

We have deliberately limited the scope of this book to children under the age of thirteen, thinking, first of all, that there are currently many books for parents of adolescents, and secondly that the problems of teenagers can be rooted within the years that come *before* adolescence. Parents often need to begin early on with their education about child behavior, its meaning, and how they might hope to influence their children as they happen to encounter behavioral or social problems.

We had several major goals as we set out to provide a book that was accurate, succinct, and practically useful to parents who may not have extensive background or formal study in the methods or theories of child behavior. First, we sought to offer parents up-to-date information about what is normal versus atypical child behavior—something that is often determined by the age or developmental level of the child, or the recognizable characteristics that can be found in the child, the situation, or both. Second, we wanted to highlight those behaviors that may be signs or symptoms of more serious problems down the road. Third, we attempted to examine behaviors that appear to be transitional or short-lived, versus those that become pervasive and inhibiting of child development. And finally, we wished to equip parents with basic knowledge that might help them know when to seek consultation or help from qualified mental-health professionals.

One bias that pervades this book is that parents will often know much more about their children than they may realize. Most of the parents who read this book—although they might need assistance from time to time from an expert or an objective observer—are able to understand and positively influence their children's behavior in significant ways. Parents are, after all, ideally situated to observe, understand, and even shape their child's behavior amid changing family or life situations and the inevitable transitions across various developmental stages.

It is our hope that this book will serve as a useful reference for parents who have common, and not-so-common, concerns about their children's behavioral and social development.

WILLIAM GARRISON, PH.D.   DAVID MRAZEK, M.D.
Chairman of Psychology   *Chairman of Psychiatry*

Children's National Medical Center
Washington, D.C.

Parenting Skills
Introduction

"At the onset, faith in one's child springs as naturally as the love we feel for a new baby ... such a flawless, vulnerable, and utterly mysterious little creature with such perfect skin, equipment, and such trust in her eyes ... Then, inevitably, comes the day of revelation in the neighborhood playground, when little Bronwyn thumps another child in the sandbox with her shovel, and without provocation. How can this child, whose environment has been so full of lullabies and entrancing crib mobiles be so antisocial? We rush to her side, pry the shovel from her hand, and give a lesson in sandbox ethics. Where, we ask, did we go wrong?

"Well, I suppose every parent goes wrong by producing other human beings who have strengths, weaknesses, and an uncanny ability to dash our plans for their character development. And that is when we need to remember how it felt to be a child."

—Phyllis Theroux in *Night Lights: Bedtime Stories for Parents in the Dark*

No matter how well we think we know our children, they can still worry, amaze, baffle, and even stump us with their behavior. *Why* is he acting this way? What can I do to make this transition easier for her? Is this normal for a child his age? Am I somehow causing this? These are questions parents constantly ask with varying degrees of self-doubt and concern.

Child psychotherapist Bruno Bettelheim once cautioned parents to try only to be "good enough," not to burden themselves, or their offspring, with expectations of being perfect. "Perfection is not within the grasp of ordinary human beings," he wrote in *A Good Enough Parent*. He added, however, that love and good intentions alone are not enough to raise a child well. Parents also need to develop skills in order to effectively help a child grow and develop happily.

This book is about those skills, in general and in response to specific behaviors. It should also help you understand *why* your child behaves

15

the way he does. Knowing the possible reasons behind a little human being's actions should make them less intimidating or bewildering for you. This book is designed to help you know how to respond in a way that is appropriate and beneficial to everyone concerned.

This introduction outlines some important overall parenting techniques. The *A to Z Guide* will then tell you about the developmental, psychological, physiological, situational, and temperamental roots of your child's behavior from birth to age twelve. Keep in mind that the reason for a child acting a certain way is rarely clear-cut and can be influenced by many factors. The book will also provide some advice on how to respond to normal, predictable behaviors, once you understand their causes and what a child may be trying to communicate through them. It is not, however, a replacement for professional consultation or treatment when a child needs it.

The tone of this book is deliberately nonclinical. We hope that besides relating specifics, such as how to deal with school fears, nightmares, temper tantrums, shyness, hyperactivity, or the like, this book shares insight that will occasionally serve merely to enhance your understanding and enjoyment of your children.

Parenting is about guiding, teaching. A child's self-esteem blooms best when a parent lovingly helps him achieve developmental tasks largely on his own. Parents are, after all, in a kind of long-term partnership with a child, the goal of which is to produce an independent adult who has confidence in her own resources, capabilities, and judgment. That process must be slow and careful, one of simultaneously "holding on and letting go," as psychotherapist Erik Erikson wrote in *Childhood and Society*.

Your response to each situation needs to take place within the context of a loving, encouraging, responsive home, one in which there is "unconditional positive regard," as psychologist Carl Rogers put it.

To help build that kind of flexible, nurturing environment, parents need to develop the skills and philosophies explained in the following sections: "Special time," "Active listening," "Consistent limits," and the basic ingredients of child behavior modifications: "Reward systems" and "Time-outs." (A final note on style. For ease in reading, the pronouns "he" and "she" are used interchangeably in each of the following sections and in the entries of the *A to Z Guide*.

16

Special time

Special time is just what the name implies: It is a prearranged, one-on-one block of time a parent has designated to spend with one child only. It's special to him. It's guaranteed time during which that parent will be available to a child unconditionally, regardless of how he has behaved during the day. It is probably the most important bit of groundwork a parent can do to build a warm, familiar relationship with a child.

Special time doesn't have to happen daily, although it's most beneficial if it does. Find a slot of time that is convenient for both you and your child. Then adhere to the agreed schedule. This must be done separately for each and every child in your family. If you must miss a time, be sure to reschedule. Length doesn't matter. It may be as short as ten minutes, but your attention must be undivided.

Let your child pick the activity. In this block of time, he should feel more or less the boss. (You're allowed to say no to a game that offends your dignity or empties your wallet, but try to get him to pick something else, as a second choice, that he truly wants to do.) Perhaps offer a choice among reading books, drawing, taking a walk, or playing a game.

The best thing is to get down on the floor and play. That's how therapists build rapport with a child before they even try to talk to him. Follow your child's lead and avoid the temptation to teach. If he wants to look at a book about numbers, look, don't quiz him on the numerals. If he wants to paint a purple pumpkin rather than an orange one, let him and say, "Oh, what a lovely purple pumpkin."

There should be no agenda to special time other than enjoying each other's company. The point is to create mutual respect, trust, and a high level of positive interaction, so that when there is work to be done or a problem to be addressed, it can occur within this context. A child may even bring up something that is troubling him, without your having to ask, while you're playing. He certainly won't bring his troubles to a parent he rarely sees or doesn't know well, or one who seems interested only in changing his behavior and opinions.

Active listening

Good communication comes from listening carefully, making eye contact, acknowledging what a child has said even if you don't agree with it, helping her find words to describe her emotions, and stopping to talk when she is ready. Pay close attention when your child is talking, since children typically bring up their worries in an offhanded, roundabout way.

By engaging in such "active listening" you're showing your child that you're truly hearing what she's saying, and that her opinion is valuable and legitimate, even if you disagree. Try asking, "Why do you say that?" or "What do you think?" You're helping her learn how to sort through confusing ideas or emotions. It will give her more confidence in her own ideas and more self-respect, qualities that help build self-sufficient adults. (See also *Listening, Refusing to Speak, Self-Esteem*, and *Self-Sufficiency.*)

Consistent limits

While trying to let a child strengthen his ability to think independently, parents must also set consistent limits on inappropriate behavior. That's the "holding on" part of the equation that sometimes makes parents momentarily unpopular. But limits keep a child's world predictable. He knows its parameters, how to act, what is socially acceptable and physically safe. Limits show a child that you care enough to say no, that you are the adult in the partnership, the one responsible for deciding hard issues and teaching children how to best navigate a challenging world. For all their seeming desire for permissiveness, children feel secure and cared for by parents who set limits for them.

Limits are particularly important for toddlers, who are struggling with issues of autonomy and separation and are in strong need of a reliable routine. They are also important for preschoolers, who engage in magical thinking and believe that what they wish can come true. They don't really want that kind of overwhelming power. The unchecked anger of a tantrum, for instance, can be very frightening to them.

It is essential that limits be consistent, and that parents present a united front. If the limits change from day to day, a child begins to feel that decisions are arbitrary and, therefore, inherently unfair. Inconsistency tempts a child to push a situation to see how far his parents will let him go.

That's not to say, however, that you shouldn't be flexible. If you set too many rules, children become overly dependent on authority, and fail to learn self-discipline or how to think for themselves. Similarly, if you are too protective, children may never learn to take responsibility

18

for themselves or to assess the potential danger of a situation. They won't learn from experience.

Parents, then, need to be *responsive* authority figures who can adjust limits as a child grows, evolves, and becomes more responsible and cognitively dexterous. The limits that are appropriate for one sibling may not be for another. Listen to a child's arguments for changing a house rule (no crossing the street alone, for instance). If he's ready to safely handle that challenge, bend. If not, explain why you still are saying no. Given a logical reason, most children accept parents' decisions. It also makes a child feel you respect him enough to explain.

Make sure that a child experiences "logical consequences" for misbehaving, not unrelated punishment. The logical consequence for his coloring on the wallpaper, for instance, is to clean up the mess, not to be sent to his room while you sponge down the wall. Ultimately, discipline should be about teaching. If you must use the word "bad," apply it to a child's unacceptable behavior, not to the child.

(See also the Developmental Tasks Appendix, *Self-Sufficiency, Aggression, Attention-Seeking, Temper Tantrums, Oppositional Behavior, Argumentative, Temperament, Sibling Rivalry*, and *Compliance.*)

Rewards and time-outs

Rewards and time-outs are behavior modification techniques. They are based on teaching children to act in socially acceptable ways, to help them give up unacceptable behaviors and to acquire or strengthen more appropriate ones that respect the rights and feelings of others. They hinge on the concept of reinforcement: Parents need to reward and affirm desired behavior, while ignoring or applying negative consequences to undesirable acts, such as aggression or tantrums.

By responding to good behavior with praise, approval, and attention, you encourage more of the same. If this doesn't achieve the desired results quickly or thoroughly enough, you might need to use a reward system as well.

Conversely, unacceptable behavior can be discouraged if it is ignored. This often requires some dogged patience. Rewarding inappropriate or annoying behavior with anger, impatience, or compliance to win peace can actually fuel or reinforce the act. If children don't respond to such tacit disapproval, it may be necessary to enlist a more systematic way of discouraging unacceptable behavior—a technique called "time-out."

(See also *Attention-Seeking, Temper Tantrums, Whining, Complaining, Aggression*, and *Temperament*.)

Reward systems: Rewards are used to reinforce, encourage, and enhance good behavior. Do not use them to try to stop bad behavior, because they then become more akin to bribes.

Try praise and attention first, or spontaneous reinforcement, such as, "It's so helpful when people brush their teeth without being reminded. Now we'll have time to read *two* books before bedtime." If that doesn't do the trick, set up a systematic reward. But apply this technique sparingly to keep its value intact. Target one behavior at a time, rewarding B+ performance as well as A. Making expectations too high sets up a child for failure and disappointment.

The most common method of reward is to use stickers applied to a chart so that a child can see her progress. At the end of a week (or a column) deliver the earned reward. Don't ever withhold or renegotiate it at the end.

The best rewards are time with a parent and special outings, not material goods or sweets. Think of what the child likes to do most. The reward has to be something she really desires for the system to be effective. It can be a trip to the zoo, viewing a favorite movie together, even something as simple as gardening or cooking. Young children in particular like to try out adult roles and be with their parents during their regular chores.

Keep up the system until the behavior seems to have become ingrained, but remember that the main purpose of these extrinsic motivators is to strengthen a child's intrinsic drive to do something. Piano lessons are a perfect example. Often, they begin as a parent's idea. It's fine to reward a child's diligence in practicing at first. But once she's improving and gaining some skill, she should become more intrinsically motivated to keep at it. Competency and pleasure in the activity will ultimately be the greatest motivator of all.

(See also *Motivation, Self-Esteem, Perfectionism*, and *Competitiveness*.)

Time-outs: A time-out can be a very effective technique to help modify children's behavior when used properly and sparingly. Unfortunately, it is perhaps one of the most overused and misconstrued of parenting skills.

The concept of a time-out came from the work of behaviorist B. F. Skinner during the 1940s and 1950s. It meant time out from reinforcement. Through his studies, Skinner proved that taking time out from a generally reinforcing environment can act to reduce a targeted, undesirable behavior. (For parents, that can translate into removing a misbehaving child from the attention-providing situation to a quiet, solitary place in which he receives no reinforcement and can regain his composure.)

In order for a time-out to be successful, there must first be a positive home environment, one in which a child is loved, played with, and praised—one in which his needs are heard and answered, and where parent and child share a mutual respect. If a child is in an environment where parents are constantly angry and frustrated with him, where there are few rewards and constant battles of will, the use of time-outs is destined to fail, since there is nothing for a child to miss during one.

Time-outs must also be applied discriminately. If parents use them more than two or three times a day, they will decrease their effectiveness. For example, imagine you have an employer who is generally positive most of the time, who respects and trusts you to do the right thing. It takes only one reprimand from that person to make you shape up. But with someone who nags you and constantly leaves nasty notes in your mailbox, one more reprimand means nothing. You'd probably ignore it or figure out a way to work around that person's demands. A child responds the same way.

Time-outs should be used only for excessive behaviors at first (being aggressive or destructive, for instance), those you want to discourage or at least suppress somewhat. They are less effective in enhancing behavior, like coaxing a child to eat dinner, do homework, or clean up his room. (You may use time-outs to modify destructive table manners, such as *purposefully* throwing food or plates, but not to force eating. See *Food Refusal*.) To enhance behaviors, praise and reward systems tend to work much better. (See "Reward systems," above.)

Target only one or two related behaviors at a time. Any more is too much for a child to absorb. Once those seem under control, move on to another behavior that needs work. Remember that time-outs are about *teaching* a child what is appropriate and inappropriate, and helping him develop self-control.

That said, here's how to do a time-out:

Formal time-outs, which are identified as such to a child, can start at around two and a half years old. (Before that time, you may put a child in a quiet and safe place, such as a playpen to cool down during a tantrum, but that is not a true time-out. See *Temper Tantrums*.) Use a place where the child feels safe but cannot engage others or be entertained by the environment.

Explain the concept of a time-out beforehand, that it is the consequence of a specific action. For instance: "Throwing food at the table is unacceptable behavior. If you do it, you will earn a time-out." Warn a child once: "If you continue to throw food at your brother, you will get a time-out." If he persists, apply the time-out consequence.

Always state the reason for the time-out, such as, "You are going to have a time-out because you threw your plate on the floor." Take him to the designated time-out spot and explain, "Time-out is over when you hear the bell." Use an external device such as a kitchen timer so that the length of time is precise and so that you are not the clock. That prevents a child from trying to engage you in conversation by asking, "Is it over yet?" Time-outs should last no more than one minute per year of a child's age. (Four minutes for a four-year-old, for instance.) Never physically hold down or verbally threaten the child who refuses to sit still or stay put in the designated time-out spot. Give him the choice of sitting there or losing something he values (TV-viewing, for instance). If he persists in getting up, seek the advice of an expert.

When it's over, it's over. If a child has thrown something on the floor, ask him to help you clean it up. But don't continue to talk about the incident or to be angry with him. If you wish to finish dinner together and he again throws his plate, you must repeat the consequences. The hope is that after one night of repeating the cycle several times, he won't engage in the behavior again. He should have learned, through trial and error, that it is unacceptable and that you will not tolerate it.

Once dinner is over, spend some quiet time together, doing something you both enjoy, as positive reinforcement of his now good behavior.

A few final words of advice: Keep your sense of humor. Talk to older, veteran parents to remind yourself that they, too, have traversed these stages and survived. If you're worn out from caring for a newborn or a demanding toddler and your patience is slipping, ask someone to baby-sit to allow you time to refuel.

Model any behavior you want to instill. Apologize when you're wrong. Admit your mistakes and faults so that children can see that everyone has imperfections. Display an attitude that tomorrow always offers a new, fresh chance to improve the situation.

Show respect for your children and the rights of others. Encourage them. Express interest in their lives and friends while at the same time acknowledging their individuality and privacy. Show a sense of balance, that life is made up of both work and play, success and setbacks, relationships and individual triumphs.

Finally, take care of yourself. Address your own problems or marital conflicts. A child's environment is, after all, largely composed of what's happening personally and emotionally to his parents.

Accident-Prone

As they grow up and play hard, all children will suffer some bumps, bruises, scrapes, and sprains. Many will visit the emergency room for stitches. These injuries often strike terror in parents, but minor accidents are inevitable.

This is especially true for toddlers, who are curious and constantly on the move, without prior experience to give them some caution. Because toddlers are just beginning to perfect their walking and running abilities, they can also be clumsy. But generally, they get right up and go on their exuberant way. Parents have to learn not to overreact to inconsequential tumbles lest they frighten their child, who may not have been bothered by the spill at all.

Between the ages of four and seven, some children will become very alarmed when they are hurt. As they become increasingly aware of themselves, they may believe that a scrape on the knee somehow mars their bodily perfection. This is another time when it's important to remain reassuring and calm as you clean and dress a cut.

Most children will escape their mishaps with little more than a scab or a scare. It is critical to know, however, that preventable injuries (nonintentional injuries) are the number-one killer of American children. According to the National SAFE KIDS Campaign, each year 8,000 children are killed and another 50,000 permanently disabled by accidents that could have been avoided.

The five leading risk areas are traffic injuries, drownings, burns, choking and poisoning, and falls. Use safety seats properly; never leave a child alone in a bathtub; teach him how to swim; use smoke detectors; turn pot handles toward the back of the stove; secure second-story windows; and lock up toxic substances, including liquor and all medications, even aspirin and vitamins. Parents of young children might also want to get down on their hands and knees and crawl about to see, with their child's perspective, all the potential trouble spots.

Check your yard for sharp objects, fill in holes, and repair broken driveways or sidewalks. Make sure your child wears a helmet while bicycling.

Parents need to help young children learn to recognize danger, and condition them to stay away from certain things. Say a very firm no when a toddler eyes an electrical socket, the stove, or a street corner. He can't yet understand an abstract notion of danger, and you certainly don't want him to learn about stoves or moving cars from experience.

At this stage children (preschool and younger) stay away from dangerous objects to please parents, not because they know better themselves in an abstract way. Often, then, it is only your displeasure (given within the context of a loving relationship) that keeps them from exploring potentially harmful places. (See *Risk-Taking*.)

For further information contact the National SAFE KIDS Campaign, 111 Michigan Avenue, NW, Washington, D.C. 20010 (202-939-4993). Recommended reading: *The Childproofing Checklist: A Parent's Guide to Accident Prevention*, by Mary Metzger and Cinthya Whittaker (Doubleday); *The Perfectly Safe Home*, by Jeanne Miller (Simon & Schuster).

If a child is excessively accident-prone, hurting himself far more often than his siblings or friends, try to pinpoint the reason. He may just be an unusually adventuresome child having a string of bad luck. (See *Impulsivity*.) Or he may need glasses. Or there may be physiological reasons for his clumsiness. (See *Clumsiness*.) Accident-prone behavior has also been related to hyperactivity. (See *Attention-Deficit Hyperactivity Disorder*.) Take a child who is persistently prone to mishaps to a pediatrician for evaluation.

He may also be emotionally troubled by something. Many mental-health professionals speculate that excessive risk-taking is actually "masked depression." A child with low self-esteem may not think himself worth taking care of, or he may feel insecure in his relationship with his parents and is testing them to see if they really do care about his safety. If either scenario seems to be the case, consider seeking the advice of a mental-health professional. (See *Depression* and *Self-Injurious Behavior*.)

Achievement Issues

The issue of achievement generally comes up if parents are dissatisfied with their child's performance, either in school, sports, or extracurricular hobbies, such as dance. One of the more delicate tasks facing parents is that of helping to motivate a child to achieve without pushing him beyond his capabilities.

That requires parents to be hopeful and encouraging yet realistic about a child's potential and desire. "Is he working hard and doing his best?" is a very different question from: "Is he the best?" Parents also need to separate their own ambitions from their child's and let him "individuate," choose what interests him (which may be *very* different from what fascinates a parent).

Parents who reward and praise a child for diligence and hard work, and help him learn methods of doing things (such as studying better) can promote family unity. Such active involvement clearly demonstrates to a child how much his parents love him. Doing a child's work for him, on the other hand, may erode his self-esteem, confidence, and motivation.

Every parent wants his child to do well and be happy. Try to remember, however, that enjoyment is the greatest motivator and that achieving something on one's own is the biggest booster of self-esteem.

(See *Self-Esteem*, *Motivation*, *Perfectionism*, *Procrastination*, *School*, *Cheating*, and *Lying*.)

Adaptability

Adaptability is one of the nine temperamental traits first described in the 1950s by Drs. Stella Chess, Alexander Thomas, and Herbert Birch of New York University, in their New York Longitudinal Study, one of the most famous scientific chartings of temperament in modern times. The

27

trait has to do with a child's ability to make transitions and to adjust to new environments, such as schools or neighborhoods, people, and things. (See *Temperament.*)

Children who are uncomfortable and afraid in new situations are often described as being "slow to warm." Poorly adaptable children also tend to be rather inflexible and picky about food and clothes; they notice even minor changes in routine or environment, writes one expert in temperament, Dr. Stanley Turecki, in *The Difficult Child.* They do not make transitions cheerfully or without some level of anxiety.

These children require extra patience and reassurance. Toddlers and preschoolers, who are at a developmental stage in which they are very dependent on predictable, familiar surroundings and schedules, can become anxious even during happy events, such as vacations or going to a new playground.

Prepare a poorly adaptable child as thoroughly as possible before such trips. Tell her about the place and who will be there, show her pictures, if possible, or drive her by *before* going. Some parents make little picture books detailing the chronology of an impending vacation or trip. The books needn't be complicated, even stick drawings will do. They work well because a young child has difficulty processing new information in the abstract. With a set of pictures, she can look at it, think about it, look at it again, and learn what to anticipate.

If you plan to take your child and her favorite playmate to a new playground, take your "slow to warm" child to explore it with you the night before, so she doesn't have to perform there in front of her friend for the first time. After investigating all the new (perhaps bigger and more intimidating) swings and tunnels with you supporting her, she'll be more comfortable and able to enjoy herself the next day. This technique is called "progressive desensitization."

Try to strike a happy medium during your visit: Don't push her to climb a ladder that frightens her, but if she's interested, reassure her that it's perfectly safe and that you'll be at the bottom watching. Remember that if you seem hesitant, she will be, too.

Sometimes with an easily upset child the temptation is to avoid discussing an upcoming event until right before it occurs. This can be a mistake. In the long run, you probably will not help a child by such avoidance. She will have learned nothing about coping. Feeling a little anticipatory anxiety and then seeing that she can succeed (who knows, maybe even enjoy the event) is a valuable lesson for her to learn. Small doses of anxiety, with you there literally holding her hand and talking her through it, will teach her coping skills to face the larger challenges that life will inevitably bring.

Before leaving for a day trip, allow plenty of time to dress and drive, so that you're not rushed. A parent acting harried or distressed is guaranteed to set off a poorly adaptable child. Her most effective method of avoiding the outing is to lie down on the floor, scream, and refuse to budge or dress. (See also *Dressing*.)

Expect some hesitancy once you're there. Whatever you do, don't push a wary child to jump right in. You might inadvertently lower her self-esteem if you seem disappointed or annoyed by her reticence. A child who is slow to warm often needs a little coaxing, and some time on the sidelines to adjust to a situation and assess its elements and players before she ventures in. She may even need to touch you physically, to lean up against you as she watches. When she's ready and checks your face for that final reassuring smile, say, "Go ahead, it looks like fun," and let go of her hand. (See also *Making Friends*.)

Some children with poor adaptability have another temperamental trait that can be difficult for parents to handle: unpredictability in their sleeping, eating, and elimination patterns. Children who lack internal rhythm typically need you to establish a reliable, external schedule for them. Help prepare them for transitions within that schedule (from playtime to dinner, for instance). Give them plenty of warnings of the impending change. Avoid doing anything abruptly.

At 5:30, tell a child that at 6:00 it will be *dinner*time. At 5:45 tell her to finish up her puzzle or game, that *dinner*'s coming. At 5:55 say "Let's wash our hands and come to the table *for dinner*." If she's learning to tell time, point to the clock and explain what 6:00 looks like.

Better yet, involve her in the process. Even a two-year-old can put napkins on the table. Praise her for being such a good helper.

These precautions do seem like extra work, but they are far easier than dealing with stubborn (anxiety-produced) resistance or a full-blown tantrum that results from a child being startled, afraid, or unsure. They are also far more pleasant for your child and beneficial to her fledgling self-esteem. And they should make your interactions much more productive and happy.

* * *

Recommended reading: *The Difficult Child*, by Stanley Turecki, M.D., with Leslie Tonner (Bantam); and *Know Your Child*, by Stella Chess and Alexander Thomas, M.D.s (Basic Books).

Aggression

More than most behaviors, aggression finds its meaning in the eye of the beholder. To one parent, a forceful tussle over a toy is the act of a bully, to another the makings of a fine competitor.

Almost all completely normal, emotionally healthy children between the ages of one and four will experiment with some form of aggression—biting, hitting, kicking, throwing objects, yelling, name-calling. It's their instinctual way of expressing displeasure or achieving what they want. Aggression is a problem, however, when it threatens the safety or feelings of other children; when it is destructive in intent; or when a child repeatedly fails to respond to limits set by his parents, teachers, or peers.

Toddlers and Preschoolers

In toddlers and preschoolers, aggression is typically "goal-directed," a method of getting things from people, of getting their own way. Developmentally, children this age seek immediate gratification of their needs. They have not yet learned patience or the more subtle conversational methods of influencing people. In the case of an eighteen-month-old, who is just learning to talk, he has the added frustration of not being able to verbalize his wants. Subsequent physical outbursts can be common and are understandable.

Toddlers and preschoolers might also just be "feeling their oats." They are making tremendous strides physically and cognitively. Physical roughness is often simply a component of that growth spurt.

At this age, aggression may be a method of control, especially as young children vacillate between feeling dependent on parents and wanting to establish some autonomy. Such seesaw emotions can be frightening and anxiety-producing for them. On the other hand, many children just enjoy being dominant. King of the hill is an age-old game played by children and adults alike in a variety of forms. As such, aggression may be partly determined by temperament. Some children, particularly boys, may simply be born with more assertive personalities. No one knows why for sure. It may be the function of testosterone or genes, although it is entirely possible for a highly aggressive child to be born of two very passive parents.

Yet aggression is rarely the sole result of nature or biological processes. Environment exerts powerful influence as well and often serves to fuel innate behavior. Our culture encourages boys to "be tough" in sports and in life. Physical agility and superiority are afforded high economic and social status. Many television shows and cartoons feature on-screen fighting that can't help but suggest certain physical acts for playtime. Some studies have shown that children already prone to aggression may be more susceptible to being stimulated by televised violence.

A child's home, however, is likely to be the most profound teacher of aggression. If older siblings or parents settle their arguments by force or intimidating language, so, too, will a child. Even heated arguments or the shoving of a chair in frustration over a bad workday can be interpreted by a preschooler as out-of-control, violent behavior. He may not be able to discern the difference between that and slapping a playmate.

By kindergarten he should know better. By then he can understand rules about behavior and that hurting someone is not nice. He has begun to be socialized through playgroups or nursery school to learn how to get along with others, and what society will tolerate or condemn. In many ways, his own friends provide him with the most stringent guidelines. They'll say, "I won't play with you unless you're nice" and mean it.

School-Aged Children

If peer pressure plus gentle, consistent parental guidance haven't modified a child's aggression by the time he's in first or second grade, he is atypical. At that point, parents probably need to seek professional guidance, especially if that child is also extremely active, impulsive, and distractible. (See *Attention-Deficit Hyperactivity Disorder.*) Children this age generally believe in the sanctity of rules, in fairness, and in the rights of others, so that the overwhelming majority of them behave in socially appropriate ways at school and in play. (See also *Bullying*.)

Preteens

Often there is a resurgence of physical aggression around ages eleven or twelve, during junior high school. Just as in the toddler and pre-schooler, aggression is fairly normal at this time. It is also when aggression most typically surfaces in girls, although the incidence of physical assertion appears to be on the rise among girls in all age brackets.

The usual pattern is for preteens to associate themselves with cliques. These groups argue with one another. Underlying this group-to-group aggression are the issues of loyalty and personal honor, among others. Athletics and physical prowess are also becoming more important as a talisman of success. (See *Popularity*.)

Hormones, which clearly influence behavior, are fluctuating at this age, and preteens are at a developmental stage in which they're supposed to test limits and authority. Many are rebellious on principle. By the time they are sixteen or seventeen, however, physical aggression should have again receded.

What to Do

Parents will be doing their child a favor by helping him learn to control his impulses and to express feelings verbally instead of physically. Not only will he have gained some vital self-discipline, he'll have learned to think more creatively and empathetically as well.

He will have more friends. No one likes a bully, and the child who is ostracized by his peers or his peers' parents because he is unpredictable, selfish, or dangerous may find himself in a vicious cycle of trying to grab attention through inappropriate means. Eventually, he may grow hostile, have trouble with teachers and classmates, and develop low self-esteem, the forerunners of more serious psychological problems. (See *Conduct Disorder*, *Depression*, and *Bullying*.)

For the toddler, distraction from that tempting toy is often the best way to avoid further trouble. If he does push or grab, firmly say no and gently move the child away from his offended playmate, teaching him that there are consequences to his behavior.

Do not reward the aggression by giving him what he was trying to snatch away in the first place. Tell him to "use words" or "ask" to encourage language development as a method of achieving goals. Convey the idea that emotions, even strong and scary ones, are fine to feel and to admit, but acting them out physically is not. Say, "I understand you're angry, but pushing is not OK." (See also *Anger* and *Temper Tantrums.*)

Avoid overreacting, as attention might be the very thing the child is seeking. If "look at me" seems to be his consistent motivation, you might rethink the amount of time you spend with that child or if you adequately compliment his good behavior. (See "Special Time" in the Parenting Skills Introduction and *Attention-Seeking.*) Or perhaps there has been a shift in a child's routine that has unsettled him. That change can be as major as death or divorce or as seemingly unimportant as a change in Saturday-night baby-sitters. (See *Reaction to Loss.*)

After the age of two and a half, children can be taught a simple rule: No hurting. That covers a wide range of activities and promotes the idea of respecting other people's bodies, space, property, and feelings. Try to assess the intensity and intent of the child's action. A haphazard shove on the playground between two children running after a ball is different from a child methodically picking up an object to use in whacking another playmate. If a child has been warned and still engages in hurtful aggression, he can benefit from a properly administered time-out. (See "Time-Outs" in the Parenting Skills Introduction.) Be sure to label the behavior, not the child, as bad.

Some people suggest hitting a child back to demonstrate to him how painful a blow can be. This probably serves only to model aggression, however, for we do know that violence begets violence. Better to discuss with him how he would feel if someone hit him. Ask him in a matter-of-fact fashion. Don't scold, moralize, or threaten. Don't overtalk the situation. A preschooler cannot absorb it all. Remember to compliment him the next time you see him sharing or asking for a toy.

If you are the recipient of his hostilities, say, "I don't like this behavior. I will not let you hurt me." Then, without further comment, move out of arm's reach. Resume play as soon as he behaves appropriately.

For an older, school-aged child, thinking through the logical consequences of his behavior can be helpful. Ask, "If someone hit you, how would you feel? Would you want to keep playing with him? Do you think Bobby is going to want to play with you now?" Suggest he find his friend and apologize, teaching him that resolving conflict is important. Then leave the situation alone. If the child has broken something, have him try to repair it or clean up his mess, not as a punishment but as a responsibility. (See *Insensitivity* and *Making Friends.*)

When a child is aggressive in one setting but not in another, it's a strong indication that there may be something peculiar to that particular situation that promotes his aggression. Perhaps his playmate is hitting him and he is responding in kind out of self-defense. Or perhaps limits aren't being set consistently, or another adult authority may be saying one thing but doing quite another, sending mixed messages to the child.

Situation-specific aggression can actually be a good sign. It means given the right circumstances a child can control himself, inhibit his aggression, and respect the rights of others.

Reading for children: *I Want It: A Children's Problem Solving Book*, by Elizabeth Crary, illustrated by Marina Megale (Parenting Press, Seattle); and *Our Peaceful Classroom*, by Aline D. Wolf, illustrated by Montessori school children (Parent Child Press, Altoona, PA).

Allergies and Behavior

According to the National Center for Health Statistics, more than 21 million Americans suffer from allergies. Sneezing and itchy skin result from the body's natural defenses against invaders, such as pollen. In the case of allergies, the body overreacts, producing too much of an antibody called IgE, Immunoglobulin E. Allergy sensitivity is hereditary. The child of a parent who has an allergy has a much greater chance of developing one as well.

The most common allergy is hayfever, an intolerance to seasonal pollens. Other common irritants, or allergens, include dust, mold spores, animal dander (most often of cats), smoke, and food. The areas of our bodies most susceptible to reaction are the respiratory and gastrointestinal systems and the skin.

In some children, behavior is affected by allergies. It is not known exactly how or why yet because of the difficulty in studying the central nervous system. But in a small percentage of allergic children, the response to allergens brings increased levels of activity; difficulty with attention, concentration, and sometimes sleep; plus irritability. It may also trigger asthmatic attacks. (See *Asthma.*)

When allergies are the cause of these behaviors, food is often the culprit. Dairy products, eggs, peanuts, soy, and wheat products are the five leading causes. Shellfish, corn, and food additives can also be offenders. And although many parents might suspect that sugar causes extreme activity, this belief has not been borne out by scientific study. However, sugar is clearly associated with cavities and obesity—two good reasons to moderate a child's intake of sweets.

What to Do

See your pediatrician or an allergist certified by the American Board of Allergy and Immunology to do "prick testing" on the skin or a "food challenge" to determine the exact causes of allergies. It's sensible to avoid foods you suspect may exacerbate behaviors. To be thorough, read food labels carefully for "hidden" ingredients. For instance, wheat is found in malt, MSG (monosodium glutamate), and graham flour. Eggs may be listed as albumin and vitelline. Tell school staff and friends which allergies your child suffers from, and ask them to avoid exposing your child to these allergens.

For further information contact the American Academy of Allergy and Immunology, 611 E. Wells Street, Milwaukee, WI, 53202 (1-800-822-2762), or the Asthma and Allergy Foundation of America, 1125 15th Street, NW, Suite 502, Washington, D.C. 20005 (1-800-7-ASTHMA).

Allowances

Allowances are certainly not essential, and parents handle the matter in different ways. For some children, receiving money only for special treats is fine, and they don't seem to need more. Others may need a more structured system.

Having an allowance does help children learn about money management. The amount should be fixed, probably weekly, and determined mostly by what he really *needs* to spend or save during that time. Include lunch or bus fares as the baseline and perhaps add a little on top of that. Ask a child to make a list of his regular weekly expenditures and needs, then discuss it.

Allowances should not be tied to regular household chores, such as making beds, helping with the dishes, or walking the dog. Those are things you should require a child to do as part of teaching him teamwork, responsibility, and that certain things just need to be done on a regular basis. (See *Chores and Cleaning Room.*) If a child really wants an expensive toy or item, you might consider helping him earn money to purchase it through paying him to do extra household jobs, such as raking the leaves or helping to clean out the garage. (See *Materialism* and *Stealing.*)

Aloofness

Some children are simply more innately affectionate. They seem born to hug, kiss, and cuddle with their families. Other children, by nature, are more reserved and restrained, perhaps appearing aloof. They may be shy or "slow to warm." (See *Temperament.*)

These are all personality styles, probably present at birth, that can be modified to some degree by the environment. If parents easily show their affection with one another and with a child's siblings, he is likely to grow more receptive to displays of affection. If parents are hesitant to hug or kiss children, particularly their boys, it may reinforce a child's restraint. You can coax an unaffectionate child into your embrace by respecting his initial shyness, and by first engaging in some quiet time together. Sitting on the couch and reading is a perfect way to instill a pleasant association with physical proximity.

A previously affectionate child who suddenly becomes withdrawn is the child who should concern parents. He may be experiencing feelings of depression. Try gently to find out what the cause is. (See *Reaction to Loss, Reaction to Parental Conflict,* and *Sadness.*)

If a child shows an extreme aversion to a particular individual, his parents need to explore why. It is a sad but true fact that sexual abuse occurs most often with relatives and family friends, not strangers. (See *Sexual Abuse.*) In another case of extremes, when a toddler has seemed truly distressed by any physical contact and shows no interest whatsoever in relationships, he may have some of the classic features of autism. (See *Autism.*)

Anger

Anger is a normal human emotion. Suppressing or denying it may cause far more problems than it could possibly solve. But as your child matures, he should learn to understand and control anger, and eventually to verbalize it appropriately and productively.

It's normal to see anger in toddlers and preschoolers as they struggle to express themselves, to contain their impulsiveness, to separate from adults, and to find socially acceptable ways to negotiate disagreements with peers. (See *Aggression* and *Temper Tantrums.*)

Public outbursts of anger or out-of-control rage common to toddlers or preschoolers are unusual in the school-aged child, six to eleven years of age. They should have learned through trial and error and peer pressure what is acceptable in social settings (although they may still show anger at home with their family). Freud called this stage (six to eleven years) the latency period, when emotions become more controlled, allowing children to concentrate on school and improve their skills. Frequent outbursts of anger in school-aged children may suggest behavioral problems or situational stress. They could be trying to cover up some unsettling emotions, such as fear, grief, or hurt. (See *Oppositional Behavior*, *Conduct Disorder*, *Attention-Deficit Hyperactivity Disorder*, *Reaction to Loss*, *Reaction to Parental Conflict*, and *Depression*.)

Angry outbursts become more common again around twelve years of age, as children enter adolescence. Hormonal surges and the desire to establish an identity separate from parents may contribute to the emotional volatility of preteens.

What to Do

Help children put names on their emotions while you teach acceptable ways of voicing them. To a toddler or a preschooler, say, "I understand you are mad. It's okay for you to be mad. But hurting me [which covers hitting, kicking, biting, etc.] is not okay. Use words to tell me what you're feeling." (See *Temper Tantrums* and *Aggression*.)

By saying it's okay to be mad, you're telling a child that you understand and that his feelings are legitimate. This is particularly important for young children, who may be frightened when they first feel rage. Show them that their feelings are normal. Preschoolers, who engage in magical thinking, may worry that their bad thoughts about someone could come true. After the storm has passed, give a preschooler a big hug so that he knows he can't drive you away with his anger.

With older children, say, "I won't talk with you while you're yelling or calling me names. Count to ten and then tell me what you're so angry about." Neutralize anger and prompt a discussion by saying, "I know sometimes I get angry when I'm embarrassed or my feelings are hurt and I don't want to admit it. Is something like that making you angry?" Have family meetings and revise household rules that anger or frustrate a child if he really has progressed to a level where more freedom is appropriate. (See *Self-Sufficiency*.)

Finally, practice what you preach. And keep in mind that children learn most about anger and settling disputes by watching their parents. Just as you would with a child throwing a tantrum, allow yourself a time-out to cool down if you and your spouse begin to raise your voices either at your children or at each other. When you're rational and ready to talk, let children witness you discussing your differences and negotiating a peace. (See "Arguing" under *Reaction to Parental Conflict*.)

* * *

Recommended reading for young children: *Sometimes I Get Angry*, by Jane Werner Watson, Robert E. Switzer, M.D., and J. Cotter Hirschberg, M.D. (Crown Publishers, Inc.); and *Alexander and the Terrible, Horrible, No Good, Very Bad Day*, by Judith Viorst (Macmillan).

Anhedonia

(See *Pleasure, Lack of*)

Anorexia Nervosa

(See *Eating Disorders*)

Antisocial Behavior

Antisocial behavior can be defined as behavior that violates the basic rights of others or accepted societal norms. Stealing, fire-setting, cruelty to animals, vandalism, and criminal violence are antisocial acts. This behavior indicates a general irresponsibility, lack of concern for others, hostility, and aggression. A child who shows antisocial behavior has failed to learn from peer and parental disapproval what is acceptable and what is not.

Other, less serious behavior probably existed long before a child engages in these extreme activities. Parental intercession at those more innocent times can help avert more ingrained undesirable conduct.

(See *Aggression*, *Bullying*, *Stealing*, *Lying*, *Cheating*, *Insensitivity*, *Oppositional-Defiant Disorder*, and *Conduct Disorder*.)

If your child is engaging in antisocial acts, you should seek the advice of a mental-health professional. Do not ignore these symptoms!

Anxiety

Anxiety is a common human emotion, causing apprehension, worry, and discomfort. It's best thought of along a sliding scale. Its severity can range from low-grade uneasiness or anticipation to physical distress. At its height, anxiety may feel like acute fear or panic. Its intensity also seems influenced by a person's innate temperament. For instance, children who are born wary, shy, emotionally volatile, and slow to make transitions are likely to be more anxious than others. (See *Temperament*, *Shyness*, and *Adaptability*.)

At each developmental stage, certain anxieties are predictable and normal. Babies and toddlers are subject to separation anxiety and stranger anxiety. These two fears result from a mixture of sometimes conflicting developmental issues: Once they develop a strong attachment to their parents and learn to trust their home environment, children must then try to establish their own autonomy. Unfortunately, they lack the calming, intellectual powers that tell them parents will continue to exist even when out of sight.

Your preschoolers may feel anxious when required to separate from you for longer periods of time at nursery school, or when left with the baby-sitter. A school-aged child may have performance-related anxiety, especially if she has a learning disability or Attention-Deficit Hyperactivity Disorder (ADHD). And preteens, who are so concerned with peer approval, are prone to social anxieties and extreme self-consciousness. These fears are fueled by comparing themselves to others and worrying about their friends' superior talents or beauty, and their own limitations.

Anxiety should not be a problem if you acknowledge your child's worries, reassure him, and help him find ways to cope with or overcome them. For example, you may promote self-soothing techniques: Allow a young child to have comforting "transitional objects," such as blankets or stuffed animals, or help him practice and improve skills that are the source of his concerns.

Anxiety is a serious problem when it prevents a child from attending school or developing emotionally at the same pace as his peers. Sometimes serious anxiety will manifest itself in chronic physical ailments such as headaches or stomachaches, and requires treatment. (See *Anxiety Disorders.*)

Infants and Toddlers

In his first year of life, your baby is trying to accomplish an incredible amount. Physically, he is learning to focus his vision, kick, reach, turn over, and sit. At the same time he is developing emotionally, cognitively, and socially. His first psychosocial task is to develop a strong attachment to you—his parents (particularly his mother, if she is the primary caregiver)—and to depend on you for all kinds of sustenance.

Erik Erikson described this critical first stage, from birth to around eighteen months, as "trust versus mistrust." If a child's cries and needs are answered, he develops trust, a sense of security and self-confidence that he can affect his world positively. If his needs go unsatisfied or he cries for long periods without a parent responding, he may feel helpless and begin to mistrust.

Ironically, while achieving a reliable, strong, loving bond with parents and caregivers, a baby also begins to experience *separation anxiety*. Around six to eight months of age, a baby may cry when his primary caregiving parent, again typically his mother, leaves a room. He experiences her absence as a terrible loss, because he doesn't know that she still exists to return. He doesn't yet have the cognitive ability to recall her image. If she's out of sight, she ceases to be. He feels all alone in the world. No wonder he cries.

Generally after eight months of age, a baby begins to develop *object permanence*. He's learning to recognize that a thing has independent existence, whether he sees it or not. If he drops a ball, for instance, he will look down to find it, rather than searching his hand for it, believing it just vanished for good. That's why babies are delighted by a game of peekaboo.

Eventually, when a child is around two and a half years old, object

41

permanence changes into *object constancy*. Then, a child can keep and recall an internal image of a person, so that she remains real and in existence, even if he can't see her. He now knows that mother will come back.

But it can be a slow process. Children who are, by temperament, more intense, shy, or generally anxious may have a particularly difficult go of it.

Separation anxiety typically reaches its peak intensity during toddlerhood. It affects a great deal of his behavior, even his sleep. For instance, it is not unusual for parents to report a child's first sleep disturbance around this time. "He used to sleep through the night," they say. "Now he wakes up in the dark, realizes he's alone, and gets scared." This is because he can't yet remember that his parents are right down the hall and settle himself back down to sleep. (See *Sleep*.)

Toddlerhood, the "terrible twos," is simply an age when whining, clinging, and temper tantrums represent anxiety. Much of it stems from his new physical agility. A child wants to be autonomous, to pursue his own interests, but at the same time he is afraid of being detached from you. If you don't applaud your toddler's growing independence or are overtly saddened by it, he will tend to become anxious. Erikson called this stage, between eighteen months and three years, "autonomy versus shame and doubt." (See the Developmental Tasks Appendix.)

Imagine your toddler walking. He is now able to cross a room easily at will. He's delighted with himself and looks back at you for approval. And there you are, yards and yards—a terrifying distance—away. He may run to you and wrap himself around your knees. If he has moved out of sight, he may even panic a bit as he runs back.

It seems contradictory, but this seesaw pattern between independence and neediness is the hallmark of the age. "Let me do it" is yet another toddler battle cry often followed closely by crawling into your lap for some reassuring babying.

Stranger anxiety is a little different from separation anxiety, although they first occur around the same time and have some overlap in cause. Stranger anxiety begins when a child can differentiate between his parents and other people. Before five or six months of age, most babies will respond cheerfully to a friendly adult who gently changes, feeds, or comforts them. By eight or nine months, however, a baby may suddenly scream hysterically when held by Grandma, even though he always seemed to like her before. She's not Mommy and he wants Mommy.

Stranger anxiety is particularly pronounced when a child has been cared for almost exclusively by one person. Children who spend more time with extended family seem to experience it less. Keep in mind, though, that consistency of baby-sitters remains an important way of minimizing anxiety.

Stranger anxiety has a lot to do with separation anxiety. Many babies are blissfully happy in a shopping mall or grocery store crammed with strangers because their parents continue to hold on to them tightly. But when a baby-sitter comes or a new person extends her arms to hold him, a baby howls. Perhaps he expects his mother to leave him with this new person.

What to Do

It is important to help your baby learn that things exist even though they are out of his sight. Try humming when you're in the next room. Call, "I'll be right there" as you come up the stairs to answer his cry from the crib. Try not to sneak out of his view, hoping to return before he notices your absence. Tell him you're going to get a drink and that you'll be right back, and then return promptly, as promised. Play peekaboo and hide-and-seek.

Don't force your child into the arms of a relative or a family friend if he's fighting it. Wait for him to warm up and let him choose whether or not he wants physical contact. Suggest they play at arm's length first, with you clearly in sight. Grandma is a grown-up and should be able to respect a baby's hesitancy. Remember that a child's instinctive wariness about strangers and physical displays of affection (if he's allowed to heed those feelings as a baby) may protect him later in life from all sorts of dangers, including sexual abuse.

Introduce your baby to a new baby-sitter gradually over a few days. If you're going out for the evening, have the sitter come early, when the baby is still awake. It can be unsettling if he goes to sleep in your presence and wakes up to a person he's never seen before or didn't know was coming. Construct a consistent exit ritual that includes a clear and cheerful "goodbye" and "I'll be back soon" (or a specific time, such as "after lunch").

A "transitional object," a beloved stuffed animal or blanket, provides a child with comfort and familiarity that help ease separation anxiety. It's actually a very healthy way of coping and shouldn't be seen as a crutch. A transitional object is something of a child's own choosing that helps him break away from you (to make the transition from dependence to independence). No longer is he reliant only upon you for solace.

(Part of what he loves about his blanket or bear is its familiar smell and touch. Be forewarned that if you wash it, it may not seem the same to him.)

Children also cope with troubling situations by including them in their play. They may "rehearse" a baby-sitter coming and saying goodbye to parents by using their stuffed animals or toys. This playacting helps them gain control over an event in which they may feel powerless. You might join in the drama, moving a stuffed animal according to your child's directions. Such "plays" are excellent opportunities to discuss whatever situation he's enacting. Ask how the animal feels about the dramatized event. Sometimes a child may talk about his feelings more readily if a toy is his mouthpiece. (See *Play.*)

Finally, assess your child's innate wariness. Try not to leave an anxious child with an unknown hotel baby-sitter when you're on a trip, for instance. (Or, if you must, be sure to have the baby-sitter come an hour or two early so that your child can become accustomed to that new person before your departure.) Recognize his limits and don't push too much beyond that, at least until he has more solid cognitive skills to help soothe him in your absence. (See *Temperament* and *Adaptability.*)

Preschoolers

When your child is between two and a half and three and a half years of age, you may decide to enroll her in nursery school for the first time. Even though she's developmentally ready for such social challenges, you can exacerbate separation anxiety, particularly if you seem tense leaving her. Even though she should have some idea of object constancy by now (see "Infants and Toddlers," above), she still has little working concept of time. A three-hour morning nursery-school session can seem like an entire day to her.

Your child will have more difficulty adjusting to this separation if she has not spent some time previously in playgroups, with other adults and children. Experts recommend finding your child a regular play-mate before enrolling her in a class to warm her up to group situations. In addition to asking her to share, follow directions, and sit quietly for circle time, nursery school requires a child to get used to a new system of rules.

What to Do

When you bring your child to nursery school, carefully prepare and forewarn her about the event. Talk about what happens there. Reassure her that it really is okay, that, yes, you will be back to get her. Describe *when* in terms she can understand. Say, "After snack [or after storytime, after you play in the playground] I'll be here to get you." Help her become engaged with a puzzle or something in the room first. Then give her your usual hug and kiss (a bigger one may actually alarm her) and a steady smile, and leave.

Of course, some children really are more anxious than others and might cry inconsolably once you've gone. If this is the case, ask the nursery school to help you gradually familiarize your child with the classroom while you are initially present, in a kind of progressive desensitization. (See *Adaptability* and *Clinging*.) Maybe she can keep her blankie or teddy or something of yours that she loves in her knapsack to hold when she's upset. If a nursery school refuses to discuss such alternatives with you, you probably need to find another place that's more child-friendly.

You might need to consider whether or not an anxious child is really ready for the challenge of nursery school. Perhaps you should wait a few months and then try it again. Ask yourself, "Am I doing something to worsen her anxiety?" The next, and easier, question is: "How can I help make a situation better for her?"

School-Aged Children

School is often fun, but it can also be frightening and anxiety-producing. Children must learn, compete, and perform academically, as well as integrate themselves socially. All sorts of things can make a child apprehensive: There's a class bully who's targeted him this week; his teacher is rigid and authoritarian; he's having trouble joining in games during recess; he's nervous about a test; or he's having trouble reading, perhaps because of an undetected vision or hearing problem, learning disability, or problems with attention (ADHD).

A child's anxiety can show up in a variety of ways. He may have trouble sleeping. He may seem distracted during class. He may even be so nervous that his stomach hurts. (See *Headaches* and *Stomachaches*.) If you're lucky, he'll talk about it. But even if he does, you might also want to discuss what's happening with his teacher. Children who are overwhelmed enough by a situation to be anxious often can't describe in detail the circumstances that worry them.

Sometimes anxiety is not so much the result of a specific environmental stressor, but of personality. Shy children are often very anxious about school or social situations. And children who are perfectionists by nature put extreme pressure on themselves to succeed, fueling anxiety. Of course, perfectionism is a quality often exacerbated at home. (See *Perfectionism*.) A child's home may also contribute to his anxiety about school if his parents are divorcing or a family member is very ill. (See *Reaction to Loss* and *Reaction to Parental Conflict*.)

In a few cases, anxiety about school becomes so pronounced that a child either refuses to attend or complains of medically inexplicable illnesses that prevent his going. The root of a full-blown school phobia is often separation anxiety disorder. (See *School, Headaches, Stomachaches*, and *Anxiety Disorders*.)

What to Do

Fortunately, knowing *what* is causing your child's anxiety can help you dispel it. Prompt a discussion by letting him know many people have similar fears and say, "I know a lot of children are worried about going to school because they're afraid of a teacher or of a mean kid. Are you worried about something like that?" Talk about alternative ways to deal with the situation.

If he's afraid of a test, help him devise a better schedule and method of studying. Maybe he'd like to have a tutor. Reduce his anxiety by asking, "What's the worst that can happen if you get a C?" Children often make a situation far more catastrophic than it really is. If he says he'll flunk school, or that you'll be disappointed, acknowledge his worry, then try to mitigate it or put it in context.

Assure him that he'll have many opportunities over the year to do better. One failed question or test doesn't mean he'll flunk out. Maybe add, "When I was in fourth grade, I was terrible at math and I thought I'd be a failure." Clearly you're not. Your admission of a weakness proves successful, functioning people can have and admit flaws. Your child will also be much more likely to come to you with his troubles in the future. The idea is to motivate a child to try hard and to do his best. If his best really is a C, you and he need to accept that limitation while finding ways to help him reach his potential. (See *Perfectionism*, *School*, *Self-Esteem*, and *Motivation*.)

(Keep in mind that if your child has a learning disability or ADHD, he needs some professional help. In the case of ADHD, medication should strengthen his ability to listen in class. Being taught how to compensate for his learning difficulties should help reduce his anxiety.)

If he's nervous about having to play basketball in gym, practice free throws at home so he'll have more confidence in his skills. Rehearse anxiety-producing events such as show-and-tell. (See *Shyness*.)

Finally, try to instill some self-soothing techniques in your child. Talk about taking a deep breath when anxious. Let a first-grader take a picture of you to school to stick in her desk to look at when she's homesick. Or tell her to think about what she likes most about school when she's worried by something there. (See *Fears and Phobias*.)

Preteens

Children aged eleven and twelve place enormous value on peer approval. At this age, children tend to run in packs, meaning they have to be accepted by a clique. They can be excluded for all sorts of ridiculous reasons. If a child doesn't have a clear sense of self or confidence in her inherent worth, no matter what other people say she is going to be even more anxious and devastated by peer rejection. Hopefully, she will have already found activities she enjoys and in which she does well so that she can define herself through those interests. (See *Self-Esteem*, *Popularity*, and *Materialism*.)

Academics also become increasingly competitive at this age. Keep in mind that your child may need extra encouragement rather than pressure to excel.

What to Do

Keep talking to your child. It's going to take more effort on your part to get her to discuss feelings at this age with you. (See *Refusing to Speak*.) Use the same techniques described above for school-aged children to ease her anxiety.

Examine your own influence on her. Do you put unreasonable or detrimental pressure on her? "Do your best" is a very different message from "Be the best." (See *Perfectionism*.) Sometimes grades slip a bit at this age because peer relationships became a focus of concern. As long as the dip isn't pronounced or prolonged, you should probably tolerate it.

Recommended reading: *Toddlers and Parents: A Declaration of Independence*, by T. Berry Brazelton, M.D. (a Delta book/Dell Publishing); *The Magic Years*, by Selma Fraiberg (Scribner's); *The First Twelve Months of Life* and *The Second Twelve Months of Life*, by Frank and Theresa Caplan (Perigee Books); and *Your Baby & Child: From Birth to Age Five*, by Penelope Leach, Ph.D. (Alfred A. Knopf).

Anxiety Disorders

In most cases anxiety is common, predictable, normal, and manageable. (See *Anxiety*.) Anxiety is a problem when it permeates a child's behavior and impedes his daily life. When a child is so anxious that he can't attend school, cannot under any circumstances separate from his parents, seems to be experiencing developmental delays or pronounced regression, or suffers from chronic physical ailments that have no medical explanation, he may have an anxiety disorder.

In its diagnostic manual, the American Psychiatric Association identifies three childhood anxiety disorders: Separation Anxiety Disorder, Avoidant Disorder, and Overanxious Disorder. Susceptibility to anxiety disorders seems to run in families and therefore is likely to have some biological basis. Sometimes, the behavior can get progressively worse: A slightly anxious child may become avoidant or have full-blown phobias if the problem is not addressed.

Separation Anxiety Disorder

Most infants and young children struggle with separation anxiety. With the development of certain cognitive abilities, socialization, and the support of parents, it generally subsides around the age of three. (See "Infants and Toddlers" under *Anxiety*.)

Separation anxiety is a serious problem when your child simply cannot be away from you because he's afraid that something terrible will happen in your absence, either to him or to you. He may not be able to be in a different room, sleep in his own bed, or play at his best friend's house without a parent, generally his mother, present. He may even show a complete disinterest in peer relationships. He may cling and whine in social situations. He feels secure only with you or at home. When there, or in an equally familiar environment, such as Grandma's house, he probably shows little if any anxiety.

Of course, many preschoolers might act this way and not have a psychiatric disorder. For them, it's a passing developmental stage. For a six-year-old, however, this behavior is atypical and problematic. It could lead to serious, perhaps incapacitating anxiety about school, even school phobia. (See School Phobia under *School*.) It could manifest itself in physical ailments, such as headaches and stomachaches. (See *Headaches, Stomachaches, Psychosomatic Disorder*.)

Other symptoms of separation anxiety include an inordinate fear of the dark, monsters, death from an accident or a catastrophe, and nightmares or other sleep disturbances. When forced to separate from parents, a child may even experience symptoms akin to those in adult panic attacks: rapid heart rate or hyperventilation.

No one knows the precise cause of Separation Anxiety Disorder, although children who suffer from it tend to come from very close-knit, protective families, and sometimes have a clinically depressed parent (generally the mother). It may begin as an inborn temperamental trait or genetic vulnerability that is exacerbated by a life crisis, such as a death, a parent being hospitalized with a serious illness, or divorce.

Avoidant Disorder and Overanxious Disorder

If a child is very anxious about a situation there are two ways he may deal with it. He can either avoid it (Avoidant Disorder) or he can take part but worry throughout the event (Overanxious Disorder). The two disorders can overlap.

If a child is diagnosed as avoidant, he is generally unsure of himself, timid, socially withdrawn, and easily embarrassed. He probably prefers to be with family. But his anxiety is different from Separation Anxiety in that it's not so much leaving his family or home that frightens him as having to interact with unfamiliar people. He may find ways of avoiding school, even with truancy. (See School Avoidance and Phobia under *School*.)

In Overanxious Disorder, a child is extremely worried, all the time, about tests, his future, peer involvement. He may fidget, bite his nails, have other nervous habits, or be unable to relax. He may be self-conscious and self-deprecating, a perfectionist, and very concerned with pleasing authority figures, such as parents or teachers. He may also have frequent headaches or stomachaches. According to APA's diagnostic manual, the disorder is more common among eldest children, in small and upper-middle-class families where there is great emphasis on achievement.

What to Do

If your child's anxiety is very pronounced and present in many different settings, talk to a professional about how you can best help your child. He may need some therapy to teach him coping skills.

If his anxiety still seems manageable, help your child calm himself in anxious moments with self-soothing techniques or by changing the situations that seem to cause his apprehension. If he's afraid of a test, for instance, help him study, devise more efficient study schedules and habits, or hire a tutor in the subject. If he's timid about gym because he can't dribble a basketball, practice it at home with him to increase his confidence. Rehearse scary situations, such as show-and-tell or book reports, the night before he must do them in class. Examine your own demands and expectations if perfectionism seems to be the root of his trouble. (See *Anxiety*.)

With Separation Anxiety, you will have done your child a great favor if you have facilitated his attempts at independence early on. (Again, see *Anxiety*.) If your child suffers from school phobia, make sure he attends. Sometimes it helps if he can call you during the day to check in. (See School Phobia under *School*, *Headaches*, and *Stomachaches*.)

If your child's anxiety is interfering with his day-to-day functioning, consider seeking the advice of mental-health professionals. It is even more essential to do so if it seems to have reached the intensity of a disorder. There are many behavior therapies and medications that have been proven to reduce the symptoms of anxiety disorders.

Argumentative

If your child is being argumentative, try to determine the motivation. Is he arguing as a way of dominating a younger sibling or family situation, or is it because he's suddenly discovered that he has a mind and he wants to debate politics with you for the intellectual thrill of it?

The latter should actually be seen as a wonderful, if somewhat taxing, opportunity. Between the ages of ten and twelve, children often like to spar with parents intellectually. It's a hint of the arguments to come in adolescence but without their emotional heat. As such, preteen debates offer a stage for you to teach children about reasoning and how to discuss divergent ideas politely. If you can listen to your child respectfully, modeling the concept that people can have very different but equally valid ideas, you will have helped create an open, curious mind.

Of course, this is easier said than done when it feels as if your child, who before was always so agreeable and interested in your opinion, seems to say "no" *just* because you say "yes." But try to take pride in your child's increasing intellectual ability and nurture that growth.

If your child seems to be arguing *only* to cause trouble or be aggressive, he may be trying to dominate your attention. Examine the family situation or your child's social behavior. If he has other inappropriate behavior patterns, there may be some underlying problem or tension. (See *Sibling Rivalry*, *Oppositional Behavior*, *Impulsivity*, *Attention-Seeking*, and *Bullying*.)

Articulation Problems

Articulation is the physical process of speaking. While it's common for toddlers and preschoolers to have some difficulty pronouncing different sounds and words as they practice and master speech, you should pay close attention if your child repeats or prolongs a single sound, syllable, word, or phrase. (See *Stuttering*.) Typical articulation errors appear in the form of omissions, substitutions, and distortions. Omission means a child leaves off part of a word as he says it ("ha" for "hat"), substitution means that he substitutes one sound with another ("wabbit" for "rabbit" or "tat" for "cat"), and distortion means that he distorts a sound ("lellow" for "yellow").

According to the American Speech-Language-Hearing Association, children learn some sounds earlier than others. *P*, *m*, and *b* sounds are usually perfected by the time a child is three years old. *S*, *r*, and *l* sounds are more difficult and sometimes not achieved until a child has been in grade school. But the Association says that children should be able to correctly pronounce all sounds in the English language by the age of eight.

Help your child learn proper speech sounds by using them correctly yourself. When he does struggle, don't interrupt or hurry him. Feeling anxious or embarrassed will only exacerbate his difficulties. When he mispronounces a word, don't obviously correct him; just use the word yourself in your response. (If he says "wabbit," say: "Yes, I see the *r*abbit. He's a very pretty *r*abbit, isn't he?")

Faulty articulation that is persistent and not part of normal development may result from physical, dental, or hearing problems, or from the brain's inability to process sounds correctly. If your child's speech seems particularly labored, have it evaluated by a professional. Undiagnosed and untreated speech and language problems may lead to behavioral, social, and academic problems. (See *Hearing*, *Language and Speech*, and *Learning Disabilities*.)

For more information contact the American Speech-Language-Hearing Association, 10801 Rockville Pike, Rockville, MD 20852 (1-800-638-TALK).

Asthma

Asthma is the most common chronic illness of childhood, affecting about 7 percent of all American children. While asthma is a medical illness, attacks can sometimes be triggered by emotional events. It can have a profound impact on the self-esteem, social adaptability, and anxiety level of children. During an attack, the asthmatic's bronchial tubes may narrow and mucus may accumulate, making breathing difficult. The child will wheeze and have particular difficulty expelling air. He may cough and feel extreme tightness in his chest.

Asthma tends to run in families. If both parents have it, a child has a fifty-fifty chance of developing asthma. Onset is typically early, with 80 percent of childhood asthmatics manifesting the illness before they are six years old. Environmental factors, such as allergies, respiratory infections, and emotional stress, can trigger a child's genetic predisposition. Cold, dry air, cigarette smoke, and exercise can easily spark an attack once a child is prone to them.

Allergies associated with asthma are caused by animal dander (most often cats'), cockroaches, dust mites, pollen, feathers, and food. Emotional stressors that set off attacks include particularly trying school situations, parental conflict, or the struggles associated with living with a depressed or alcoholic parent. Anything that represents a separation, loss, or crisis to a child may trigger an attack.

Children with asthma do have a higher risk of developing emotional problems if they and their parents have trouble coping with the condition. Severe asthma produces high levels of anxiety during sports or school. As the parent of a very young asthmatic, you may understandably want to "overprotect," but in the process your child may become afraid of leaving the safe confines of home. (See "Separation Anxiety Disorder" under *Anxiety Disorders.*)

As a result, the child may forgo outings to the zoo or sleep-overs, normal, happy events of childhood. Feeling different from other children may exacerbate low self-esteem and depression. An asthmatic child may also feel guilty about being a burden to his family, or angry about the unfairness of having to take extra health precautions.

What to Do

Fortunately, most cases of asthma are easily managed with medication, physical conditioning, and parental sensitivity. Properly treated, asthma will often remit as children grow older.

Seek medical help at the first occasion of wheezing and then follow the regimen prescribed by doctors to control future attacks. If you are asthmatic, your child runs a higher risk of developing asthma. You should educate yourself about the illness. Take precautions to avoid risk factors and to know what to do if an attack occurs. In the case of a severe attack, when a child doesn't respond to treatment, take him to an emergency room.

Manage the environment. If the asthma results from allergies, avoid unnecessary exposure. If the family pet is the culprit, for instance, find it another home or create a run for it in the yard outside. Vacuum often to remove dust. Wash stuffed animals and blankets frequently. Put filters on the furnace and air systems. Stop smoking or smoke only outside the house.

Avoid unnecessary conflict. Arguing in front of a child under five years of age can be a very upsetting event to him. He is too young to put the disagreement in context.

Likewise, use extra discretion in choosing day care or a nursery school to find one where he runs a smaller risk of catching respiratory infections from other children. Find an institution with fewer children or one that segregates sick youngsters. Make an effort to prepare him for starting day care, so that attending will not be too stressful for him. If your child is at the stage when he's afraid of strangers (beginning at nine months), try to postpone leaving him with a sitter until he is older.

Both you and your child should be sensitive to his limits, but don't keep him from enjoying life or pursuing his talents. With proper precautions, such as pretreatment with an inhaler, a child can easily participate in sports. Being in shape physically is, in fact, a good way to minimize the impact of an attack and to lower the amount of medication needed.

Finally, talk about his asthma with him. Children who understand what triggers attacks and how to work through them cope better. Admit they are a little different from their peers, but then focus on their unique abilities and characteristics. If well controlled, asthma can be an almost invisible condition.

For further information about causes, treatments, support groups, and training classes, contact the Asthma and Allergy Foundation of America, 1125 15th Street, NW, Suite 502, Washington, D.C. 20005 (1-800-7-ASTHMA); the American Academy of Allergy and Immunology, 611 E. Wells Street, Milwaukee, WI 53202 (1-800-822-2762); Mothers of Asthmatics, 3554 Chain Bridge Road, Suite 200, Fairfax, VA 22030 (703-385-4403); or the Lung Line of the National Jewish Center for Immunology and Respiratory Medicine (1-800-222-LUNG).

Recommended reading: *A Parent's Guide to Asthma*, by Nancy Sander (Doubleday); *What You Can Do About Asthma*, by Nathaniel Altman (Dell Publishing).

Attention-Deficit Hyperactivity Disorder

Attention-Deficit Hyperactivity Disorder (ADHD) is characterized by problems with inattention, impulsivity, and activity level. Children with the disorder have trouble sitting still, paying attention, following directions, and letting other children have their turn; they often act without thinking. Parents describe them as "human tornadoes" or "wind-up toys." "When he learned to walk it was like someone opened the gate to a horse, and I've been chasing him ever since."

ADHD is one of the most common reasons for referring a child to mental-health care. In its diagnostic manual, the American Psychiatric Association estimates that 3 percent of children in the United States have ADHD. The disorder often begins between the ages of three and seven (as children enter school and have difficulty fitting in because of their hyperactivity). Children with ADHD tend to be boys, at a ratio of about six-to-one.

Although no one knows the exact cause of ADHD, scientists believe that it results from an interaction of biological and environmental factors. Children with ADHD may have a chemical imbalance that affects the way their brain regulates attention and motor skills. Usually there is someone in the family who has had ADHD, or "minimal brain dysfunction," as the disorder was called during the 1940s and '50s, suggesting that the disorder is passed genetically.

Most children with ADHD are born with a predisposition or biological vulnerability to the disorder, which can then be triggered or exacerbated by a child's environment, his life's events, and his parents' response to his hyperactive behavior. There are also children who may have a genetic susceptibility but who never exhibit ADHD.

It's important to remember hyperactivity is often found in children who've undergone some emotional stress, such as a divorce, death, or job loss in the family. Children can be distracted for reasons less serious than ADHD as well: They're afraid of the child sitting next to them in school, they have a headache, or they've just noticed that they have on mismatched socks and are worried they'll be teased. There are also children who are just temperamentally more active and impetuous. (See *Temperament*.)

ADHD is diagnosed by looking at fourteen behavioral characteristics listed in the APA's diagnostic manual. A child must exhibit eight of those symptoms over a period of six months before the age of seven to qualify for the diagnosis. As described by the APA, these include: fidgeting and squirming; being easily distracted; having difficulty remaining seated, awaiting his turn in games, following instructions, or sustaining interest in a task; blurting out answers to questions before being asked; often jumping from one uncompleted activity to another; an inability to play quietly; excessive talking; interrupting others; difficulty listening; often losing things; and taking dangerous risks (out of impulsivity, not for the purpose of seeking thrills).

The behaviors must also be analyzed according to the normal development of a child's age. A three-year-old, for instance, shouldn't be expected to sit still for a twenty-minute lecture, while an eight-year-old is regularly asked to do so in school. It's having a marked difference from other children his own age that suggests trouble. The characteristics often occur across contexts. If a child acts impulsively only in the classroom, not in the playground or at home, there may be something about that situation that is causing his ADHD-like behavior.

If you suspect ADHD in your preschooler, look at his ability to do different things. If he seems mostly to run, jump, climb, and ignore all caution but can also sit quietly by himself and finish a puzzle, the issue of whether or not he has ADHD is less clear and is best determined accurately only by a professional. It's a child's ability to concentrate, to comprehend the intent of an activity, to tolerate frustration, and to finish a task and then move on to a different activity that helps distinguish a child who is merely highly active from one who might be diagnosed with ADHD.

Other behaviors that have been associated with ADHD include: resisting behavior modification or peer pressure; having a hot temper; a complete disinterest in pleasing adults; and poor eye-hand coordination.

What to Do

If you suspect your child has ADHD, seek professional counseling early on. Left untreated, ADHD usually results in serious difficulties with school performance and with peers. ADHD children have trouble absorbing information. They tend to irritate teachers and classmates with their disruptive behaviors, which can lead in turn to low self-esteem and more behavior problems. Associated diagnoses include: learning disabilities (perhaps as many as 40 percent of children with ADHD also have learning disabilities); oppositional behavior and conduct disorders (up to one-half of all children with conduct disorders have ADHD); depression; and anxiety disorders.

There are basically three medically accepted treatments for ADHD: medication; retraining parenting skills and behavior modification; and cognitive therapy. And, although there is little scientific data to support it, some parents firmly believe that diet manipulation helps calm their hyperactive children.

Research has shown medication to be effective for the majority of ADHD children. Ritalin (methylphenidate) is the most commonly prescribed, followed by Dexedrine (dextroamphetamine) and Cylert (pemoline). These drugs increase attention while reducing impulsivity. They should make listening to teachers and concentrating on schoolwork easier.

They can also help with social interactions. Think of a game of baseball, for instance, which has been studied in association with ADHD children. A child who just can't wait until someone hits the ball to run to a base, who constantly throws the ball to the wrong person, or who doesn't pay enough attention to see a fly ball coming his way isn't going to be too popular with his peers.

As with any kind of medication, drugs used to treat ADHD must be prescribed and carefully monitored by your physician to gauge effectiveness and any possible side effects.

These medications are best given in tandem with counseling parents how to better manage their ADHD children. Therapists can teach you how to give directions and how to use praise, rewards, and time-outs more effectively to help your ADHD child control his actions. These children can be difficult handfuls, and you can easily fall into a self-defeating cycle of unacceptable behavior followed by punishment, which is followed by more bad behavior and increased frustration and anger on your part.

Once you've learned to accept your child's behavior as part of his temperament or as part of a disorder (rather than *intentional* destructiveness or disobedience), it will be easier for everyone to remain calm and to react productively. Remain consistent as a couple. If one of you is permissive while the other tries to set limits, you'll confuse any child, but particularly one with ADHD.

Finally, with the use of cognitive therapy, you can teach your child problem-solving techniques. The goal is to make him more reflective, so that he'll think through his options and the consequences of his choices rather than just act impulsively.

For further information contact the National Attention-Deficit Disorder Association (ADDA) (1-800-487-2282); or Children with Attention Deficit Disorders (CHADD) (305-587-3700).

Recommended reading: *A Parent's Guide to Attention-Deficit Disorders*, by Lisa Bain for The Children's Hospital of Philadelphia (a Delta book / Dell Publishing); *Your Hyperactive Child: A Parent's Guide to Coping with Attention-Deficit Disorder*, by Barbara Ingersoll, Ph.D. (Doubleday); and *Attention Deficit Hyperactivity Disorder: A Handbook for Diagnosis and Treatment*, by Russell Barkley (The Guilford Press).

Attention-Seeking

It is perfectly normal—healthy, in fact—for your child to want your attention. He thrives on your hugs, acceptance, praise, and those moments of undivided focus. Your challenge is to try to give the child all that attention properly—during daily "special time" (see the Parenting Skills Introduction), meals, bedtime, and playtime, and when he asks for help—not just when he misbehaves.

Children will try to get attention by whining, clinging, complaining, interrupting, and throwing temper tantrums. Young children—preschoolers and toddlers—will most typically engage in this nasty repertoire when you are least able to respond: when on the phone, at the grocery store, or at Grandma's house.

Even in such embarrassing or inconvenient moments, it's important to remain committed to helping children learn appropriate ways of asking for things. They can't negotiate the outside world without that knowledge. And remember, children are smart enough to play the odds; if you do intermittently give in to tantrums or whining for the sake of peace, children will probably push and push to see if this is one magic time when they can get their way. Why give up whining if it works? It's your job to help your child learn some patience and better methods of asking, or he may become stuck developmentally.

Toddlers and Preschoolers

Toddlers and preschoolers are normally demanding. For one thing, they haven't yet developed an ability to delay their need for gratification (they want what they want right now). Since their vocabulary is not very sophisticated, they become frustrated and impatient. They also are in an emotionally volatile, contradictory stage of trying to separate a bit from parents and establish some autonomy. Attention-seeking, then, often has to do with being uncomfortable in a new situation that requires more independence, especially if a child is innately hesitant or easily upset. (See *Anxiety*, *Temperament*, *Adaptability*, and *Clinging*.)

But because a child this age is trying to establish some authority in his own right, whining and temper tantrums can also be simple power plays. That's especially true if he misbehaves at a time when your attention is focused, out of necessity, on something else (answering the phone or tending to a new baby, for instance). There is nothing insidious about this behavior; it's just a reality that you must keep in mind. (See also *Interrupting*.)

Also remember that young children faced with sharing Mommy with a new sibling may regress a bit and act younger than their age. (See *Regression*.) Usually, such regression passes if it is handled empathetically and you reassure the child by giving him lots of attention when he's *not* misbehaving. (It's a problem when a child seems satisfied only if you yell at him; then he's seeking negative rather than positive attention. Such children may have low self-esteem or feel neglected. Ask a professional for advice in this scenario.)

What to Do

Remain dispassionate even in the face of a tantrum. Responding with anger or shouting only fuels a child's thrashing or crying. You will take the power out of a fit by answering calmly. Don't respond to the child's request until she makes it appropriately.

If a child is learning to talk, tell her to use words instead of screaming. When she's whining, say, "I won't respond while you use that kind of voice." (See *Temper Tantrums* and *Whining*.) Tell a preschooler who's interrupting dinner to count to five (you may need to count it out for her) and that then you can help her. (See *Interrupting*.) At five years of age, she may even respond well to a little humor. She may laugh and stop if you mimic her whining, as long as you do it as fond teasing, not belittlement.

One of the most difficult aspects of trying to modify developmentally inappropriate attention-seeking is helping a child to learn some patience, tolerate frustration, and delay gratification of his impulses. There is no quick fix. It takes a child's cognitive maturation and parents setting limits consistently.

Look for gradual improvement and recognize that if you cave in after five minutes of whining, the process will be even slower. You have to steel yourself to tolerate and ignore whining, for ten, fifteen, twenty minutes at a time without finally throwing up your hands and saying, "All right, all right." Your child will have won that particular battle and slowed down his socialization in the process.

When children word their request in an appropriate voice, respond.

If you honestly can't do what they want right that very second, try to get a preschooler to count to three (as you put that roast in the oven). Next week he'll be able to make it to the count of five, if you stick to your guns.

If tantrums take place consistently in the grocery store or shopping mall, ask yourself if you are taking him there too often or for too long a stretch. Young children can tolerate only so much, especially if it's close to naptime. After that, the first line of defense is distraction and involving a child in the process. Try, "Hey, what aisle is dog food in? Do you remember? Let's see if you can spot it for me."

Give yourself and your child credit for improvement. If tantrums give way to low-pitched whining, things are getting better. If not, take the power out of a child's hands. Leave the store or the party where he's throwing a fit. Then, the next time you go, don't take him. Say as you're leaving, "I would take you, but last time you misbehaved. I'm going again next week and you can come with me then as long as you behave." Although he may put up a considerable fuss, he will have learned a valuable lesson about the consequences of his own behavior as well as about your ability to do what you say you will.

School-Aged Children

Fortunately, most problematic attention-seeking will disappear around the time a child turns seven. That's largely due to a development in cognition that is as profound as the shift from preverbal to verbal abilities in a toddler. Swiss psychologist Jean Piaget called this "concrete operations," meaning that a child is now capable of thinking through cause-and-effect sequences, of recognizing that there are multiple ways of solving a problem. (See the Developmental Tasks Appendix.)

Older children should ask for things in more appropriate ways and at more appropriate times. Whereas a four-year-old is not tuned in to his mother's mood and will often interrupt her with a demand at the most inconvenient moment, an eight-year-old is more careful. He will take a reading on Mom's circumstance and consider the likelihood of his getting what he wants at that moment. He's more likely to wait (and is capable of doing so) until she's accessible to ask for something. And then he'll probably accept a refusal if she has a logical, fair reason for it. He is now more likely to understand and believe in reasonable rules.

What to Do

Be sure to discuss your reasoning for granting or denying a school-aged child's requests. That helps teach him logic and shows that you respect him enough to explain. Hear out his arguments, even if the answer remains no.

It is unusual for a school-aged child to have great difficulty checking his impulses or anger. Have you set enough limits for such a child? Do you spend enough time with him or put too much pressure on him? Is the situation exacerbating his behavior? (See *Oppositional Behavior, Aggression, Reaction to Parental Conflict*, and *Conduct Disorder.*)

Preteens

While children aged six to eleven are more emotionally tranquil, preteens are moving into a time of hormonal surges and identity crises. Just as toddlers and preschoolers did, preteens are more likely to test you for the sake of establishing autonomy. They also have developed intellectually so that they might want to debate, again just for the fun of it. (See *Argumentative.*)

For all its seeming defiance of authority, much of preteen behavior is unconsciously designed to grab your attention, especially if preteens feel neglected or under too much pressure to excel. At eleven and twelve years of age, children still want to know what Mom and Dad think.

What to Do

Keep your sense of humor and wits about you. View arguments as discussions and the opportunity to teach a child about polite debate. Just as you would with a preschooler, refuse to answer or respond if a child is yelling. Remember, a calm response diffuses the power of anger. Say, "I'm not going to talk to you until you count to ten and speak in a normal tone of voice and explain to me why you're so angry." Practice what you preach.

Have regular family meetings to discuss problems before they grow into emotional confrontations. Spend time with your preteen and look for opportunities to discuss difficult issues when he presents them. (See *Self-Esteem*, *Refusing to Speak*, and the Parenting Skills Introduction.)

Autism

Autism is a serious, pervasive developmental disorder that affects about four in every 10,000 children. More males than females are afflicted, at a ratio of four-to-one. The critical symptoms are a persistent lack of interest in social relationships, even with parents, and abnormal language development. (Autistic children may know only three words at age three; tend to repeat the last words of a question by way of answering; reverse pronouns, saying "you" when they mean "I," for example; or seem to devise a confusing language of their own.) To be diagnosed with autism, a child must exhibit these symptoms before reaching thirty months of age.

As babies, autistic children may have stiffened and arched when held, seeming to dislike physical contact. They often refuse to make eye contact and seem unaware of other people's emotional responses to them. As they grow older, autistic children prefer to play by themselves and seem unable to interact with others. They may stare into space during social gatherings.

Other symptoms include abnormal body movements, such as continually clapping or flicking their hands, whirling their bodies around, and flapping their arms and hands. Autistic children may spin plates at the table or become obsessed with parts of objects. They throw intense tantrums when their routines are changed or household objects are moved. Some are highly sensitive to sound. Other autistic children may rock, bang their heads, or engage in extreme, self-injurious behavior, such as poking their own eyes.

Studies indicate that many autistic children are hyperactive and inattentive. Three out of four are also mentally handicapped. More than half of autistic children will develop seizures.

Autism can result from genetic abnormalities or exposure to viruses such as measles or rubella in utero. In the 1940s and '50s, when autism was first studied, clinicians believed that cold, aloof parenting— "refrigerator mothers," they were called—caused autism. This theory has been disproven. Parents' personalities and child-rearing styles cannot cause autism, but knowing how to relate properly to an autistic child can greatly facilitate his adaptation.

What to Do

Children who display autistic features should be evaluated by an experienced psychiatrist and neurologist. Autistic children should be enrolled in preschool/elementary programs that use appropriate behavior modifications designed to help them maximize the abilities they do have.

There is no medication to cure autism. There are, however, drugs that alleviate the severity of symptoms, particularly the hyperactivity, which makes managing autistic children within a family so difficult.

Recommended reading: *Autistic Children: A Guide for Parents and Professionals*, by Lorna Wing (Brunner-Mazel).

Avoidant Disorder

(See *Anxiety*)

Bed-Wetting

Bed-wetting, or nocturnal enuresis in medical terms, is a common childhood problem. Twenty percent of five-year-olds and 10 percent of six-year-olds routinely wet their beds. This is a physiological not an emotional condition and has to do with the maturation of the bladder. Suspected causes include a smaller-than-normal bladder, deficiencies in hormones that regulate the bladder, and immature neurological connections between the bladder and the brain. Bed-wetting tends to run in families.

In a few cases, more serious medical conditions—urinary infections or diabetes—are the underlying cause. These children typically wet themselves during the day, as well. (See *Day-Wetting*.) Your pediatrician should run a simple urinalysis to rule out such causes. There is also the possibility that emotional stress has triggered a child's physical predisposition to flare, but typically this child has secondary enuresis: He's been dry for a substantial period of time (three to six months) without incident. Such environmental stressors may include the birth of a sibling, serious parental conflict, school pressure, or a death in the family. (See *Regression, Reaction to Loss*, and *Reaction to Parental Conflict*.)

Two out of three bed wetters are boys. Left untreated, the vast majority will grow out of the problem, especially after their sixth birthday. Only 2 percent of fourteen-year-olds still wet their beds.

But the bed wetter usually doesn't want to wait for the problem to go away on its own. His friends are having sleep-overs, which he may be reluctant to attend for fear of embarrassing himself. His wetting is sure to be causing some parental aggravation, as well. Siblings may tease him. And no matter how educated he and his family are to the fact that he is not purposefully doing this, that his bodily functions are simply still maturing, a child's self-esteem is going to suffer if wetting continues over the long term.

What to Do

First, visit your pediatrician for a thorough exam. Don't let the doctor entirely dismiss the problem with, "Don't worry, he'll outgrow it." He may, of course, but you can help him speed the process.

Treatment involves behavior modification techniques that are easy and effective. They work best when the child himself is motivated to change. You may start using these therapies as early as four years of age if the problem has started to bother the child.

To train your child to wake up and relieve himself in the toilet when his bladder is full, have him practice the process when he's awake. Have him lie on the bed, imagine what a full bladder feels like, then get up and go to the bathroom. Be sure to have night-lights in place so he can find his way in the dark. Or he can do bladder-retention training exercises: stop the flow of urine to promote control, and drink lots of water then hold on as long as possible to stretch the bladder. This approach has moderate success—a little more than half of all bed wetters show some improvement through it.

The most effective behavioral technique is the use of small, strap-on body alarms. The alarm sounds at the first few drops of wetness so that a child can wake, get up, and finish urinating in the toilet. Alarms are run by tiny hearing-aid batteries, so there is no danger of electric shock. After a month or so of use, a child gradually becomes conditioned to wake up on his own when he senses his bladder is full. About three out of four children have long-term success with these alarms, which cost between $45 and $65. Be prepared to get up with a child, particularly one under five years of age, during the first weeks of use.

While your child is developing night control, remain supportive and sympathetic. Don't punish, lecture, or tease as he tries to train himself. Reward him in a way that allows him to mark his own progress, such as stickers to put on a calendar. Never discuss the problem in front of him with family or friends. He is vulnerable to embarrassment about his wetting. Make sure he bathes after an accident, so there is no telltale scent to invite comment from schoolmates.

With children over the age of six, taking responsibility for themselves, changing their own beds and laundering the sheets motivates them to stick to their exercises and alarms. On a sleep-over, let the child take a sleeping bag, so in case of an accident he can roll it up in the morning before his friend notices.

Medication is also an option. Drugs can be used in tandem with or instead of behavior modification therapies. Medications can help protect a child during a sleep-over, or provide increased control.

Researchers have discovered that the body naturally secretes an antidiuretic hormone (ADH) during sleep to enable kidneys to concentrate urine. Some bed wetters may have an ADH deficiency, which can be counteracted by hormone therapy. An antidepressant may also happen to increase bladder capacity. Always ask your doctor to outline any kind of potential side effects of otherwise helpful medications.

Recommended reading with sections for both parents and children: *Dry All Night: The Picture Book That Stops Bed-wetting*, by Alison Mack (Little, Brown).

Biting

Biting is common among toddlers. It is generally no more malicious than a push or slap spontaneously made when trying to grab a toy away from a playmate. However, biting seems worse because it has an animalistic quality to it, and teeth marks are more alarming than a simple bruise.

Clearly you need to teach your child that biting causes pain and isn't acceptable behavior, rather he must use words to express his feelings. Contrary to conventional wisdom, never bite a child to show him how much it hurts. (See "What to Do" under *Aggression*.)

Because biting is typical of a young child, you can help by trying to defuse a situation before trouble occurs. Become aware of a toddler's behavioral cues, such as whining. If he's tired, hungry, frustrated, or overexcited, he's far more likely to be aggressive. Lunch, a nap, a quiet, calming-down period, or simple distraction can often decrease biting behavior. (See also *Temper Tantrums.*)

A nursing infant or a twelve- to eighteen-month-old may bite a parent accidentally or out of affection. Even so, it is appropriate to say, "Ouch, that hurts," and put the baby down. Avoid overreacting, which can teach a child a quick and effective way to get your negative attention. (See also *Attention-Seeking*.)

Persistent biting behavior in a child over the age of three or four is atypical and you should seek professional consultation.

Boasting

Boasting is another way for a child to garner attention. It's less of a problem in the preschooler, who is probably just engaging in magical thinking and fantasy play. (See *Play* and *Lying*.) But boasting can get a child older than seven years of age into trouble with his peers. At this point, he knows the difference between reality and fantasy, and his friends will be able to pick out his embellishments. He runs the risk of receiving a reputation for lying or being conceited.

Children boast either because they are full of themselves or because their self-esteem is low and they're trying to hide what they see as inadequacies. Boasting seems to occur most frequently in the seventh and eighth grades, when children are often unsure of themselves and peer acceptance is so critically important. They often exaggerate to win acceptance into a clique.

Help a child understand that boasting is no way to make friends. If his self-esteem is low, try to find ways to help him compensate for or overcome his insecurities. (See *Self-Esteem*.) Help him think of ways to befriend other children. (See *Making Friends*.)

If he's bragging about very real talents, teach him about humility and empathy. Ask, "How would you feel if you weren't very good at soccer and your friend kept showing off?"

Also discuss the importance of taking turns and letting other people talk about themselves during a conversation. (See *Talkativeness*.) Then practice what you preach.

Bossiness

Toddlers and preschoolers are infamously bossy. As they develop some autonomy and better language skills, they test out giving directions, just like the ones their parents so often hand down to them. Parents can be mortified to hear their edicts come right back at them. You might hear your eighteen-month-old emphatically saying "No, no, no" to her doll and eventually, "If you keep on, you'll get a time-out."

If your child's tone is really unpleasant, say, "I think there is a nicer way to say that. Try *please* [for instance]." Sometimes children pick up bossy statements from friends, but mostly they come from home. If your child is constantly bossy, examine your own way of talking. It's always best to try to enlist cooperation rather than demanding a child do something. Try statements such as: "It's time to brush your teeth" rather than "Go brush your teeth." Add: "When you've brushed your teeth, we'll be ready for bed and can read a book," or "Boy, it sure is helpful when people brush their teeth. Now we have time to read *two* books."

If children receive too many instructions during the day, requests lose their impact. Try to give choices when it's possible, and save a directive for essentials. Finally, remember that if you want your child to say *please*, he will learn more quickly if you use it, too.

Preschoolers are often bossiest in their play. Try to follow a child's lead in her tea-party scenarios while still reinforcing politeness and cooperative interaction. If you do absolutely everything a child requests (make the bunny do this, make the giraffe say that), she will have a hard time playing with her peers, who will have their own distinct ideas about how a drama should unfold. (See *Play* and *Making Friends*.)

Finally, older siblings often boss younger children. As with most sibling interaction, it is best to let them work out their differences themselves, unless it is hurting someone's feelings or endangering his safety. (See *Sibling Rivalry* and *Teasing*.)

Breath-Holding

It is not all that uncommon for a two- or three-year-old to hold his breath during a temper tantrum. Like screaming or kicking, it's probably meant to attract your attention. Of course, it is far more frightening for parents to watch, especially since some very determined and stubborn children are capable of holding their breath until they turn blue, make themselves nauseous and dizzy, or actually faint.

Be reassured that a child cannot kill himself by holding his breath. Even in the worst-case scenario—he holds his breath long enough to pass out—his body will automatically start breathing as soon as he loses consciousness. Still, tell your pediatrician about the first breath-holding incident so he can rule out the possibility of a febrile seizure.

After that checkup is completed, try to ignore further breath-holding, just as you would a purposeful temper tantrum. Some tantrums are designed to be manipulative while others are more an involuntary result of temperament. (See *Temper tantrums* and *Temperament.*) Try not to become too upset if he does manage to make himself sick. Clean him up with little comment and in a businesslike fashion. If you seem overly concerned or shocked, he will have achieved his goal.

Breath-holding is unusual in an older child. It typically fades as does other attention-seeking behavior as a child becomes more verbal and aware of what behavior is acceptable. If it continues, instigate consequences for his bad behavior. Say, "If you do that again, the following [usually a time-out] will happen." (See *Temper Tantrums* and "Time-outs" under the Parenting Skills Introduction.)

Although you'll be tempted to avoid an episode at all costs because they can be so frightening, do not overprotect or indulge a breath-holder as that will only encourage him to continue. (See also *Impatience*, *Demanding*, and *Attention-Seeking.*)

Bruxism

(See *Teeth-Grinding*)

Bulimia

(See *Eating Disorders*)

Bullying

Bullying is not the normal or occasional hitting or shoving that occurs between playmates. Instead, it is a recurrent pattern of extreme, antisocial aggression that has resisted modification by parents, teachers, or peer pressure. Most children have stopped acting out physically against their playmates by the first or second grade. They have learned self-control, can resolve conflicts through words, and know what is acceptable to their friends. The third-grader who still intimidates or hits classmates is in trouble.

Bullies tend to pick out victims and persecute them repeatedly, by knocking them down, taking their lunch money, or other such actions. Their behavior has a ritualistic quality to it. It is their way of relating to other children. In an odd way, a bully's victims are his friends. But this method of social interaction is self-defeating. The bully is not liked. He is avoided. Consequently, he is vulnerable to developing low self-esteem. Typically, he does poorly in school and can be chronically oppositional with teachers. Such a child is at risk of developing a serious conduct disorder. (See *Oppositional Behavior, Oppositional-Defiant Disorder*, and *Conduct Disorder*.)

71

What to Do

Parents of bullies often don't recognize the problem. It's usually the parents of his victim who call to complain. If their accusations are confirmed by the bully's teacher, you should seek some professional counseling for your child and then examine the methods of communication you are using at home. Is it possible that you are encouraging his aggression by praising him for being tough, dismissing it as "boys will be boys," or insisting that he be stronger than his peers?

Bullying doesn't mean a child is destined to grow up to be a criminal. But it does mean he is deficient in his ability to interact socially and to think through behavior options. Without corrective guidance he may have long-term difficulties fitting in or succeeding academically and professionally. His victims will also continue to suffer from his abuse.

(See also *Aggression*, *Insensitivity*, and *Making Friends*.)

Cheating

Look up "cheat" in the dictionary and you'll find an unsettling list of meanings: to defraud, swindle, deceive, victimize, dupe, violate rules, or be an impostor. These are the attributes of villains, and it's almost impossible to imagine they could apply to children.

In most cases such extremes don't. Children may cheat at games or on tests. Often they do so because they haven't really learned the sanctity of rules or because they panic and suddenly look at a classmate's test paper. Isolated acts of cheating shouldn't be viewed as unpardonable offenses (although parents often act self-righteously shocked when they discover their child has cheated) but as opportunities to help a child build a code of ethics and moral judgment. These lessons will help prevent future dishonest acts.

Cheating at games is common for five- to six-year-olds. They really don't understand rules yet or that breaking them is wrong. When they change rules to suit themselves, it's not with the intention of fooling others or of winning; they simply aren't yet capable of thinking through methods of achieving a goal.

That kind of logic—an awareness and understanding of cause and effect—doesn't come until around the age of seven, when children develop the ability to reason. After achieving this ability, children understand rules and consequences and the concept of right and wrong. (See the Developmental Tasks Appendix.) Cheating at games should subside, especially since children this age are predisposed to respect authority, are more aware of what is acceptable and unacceptable behavior, and are responsive to peer pressure. Children don't like to play with "cheaters."

If children don't respond to these natural censors, they may have impulsive or aggressive personalities or have difficulty understanding instructions. (See *Impulsivity, Aggression, Attention-Deficit Hyperac-*

73

tivity Disorder, and *Language and Speech*.) Perhaps the cause is situational—something about the game or event tempts him. Perhaps a child is under excessive pressure, at home or at school, to be a "winner." (See *Perfectionism* and *Competitiveness*.)

Academic cheating often has a similar situational overtone. A child is afraid of failure, or is expected always to get A's. On the other hand, there may be something about a child's personality that drives him to achieve. He might cheat because *he* (not his parents) insists on "being the best" in his class. He may also have the opposite problem. He may have an undetected learning disability that is causing him to lag behind his peers, and in frustration he looks at someone else's test paper. (See *Learning Disabilities*.)

In any case, cheating in elementary school should be taken seriously because it is so out of character for the age. Schoolwork is not really that difficult yet and children generally are very in touch with what constitutes fair play.

A pattern of cheating may also be a cry for attention. Sometimes when children experience a loss, they show their sadness or anger by defying authority and societal rules. (See *Oppositional Behavior*, *Reaction to Parental Conflict*, and *Reaction to Loss*.)

Academic cheating is, unfortunately, commonplace with teenagers as they become more aware of its specific short-term benefits. Good grades bring good colleges. (A 1989 Girl Scouts survey on the beliefs and moral values of America's children found 65 percent of high school students would cheat on an exam.) Teachers usually first report cheating during junior high school. This is, of course, the time children become painfully aware of how they compare with their peers, academically as well as socially.

What to Do

Don't overreact, especially if your child admits cheating on his own volition. Your first thought might be that you've been a failure as a parent, but you're doing very well if your child feels safe coming and telling you about wrongdoing. That's particularly true of a ten- to twelve-year-old, who by virtue of his developmental stage is far more secretive and interested in his peers' opinion than in yours.

Ask why he cheated. His answer will tell you what to do. Don't settle for "I don't know." Keep probing in a gentle, supportive way.

If it was situational—he felt inadequately prepared for a test and was afraid of flunking—help him find alternatives. Arrange for a tutor in the subject, help him study, or structure homework time more carefully within the family schedule. Cheating is often a shortcut or a spur-of-the-moment act of desperation. Using prepared crib notes is a far more serious act than glancing over at another's paper, since it shows intent. (See *Motivation* and *Procrastination*.)

If he cheated because he wanted an A rather than a B, examine how much pressure you or the school put on him. Are those expectations realistic? His actions may also be a result of low self-esteem. In that case, give him more positive feedback. You must walk a delicate line between recognizing your child's limitations while still encouraging him to achieve all that he can. Tell him a B is acceptable if it reflects his best efforts. But if you suspect your child is performing below his potential, seek guidance and more information from his school. (See *Self-Esteem* and *Motivation*.)

Avoid moralizing or harsh punishments. If your child has been caught cheating, he has already received some consequences: He's been embarrassed and knows that he has disappointed you. Being punitive or derisive will probably drive the behavior underground. View this as an opportunity to help your child better understand himself, his motives, and his responsibilities. If you handle a relatively innocent and isolated incident well early on, you'll help prevent further, and more profound, ethical mistakes.

Finally, watch your own behavior. Constantly doing your child's homework or science projects for him says that you don't think his work is good enough and that turning in someone else's work as one's own (i.e., plagiarism) is okay.

Chores and Cleaning Room

Assigning a child a reasonable number of household chores helps build his self-esteem. It makes him feel like a competent, responsible, trusted member of a team (your family). He'll feel good about himself when he sees that he has helped you. We all like to feel useful and needed, and chores give a child a sense of accomplishment, especially if you compliment his work. Chores will also help teach him some self-reliance, self-discipline, and that some tasks just need doing.

Of course, chores need to be age-appropriate, not overwhelming in scope, and things that really need doing, not just busywork. Keep regular chores separate from allowances or extra money. You want children to contribute to keeping house because it's their home, not because they're being paid for it. (See *Allowances*.) Paying extra money for larger jobs, such as cleaning out the garage or mowing the lawn, is another matter.

What to Do

When you want something done, be simple, clear, and direct. Don't pose a request in a question: "Would you like to pick up your toys now?" Say instead, "It's time to pick up your toys now, please." Don't fall into lengthy explanations of why things need doing, because you inadvertently feed procrastination that way.

Make your request while in the same room with the child. Even better, make eye contact. Calling to him from downstairs rarely works. Try to time your request when it has a greater likelihood of success: Don't ask a child to pick up his room when he's right in the middle of a game. (See *Listening*.)

With younger children, it's best to enlist their help and direct their work rather than expect them to do an entire job solo. Ask preschoolers to pick up the pieces to a specific puzzle while you put away their other toys, for instance. Praise them as being "such big helpers."

In fact, helping parents is fun for most children under the age of five. They don't need much motivation if you're going to be alongside them. Include them in sorting and putting away laundry, dusting furniture, or setting the table (don't give them your best crystal to carry, but something that won't matter if it's broken). Maybe have a broom that's just their size to help you sweep. Besides being fun for them, including preschoolers in household activities establishes helpful habits and attitudes more easily than trying to initiate them later on.

As with any activity meant to help build a child's self-esteem, set up chores so there is a greater than average chance of a child accomplishing the task. No child, for instance, is going to be able to wade into a room that's literally knee-deep in toys and organize them. Have boxes already marked to hold certain items: puzzles, Legos, crayons, cars, blocks. Get rid of the excess that really isn't played with any longer.

With younger children, work together and make it as much of a game as possible. "Can you get that toy into the chest before I count to ten?" "How many cars can you find?" "How many red things can you find?" are good questions to make cleanup more fun.

Most important, compliment a child's work and don't expect perfection. So what if there are a few spots of dust left? Don't go right back and redo or criticize. You'll not only run the risk of hurting a child's feelings and self-esteem, but also of discouraging her from even trying next time. If it is important enough to correct, do it in a positive fashion. Say, "You really did a good job over there. Thank you. Let's just finish up this last spot together." She still feels a sense of accomplishment, while learning that a task well done can still stand a few improvements. (See also *Perfectionism.*)

When children are ready to do things on their own, be explicit in your directions. Rather than saying, "Clean your room," be specific: "Hang up your clothes in the closet and put your books on the shelves."

Bestowing rewards helps keep a child motivated. Reward systems are used to increase desirable behavior (not to stop bad behavior). (See the Parenting Skills Introduction.) Build in an expectation of a 75 percent performance, not perfection. Then be sure to deliver the reward when a child earns it. If a child was promised an outing after getting seven stars, for instance, follow through. The most effective rewards are time with you or events such as a movie.

With the question of cleaning up bedrooms, be aware that there can be a fine line between asking a child to be responsible and being intrusive. It's perfectly reasonable to require a child to keep track of his things, to put dirty clothes in a hamper and clean clothes away, but don't expect him to be as meticulous as you are.

Draw the line when safety and daily functioning become an issue.

Having some toys on the floor is probably okay as long as a child doesn't stumble or fall over them; it's okay for clothes to be a little messy as long as they're not damaged and the child can find them to get dressed and off to school in the morning.

With preteens, it's probably time to show some reasonable respect for their bedroom's sanctity. The door to a room can always be closed so that you don't have to be offended by its decor.

Finally, temper your expectations while not giving up your requests. Children aren't proud of tasks left half done, no matter how much they complain in the process. Acknowledge that sometimes chores can seem dull but it's an admirable trait to finish jobs and live up to responsibilities. Then, count yourself lucky and your children well motivated if they do their chores more often than not, with minimal reminding on your part and only a small amount of whining or muttering on theirs.

Clinging

A big bear hug from a child is a great gift that shows she's affectionate and demonstrative. If she constantly clings to your leg, however, it's a different story. It suggests a child is hesitant or nervous in a new situation, or, at its worst, that she is fearful and has pronounced anxiety about separating from you.

Some children just seem to be born clingy. By temperament, they are hesitant in new situations, dependent on parents, perhaps shy or "slow to warm." (See *Temperament*, *Adaptability*, and *Shyness*.) Clinging provides comfort and a sense of safety, a reassurance that parents are physically there for them.

Many children go through predictable clingy phases: at nine to twelve months of age, when separation anxiety and stranger anxiety set in; as toddlers, when they struggle with asserting their independence all the while needing parental involvement and guidance. (A two-year-old's outburst of "No, no, no" may quickly be followed by his scrambling into your lap for a dose of security.) Preschoolers often cling as they enter nursery school and are called upon to separate for longer periods of time from their parents and to integrate into larger play-groups. (See *Anxiety* and the Developmental Tasks Appendix.)

Children cling more when they're tired or under stress. A major life-style change, such as the birth of a sibling, also causes children to hang onto parents' pantlegs. This last form of clinging is often part of an overall regression to more babyish behavior, when a child suddenly whines more, refuses to separate or do for himself what he had been doing alone for quite some time. (See *Regression*, *Attention-Seeking*, and *Sibling Rivalry*.)

What to Do

Try not to push a very young child away, as that may only heighten her fears that you'll abandon her. While it may sometimes be appropriate for older children who know better, scolding a young child with "You're acting like a baby" could damage her fledgling self-esteem.

It's important to recognize the difference between a "slow to warm" temperament and inappropriate behavior. Clinging is often more about anxiety than about manipulation. Give an innately hesitant child a hug and some reassuring words. Don't shove her into a new situation and immediately leave. Help her get acclimated and find something to interest her. When you take a clingy child to nursery school, for instance, help her start playing with a puzzle or a toy before leaving. Put something of yours in her pocket—maybe a handkerchief sprayed with a bit of your perfume—that she can pull out and use to remind herself of home when she feels anxious. Or let her carry her beloved teddy with her (if her nursery school allows it and her classmates won't tease her).

Remember that if you seem nervous about her growing autonomy, you may actually encourage the clinging in subtle ways. If you seem distressed at leaving her, why shouldn't she be, too? Reassure her with your facial expression and with words: "Everything is going to be just fine, really." (See *Anxiety*.)

Finally, if your child's tendency to cling increases suddenly and seems clearly a reaction to a particular event, give her time to adjust. With some added support and reassurance, most children will give up regressive clinging all on their own in a few weeks. (See *Reaction to Loss* and *Reaction to Parental Conflict*.)

As your child ages, clinging will clearly become less appropriate, but if it continues into grade school, try to discover if something specific is troubling her and consider seeking the advice of a mental-health professional.

Clowning

Clowning is a method of getting attention. Much like boasting, it's a behavior that may bespeak a lack of social skills. While some children really are popular with peers because of their wit, most children fall short of that sophisticated mark. There's a big difference between being a comedian and being a clown. A comedian may make others laugh, but a clown is often laughed at.

A little bit of clowning is probably fine, but if a child seems to be hurting his peer standing or class work, you should think about what could be motivating his behavior. Is he receiving enough attention from you at home? Is he trying to cover up something he feels is an inadequacy, maybe even a hidden learning disability? Despite his extroversion, a child who clowns may, in fact, have very low self-esteem and think people wouldn't be interested in him if he didn't "act funny." He may also have a problem with impulsivity and tend to interrupt teachers and other children.

Talk to a child who clowns about conversational skills, about being quiet long enough for others to talk, and about how interrupting people may hurt their feelings. Ask, "How would you feel if you were talking about something and someone started making faces at you?" Discuss other ways to make friends. (See *Making Friends* and *Interrupting*.)

Tell him he's not funny if he's not. Gently, of course. Compliment his non-clowning attributes: "I really like it when we can talk quietly like this." Remind him he's clowning when he lapses into the behavior, but avoid giving it too much attention as that may serve to fuel it. Similarly, lectures on the seriousness of life are sure to fall on deaf ears or promote more silly behavior.

Clumsiness

Being clumsy can be hard on a child. He may spill drinks on himself, break dishes, bump into things, and knock over siblings' precious treasures. He may be yelled at frequently because his clumsiness wreaks havoc in a household and upsets the flow of a meal or a family outing.

He'll probably fare no better at school. A child who is genuinely clumsy is at a disadvantage socially. He won't be picked for a team. A boy may be demeaned as a sissy if he can't compete athletically, a girl targeted as unfeminine if she can't skip rope or dance.

With all these factors, a clumsy child is likely to have a bruised self-esteem. You can help your child by keeping several things in mind:

Children's coordination should be viewed along a continuum. Not everyone is a ballerina, a gymnast, or a quarterback. And most eventually outgrow clumsiness.

Between the ages of two and five, children are learning to balance themselves, to run smoothly, and change direction without falling over. They are finding out, through experience, how they move through space and what their bodies must feel like. Humans learn to control their bodies basically from the head down. First, we balance our heads on our necks. Then we learn to hold our torso steady as we sit. Perfecting our ability to walk, throw a ball, or run takes time and a lot of practice. There will be mishaps along the way.

Coordination also improves with physical maturation of the brain. During the stage between two and five years of age, many vital neuronal interconnections are still being established. (Neurons pass information within the brain. We are born with all our neurons, but many of the communication pathways among them—the electrical wiring, as it were—must still be laid down.)

Try to keep this in mind if you have a clumsy preschooler. Within a year or two, his coordination should improve. Chiding him now for overturning his milk will only make him self-conscious and unsure of himself. Help him achieve physical challenges safely to improve his confidence. Stand close by as he climbs up a tall slide. Give him big, easy-to-see balls to kick or throw.

As he gets older, don't push him to join a highly competitive soccer or baseball team if he doesn't want to, even though participating can improve coordination. For others it might make them more anxious and consequently even more clumsy. Perhaps try a less competitive league first or more individualized sports such as swimming or riding instead.

Watch to see if he appears nearsighted. Eye-hand coordination is obviously enhanced by good vision.

If a child continues to be *remarkably* clumsy, he may have a malfunction in how he processes information. Many clumsy children don't analyze things well visually. They may have trouble learning their ABCs, for instance. Clumsiness can be associated with learning disabilities and reading problems. Language-based learning disabilities are probably the result of the brain's faulty processing of information, *not* a careless or poorly motivated personality. (See *Learning Disabilities.*)

Finally, some children who are extraordinarily clumsy have motor sequencing problems, which may also show up as poor handwriting. Again, like learning disabilities, such difficulties may result from faulty communication between the brain's neurons. Indiscernible handwriting can also lead to poor motivation in school. If your child's poor handwriting is caused by motor-sequencing / output problems, talk to teachers about recognizing the difference between content and quality of writing. A mental-health professional who specializes in learning disabilities could help make that determination.

In general, severe persistent clumsiness should also be evaluated by a pediatrician.

Colic

Babies who suffer from colic sleep fitfully, can't be soothed, pass a lot of gas, and truly seem to be in physical distress. Colic usually happens in the evening and during the first three months of an infant's life. In most cases, it seems to stop miraculously around a baby's fourth month.

No one knows the exact cause of colic. Its root may be related to either neurological or gastrointestinal immaturity. A baby goes through incredibly rapid physiological changes during his first three months.

His digestive system is immature, which may lead to muscle spasms in his stomach and intestines. There is also some evidence that colic may be exacerbated by cow's milk.

What to Do

Talk to your pediatrician to make sure your baby doesn't have a medical condition. The doctor may switch the baby's formula or suggest changes in your diet if you're breast-feeding.

But the real aid for colic is vibration and motion. Many parents report that taking an infant for a ride in a stroller or a car, carrying him around in a Snugli so that he feels the sway and warmth of their body, or putting him in a baby swing helps.

To prevent the severity of the nightly bouts, make sure a baby burps adequately after feeding. Hold him upright for longer periods than you would a noncolicky baby. Avoid overstimulating him after dinner. If a baby is very tired, he will sleep badly and become irritable, which in turn will worsen his colic. This is a common problem since a working parent usually comes home in the evening and wants to play. But if the exchange seems to make his colic worse, forgo it for a while. If it's classic colic it will disappear by the time a baby is four months old.

If it doesn't, a baby may simply have a fussy temperament. (See *Crying* and *Temperament*.)

Recommended reading: *Cry Babies, Coping with Colic: What to Do When Your Baby Won't Stop Crying*, by Marc Weissbluth, M.D. (Berkley Books).

Competitiveness

Competitiveness is probably a basic survival instinct. It is also a cultural value in Western societies such as ours. Our free-market economy certainly has an element of only the fittest shall survive (or at least climb to recognition and affluence).

A little bit of competitiveness in a child will make his adjustment to challenges go more smoothly. It will help motivate him to improve himself, to work hard, to test his limits, and to constantly move forward. If a child has no "competitive drive," he may never realize his potential. And it is through recognizing and honing skills that a child's self-esteem grows.

A particularly fierce sense of competition, however, may result in problems. Too much may mean he never does anything—plays a game, for instance—for the sheer pleasure of doing so. He does it only to win. What if he fails? What happens to his self-esteem and confidence if he can accept nothing but being the best? No one can be the best all the time. (See *Self-Esteem* and *Perfectionism*.)

Being too competitive also means a child probably studies not to learn but to get that all-important A. Such a means-to-an-end attitude about academics may promote cheating, cutting ethical corners, or lying to parents if he fails. A fanatically competitive child may also have difficulty working cooperatively on projects, playing on a team, or making friends. Who wants to spend time with someone who *has* to win a game or throws a fit when he loses?

Such competitiveness can also exacerbate sibling rivalry. Some rivalry between siblings is normal, of course, and probably healthy. It will be strongest when children are the same sex or close in age, or if one has a particular and outstanding talent.

As parents, you can make rivalry counterproductive, however, by comparing your children unfavorably. It drives a wedge between them. Remember that someday you won't be around, and that your family will then be defined by your children's relationships with one another. (See *Sibling Rivalry*.)

Another common form of childhood competition manifests itself not in contests against a child's contemporaries or siblings, but in fighting the parent of the same sex for the attention of the opposite-sex parent. This is part of Sigmund Freud's famous Oedipus complex theory. A century ago it was considered outrageous, but today the fact that a three- or four-year-old boy "falls in love" with his mommy (or a girl with her daddy) is considered to be about as normal and nonthreatening as learning to ride a tricycle.

Your best response is to recognize the family triangle, accept your child's behavior and attention with good humor, but don't encourage it. A little girl is *not* her daddy's "little girlfriend." Children do not have that kind of relationship with adults and using such phrases may confuse a child and render her vulnerable to inappropriate approaches from older people.

What to Do

If your child has a worrisome competitive streak, first examine the pressure you put on him. Could he feel that your love or approval is contingent on his winning?

Temper unhealthy competitiveness by playing games at home without keeping score. Introduce the concept of "personal best," helping him to judge himself against his past abilities. Is he improving? That's achievement rather than competition.

Praise him for *trying* his hardest. That's different from being the best. Praise him, too, for being a good sport if he loses a match. Reassure him that tomorrow is another day, with another chance to improve himself. Life is full of wins and losses, and it's important that a child be able to cope with both experiences and still value himself.

If you feel he has the opposite problem, that he's not competitive enough, again examine yourself. Are the goals you have for him realistic? Does he share them? Or are you projecting your own unfulfilled ambitions on him? Some children are temperamentally less driven, less competitive. Remember, not everyone can or should try to be a star.

(See also *Self-Esteem, Perfectionism, Motivation, Procrastination,* and *School.*)

Recommended reading: *Children of Fast-Track Parents: Raising Self-Sufficient and Confident Children in an Achievement-Oriented World,* by Andree Aelion Brooks (Viking Press).

Complaining

Complaining is really just a more verbal form of whining, and you can respond to it in a similar fashion. Give children the clear message that it doesn't work and that they should find more appropriate ways of expressing their wants or needs. Don't respond with anger, even at a very common complaint: "You never give me anything." You can defuse the power of such a statement by answering dispassionately, "That's not true. You're going to have to find another way of telling me what you're feeling."

Temperament is something that may affect a child's level of complaining. A fussy baby, who was always quick to become upset and hard to console, is more likely than a calm baby to grow into a preschooler who whines and complains. Still, you can help a child learn more constructive, acceptable ways of expressing his discomfort or anxiety. (See *Attention-Seeking*, *Demanding*, *Bossiness*, *Whining*, and *Adaptability*.)

School-aged children are cognitively capable of being reasoned with if you have already set the stage by not giving in to temper tantrums during toddlerhood. Discuss the feelings behind complaints, once they are properly voiced to you. Then explain your reasons for granting or denying a request. (See *Argumentative*.)

Finally, remember that children learn through your example. If they hear you constantly complain about work or relatives, they are likely to follow suit.

Compliance

Like many other personality traits, a child's compliance may be the result of innate temperament or of conditioning. The child who is constantly reprimanded, punished, or even abused, may adopt a habit of conformity as a defense. Another child might be born with a ready-to-please personality, and is often lauded as being an "easy" baby. She probably rarely fusses, is sweet and gentle by nature, and opens her mouth like a little bird as she begins feeding. Mothers of such children count themselves lucky.

It is the extremes of behavior that should concern parents. If a child shows no initiative or *never* questions authority, explore the reasons for her passivity or actively encourage her ideas. When playing with a submissive toddler, resist the constant temptation to show her how to build a block tower, for instance. Wait patiently for her to construct something, even if it's only two blocks in a line, and say, "I really like what you did." Don't automatically set out clothes for your passive preschooler. Let her choose among two or three outfits that are suited to the weather.

Maintain reasonable flexibility in limit-setting. Listen to her reasons for wanting to do something you forbid. If they are logical and she's reached an age at which that limit may no longer be necessary, let her win the point. (See *Self-Sufficiency*.) Allow her to say no to foods she truly dislikes and to determine the amount she eats at mealtime. (See *Food Refusal*.)

Such small, progressive autonomies will give her the self-confidence to say no later in life to peers who may pressure her to try something she doesn't want to do. (See also the Parenting Skills Introduction.)

Compulsions

It is fairly common for children to develop curious rituals or food fads. Some will eat only hot dogs cut a particular way; others get dressed in a certain order, or have to count all the steps while going upstairs to the bath. These habits are normal, self-soothing control mechanisms, a way of establishing predictability and autonomy in a world largely dictated by adults and outside forces. (See *Food Refusal* and *Dressing*.)

Compulsions, on the other hand, are repetitive, purposeful actions designed to neutralize discomfort and which interfere with day-to-day activities. For instance, a child is so preoccupied with washing her hands that she can't come to the dinner table night after night, or has rituals surrounding dressing that are so complicated and lengthy that she constantly misses the school bus. Such behavior suggests underlying emotional problems. She may dread something about eating or going to school, and believes if she is not allowed to follow her compulsions something awful will happen.

The sad thing about compulsions is that they never really accomplish what they're designed to do. They do not provide calm or reassurance—that's why a person is *compelled* to repeat a behavior over and over again.

If a child is very rigid in her habits or continually throws tantrums (past the age of three) when activities can't be done in a prescribed, ritualistic fashion, she needs some help. She should also be evaluated by a child psychiatrist to consider the possibility of taking medications that have been shown to reduce and control compulsive behavior and to learn ways of helping her become more adaptable or cope with fears that often precipitate compulsions. (See also *Anxiety*, *Fears and Phobias*, and *Panic*.)

Concentration

A child's ability to concentrate and to remain attentive are closely related skills and are vital to learning. The ability to selectively focus attention is the first step. Maintaining that focus (concentration) is the second. Through concentration, a child learns and remembers information to apply elsewhere.

Some children can concentrate on a book or a puzzle in the middle of a crowded, noisy subway stop. Other children are easily distracted by sounds or by visually stimulating environments. Some have very low frustration tolerance and may angrily break off their concentration when a tower of blocks falls or a math equation won't work.

Even though the ability to sustain concentration varies according to a child's individual temperament, it is really more a trained skill than a natural talent. You can help a child improve his concentration with a few simple techniques. (Children diagnosed with Attention-Deficit Hyperactivity Disorder are going to have a much harder time focusing their attention and concentrating on a task. See *Attention-Deficit Hyperactivity Disorder.*)

First, make sure the environment suits your child's concentration powers when you want him to focus on a task. If he's easily disturbed, find a quiet place for him to study; don't fill his playroom with too many toys. Too much will overwhelm him and actually discourage his exploration. (See *Play.*)

If he's easily frustrated, help him develop patience as early as possible. When his block tower collapses, say, "Oh well, that happens. Sometimes it's hard. Let's try again." Put two up and let him finish the rest. (See *Impatience*, *Self-Esteem*, and *Play.*)

Make concentration and mental activity fun. Games let a child practice and hone his abilities without realizing it's work. Try the card game "concentration," in which players turn over cards and try to remember their location to match pairs. Play word-association games, such as naming a state or a city starting with the last letter of the place an opponent has just said. Even singing "Old MacDonald Had a Farm" and other childhood songs or rhymes will help young children develop the ability to learn long sequences. Some educational computer games are also designed to help older children sharpen their ability to focus and concentrate.

(See also *Memory Development.*)

Conduct Disorder

Conduct disorder is a persistent pattern of antisocial behavior that lasts at least six months and that violates societal norms or the basic rights of others. Stealing, running away from home, frequent lying, fire-setting, truancy, vandalism, being cruel to animals, and sexually victimizing someone are all behaviors listed in the American Psychiatric Association's diagnostic manual as belonging to childhood conduct disorders.

"Juvenile delinquency" is a legal term, meaning a child has been caught by authorities and charged with engaging in such activities. In most cases, if the juvenile delinquent is evaluated, he will be diagnosed as having a conduct disorder.

Typically these children do poorly in school, have few friends without conduct problems themselves, and can be extremely hostile and aggressive. Rarely does a child develop conduct disorders overnight. Usually, these children have shown behavior problems for quite some time and may have been previously diagnosed with oppositional defiant disorder, a less severe disorder. Conduct-disorder cases tend to be boys who have shown a pattern of aggression, hyperactivity, and impulsivity from early childhood. They often want immediate gratification and to be in control. (See *Aggression*, *Bullying*, *Lying*, *Stealing*, and *Oppositional Defiant Disorder*.)

Children with Attention-Deficit Hyperactivity Disorder (ADHD) or with alcoholic, mentally ill, or divorced parents, or those living in poverty, are thought to be at higher risk of developing conduct disorders. Conduct disorders always require professional help. (See also *Antisocial Behavior*, *Cruelty to Animals*, *Truancy*, and *Fire-Setting*.)

Confidence

(See *Self-Esteem*, *Self-Sufficiency*)

Constipation

A constipated child is one who has a marked difficulty during bowel movements. It has nothing to do with frequency or regularity. A constipated baby will show clear signs of distress while trying to have a bowel movement. He'll cry, and draw up or kick his legs. His stools may look hard and pebbly. Consult your pediatrician about methods for helping your child with constipation.

A constipated baby may have extreme discomfort when he tries to pass a stool. If he begins to associate pain with bowel movements, a baby may hold them back, setting up a vicious cycle. Withholding causes more constipation, which causes increased pain and more withholding.

Eventually, bowels can become blocked by fecal retention. If that has happened, a child will actually seem to have some watery diarrhea as fecal matter is leaking around this accumulated and painful mass. See a doctor immediately to treat this condition. (See also *Soiling*.)

A tendency to constipation is important to keep in mind when toilet training your child. Don't embarrass or scold him for a soiling accident, since he's likely to try to retain his bowel movements, again setting up a physically painful cycle that is likely to ruin any attempts at toilet training. (See *Toilet Training*.)

Allow a school-aged child plenty of time to use the bathroom in the morning at home. Many children dislike public bathrooms and may hold back bowel movements during the school day as a result.

Crawling

By nine months of age, most babies are moving forward either on their hands and knees or by squirming their bodies along the ground. Crawling is an important motoric milestone, but it's also vital to a child's psychosocial development. It's a statement of independence and curiosity as well as physical dexterity. Now a baby is mobile and doesn't have to wait for someone to carry him over to that intriguing object he wants to handle.

To allow a child to explore safely, be sure to childproof your home. It helps to get down on your hands and knees and examine the house from his perspective. You'll be shocked at the number of nails and splinters protruding from the underbellies of furniture. (See *Accident-Prone*.)

This is the age many parents give their child walkers. Some pediatricians worry that walkers may interrupt a child's natural sequence of motoric accomplishments, preventing him from first pulling himself up and "cruising" along the edge of furniture. A real danger is that a child in a walker is at greater risk of tumbling down the stairs.

Cross-Gender Behavior

(See *Playing with Dolls*, *Gender Identity Disorder*)

Cruelty to Animals

Under the age of three, children may not recognize that pulling a cat's tail hurts the cat. As a parent, you should treat animals kindly yourself to act as a model of appropriate behavior, but you should also directly teach children how to interact with animals. For one thing, it can be critical to your child's safety. An aggravated pet, no matter how passive, may eventually lash out in self-defense. Say, "No, that hurts Kitty," then take the child's hand and gently stroke the cat to show correct behavior.

After a child is three years old, he should be capable of some empathy and recognize that he's inflicting pain. (See *Insensitivity*.) If he persists in hurting animals, he may have poor impulse control (perhaps coexisting with Attention-Deficit Hyperactivity Disorder) or an aggressive temperament that needs some active behavior modification (see *Aggression*). Children who have been abused may try to regain control of their lives by abusing beings smaller than they are. If they feel neglected they may act out to try to garner attention. (See *Depression*.)

In any case, children who persist in hurting animals are at risk of

experimenting with other cruel or violent acts that are part of conduct disorders. (See *Conduct Disorder*, *Bullying*, and *Antisocial Behavior*.)

Crying

Crying is a baby's language. It tells you that he's hungry, wet, hot or cold, bored, frustrated, frightened, or lonely. After some time to-gether, you will be able to differentiate the tone of your baby's cries. You'll recognize the different messages that different cries carry, and learn how fast you have to make it up the stairs to your baby's bedroom.

Of course, some babies cry more than others because of tempera-ment. Perhaps they were born fussy, quick to become upset, and hard to calm. (See *Temperament*.) Other babies suffer colic, which usually goes away after an infant reaches four months of age. (See *Colic*.)

Around six months of age, most babies simply cry less. They experi-ence far fewer physical discomforts, and physiological changes have slowed. They are also a little more sure of their environment and have some capacity for self-soothing. You can help facilitate your baby's ability to calm himself by giving him transitional objects, such as stuffed animals, pacifiers, or blankets; calling to a baby as you come to him; or patting his bottom rather than always picking him up.

It's important that before the end of his first year a child begins to develop some ability to comfort himself, since this is when his cries will take on a new tone that's harder to soothe. He's afraid when you leave him now, and sometimes you simply must. (See "Separation Anxiety" and "Stranger Anxiety" under *Anxiety*.)

In toddlerhood, violent, loud crying is common and typically the expression of frustration. It's critical for you to recognize the difference between tears of distress and those meant to manipulate. (See *Temper Tantrums*, *Temperament*, *Adaptability*, and *Oppositional Behavior*.) As a child acquires more language, so that he can voice his emotions and needs in words, the frequency of his crying should subside.

Crying remains a natural and normal expression of pain or sadness throughout our lives. But a child who is excessively weepy for long periods is unusual and probably in need of some extra attention from parents. Frequent crying in an older child should be brought to the attention of a qualified mental-health professional. (See *Reaction to Loss, Reaction to Parental Conflict, Sadness, Depression, Anxiety*, and *School Phobia*.)

What to Do

Infants

It is difficult for parents to spoil an infant during the first four months of life. Respond to his cries quickly. Doing so builds his trust in the world, in you, and in himself. It tells him that there is a reliable someone out there to answer his needs and that he has the ability to affect the world around him. (See Erikson's "trust versus mistrust" in the Developmental Tasks Appendix.) Letting a baby "cry it out" will not teach him to cry less at this stage. In fact, some studies indicate that the more you respond to a baby's cries during his early infancy, the less he will cry overall and later on.

After four or five months of age, most babies cry less. Their neurological and gastrointestinal systems should have stabilized and evening colic has probably disappeared. This is when you can begin helping a baby learn to calm himself a bit. When you know that a baby is fed, dry, warm, comfortable, and safe (and when his cries are of the non-emergency nature), use methods other than picking him up to comfort him. Talk to him from across the room. Give him a stuffed animal to cuddle. These objects serve as "distance receptors." They tell a baby that, yes, you are still around and everything is okay.

Often a baby cries because he wants stimulation. When you can't hold him and play—dinners do need to be fixed and other children attended to—set him up in a way that he can entertain himself. Put him in a bounce seat so that he can watch you prepare the meal or see things moving outside the window or his reflection in a child-safe mirror. Give him a rattle or a favorite toy.

This is also the time to establish "place holders." Try to help him build a little bit of an ability to delay gratification (but remember that babies and toddlers are not capable of much in this regard). As you come up the

94

stairs, call, "I'm coming"; or as you fix his bottle and he can see you doing so, say, "I'm getting it." His cries should slow. At some point they may even stop as he anticipates your bringing him his food because he sees you preparing it. He's learned that sequential connection.

This is also the time to try to let a baby fall asleep in the crib, not in your arms. If he's dry and fed, don't pick him up or turn on the lights when he cries in the night. Talk to him, touch him lightly, and generally reassure him that you are there. At this stage, he just wants you and isn't afraid of the dark. That comes later. (See *Sleep.*) Of course, all these techniques have varying success depending on the personality of your baby. Temperamentally volatile babies are probably going to remain more resistant to change and need extra patience and reassurance. (See *Temperament* and *Adaptability.*)

It is easy to forget to consider the influence of physical ailments on a child's crying style. A round of ear infections is sure to make a baby more needy and clingy, and harder to soothe. Keep in mind that out-of-character or excessive irritability can be a red flag that something is medically wrong. Consult your pediatrician. Teething also causes an infant pain and is likely to make him fussier. (Try giving him a teething ring soaked in ice water.)

Colicky babies also need special attention during their fussy bouts. (See *Colic*). A gentle, swaying motion is generally the cure. Give a baby a ride in the car, stroller, or baby swing. There are even devices to vibrate his crib. Some children like being swaddled or being carried about in a Snugli. Putting a newborn crossways in the crib rather than the usual top-to-bottom position may help since all that open space is actually disquieting to him.

And all children are calmed by being held. In most traditional societies, children are simply strapped onto the mother and carried about, feeling her warmth and lulled by the rocking of her movement.

Finally, try not to blame yourself harshly if you can't immediately soothe a baby. You'll learn how to calm your baby through trial and error. Also, remember that it is only recently that mothers have been isolated in their homes to care for babies all alone. In preindustrialized societies, and ones that are less mobile than ours, childcare is a shared job among female family members. Try to arrange help so that you can take a few breaks to replenish your patience.

Toddlers and Preschoolers

Crying at this stage generally stems from a child's frustration while trying to achieve some independence but being uncertain about it, or from your imposition of limits. (See *Temper Tantrums*, *Oppositional Behavior*, and the Developmental Tasks Appendix.) It's important to handle separation from a child with empathy and calm reassurance. If you are distraught at the sight of his tears, they will only get worse. (See *Anxiety*.)

School-Aged and Older Children

Many children will cry when they skin their knees, when they get on the school bus for the first time, when a friend moves away, or when their pet dies. Occasional crying is a normal and probably very healthy emotional response. However, long periods of sadness accompanied by listless behavior, and changes in eating and sleeping habits and in friends and activities, may suggest that a child is depressed or anxious. (See *Sadness*, *Reaction to Loss*, *Reaction to Parental Conflict*, *Anxiety*, *Depression*, and *School*.)

Recommended reading: *Your Baby & Child: From Birth to Age Five*, by Penelope Leach, Ph.D. (Alfred A. Knopf); *The First Twelve Months of Life* and *The Second Twelve Months of Life*, by Frank and Theresa Caplan (both Perigee books/ Putnam Publishing).

Curiosity

Curiosity is a wonderful human drive almost as powerful as hunger. And it often seems strongest during childhood. Children want to know how something works, where it came from, and why, why, why just for the pleasure and fun of knowing. There's no chore to it. A curious child is a human being still amazed and thrilled by the world's mysteries.

That's part of the joy of being a parent, to taste that wonder again through your children.

The degree of a child's curiosity may have a temperamental basis, but it's a trait that can easily be fostered or squashed by his environment. Different cultures have differing tolerances for curiosity in children. Fortunately, in the United States curiosity is valued, and recognized as an indication of intelligence and as a requirement for science, innovation, or inventing. Most schools, book publishers, and public broadcasting stations and many toy manufacturers have responded to the need to stimulate curiosity in children.

Of course, an inquisitive toddler who rushes to pull apart everything in his excitement to learn can tax the patience and nerves of even the most attentive parent. Carefully childproof your home to ease the tension caused by such a knee-high inquisitor. Lock up harmful substances (including liquor and any kind of medication) and plug up electrical sockets. Get on your hands and knees and explore the house to see what intriguing dangers present themselves to crawling or toddling babies. (See *Accident-Prone* and *Risk-Taking*.)

The older child who literally asks "why?" about everything and in response to each answer you give can also be wearing, but try to retain the energy you need to help him learn. Avoid plopping him in front of the TV to distract him from asking questions. Science camps and trips to museums and libraries help provide him with the stimuli he seeks. Don't be afraid to admit, "I don't know the answer; let's find out together." You'll teach him about research and that learning goes on throughout life.

Some children simply aren't as curious (or as persistent about it) as others. This is no cause for alarm, unless a child shows absolutely no interest in exploring. A twelve-month-old baby who rarely reaches out to mobiles or brightly colored objects may have a problem. A complete lack of curiosity is unusual and could be an indicator of infant depression or developmental delays. Talk to your pediatrician.

97

Daydreaming

Daydreaming is an important part of creative thinking. It is a common and normal human behavior, one which is probably best judged along Goldilocks's criterion: Is it too much, too little, or just right? Too much daydreaming may mean a child misses out on important discussions at school or home; too little that he is unusually concrete and unable to entertain himself with thoughts of his own making. Just right means a child has a capacity for fantasy and whimsy, plus a healthy, intellectual ability to deal with things in his own mind.

Daydreaming often involves reliving memories or playing out wishes and alternatives. It functions as a coping mechanism for boredom. A very bright child in a tedious or unchallenging class is likely to fill in the spaces with daydreaming, since he's not receiving enough intellectual stimulation. When a smart, basically motivated child is criticized by teachers for daydreaming, they and his parents need to find ways to make schoolwork more interesting and appropriately challenging for him.

Children may also use daydreaming to block out something that makes them anxious: the teacher, the classroom bully, or the difficulty they're having in learning the material. (See *School* and *Learning Disabilities*.) Or they may use it as a way of procrastinating or ignoring directions, in which case a child might be engaging in a pattern of oppositional tactics. (See *Oppositional Behavior*.)

Daydreaming can also be a defense against unpleasant realities. Children grieving about the death of a relative, or going through their parents' divorce, alcoholism, depression, or abuse may be prone to daydreaming or seem distractible in general.

In a few extreme cases pronounced daydreaming may be a sign that a child is reliving a traumatic event in a syndrome called Post-Traumatic Stress Disorder (PTSD). Persistent daydreaming that seems bizarre and unintelligible to parents may be a sign of other, more serious problems.

Such seemingly delusional musing should be brought to the attention of a pediatrician or a mental-health professional. Likewise if a child seems to be staring blankly, completely unaware of his surroundings, and you have great difficulty getting his attention. (See *Staring Episodes*.)

Most daydreaming, however, is perfectly fine, even enriching, and should be tolerated by adults. The more a child can describe and share his daydreams, the less a parent should worry about them. If he's secretive about them, it may simply be because he feels his privacy is not respected. In a few cases, it might mean there's something disturbing in his fantasies that he's afraid to talk about or can't understand.

Day-Wetting

Day-wetting (diurnal enuresis, in medical terminology) is different from bed-wetting and from soiling (passing feces) in pants. (See *Soiling*.) Most children gain bowel control sooner than bladder control, but by the time a child is regularly using the toilet he or she should be able to stay dry most of the day.

Unlike soiling, which may have a defiant component to it, day-wetting probably connotes a physical problem. The bladder may be leaking all day without the child's really knowing it until enough liquid has collected to leave a spot on clothing. See a pediatrician if this seems to be the case.

In the psychological arena, an accident may result when an anxious child is suddenly startled, embarrassed, or frightened. Many highly active children simply forget to use the bathroom during the excitement of playtime. Frequent, carefully scheduled trips to the bathroom can help minimize the potential for accidents. (See also *Toilet Training*.)

Death

(See *Reaction to Loss*)

Defiance

(See *Oppositional Behavior*)

Delinquency

(See *Conduct Disorder, Antisocial Behavior*)

Demanding

One of parents' biggest fears is that they will produce a demanding, spoiled child. The reality is that most children are demanding at certain developmental stages (toddler and preschool years) or following a jolt to their usual routine (the addition of a new sibling). And some children are just temperamentally more prone to be colicky, fussy, and demanding of attention. (See *Temperament* and the Developmental Tasks Appendix.)

Try to survive these stages or reactions with humor, accepting them as normal while still helping your child learn what behavior is inappro-

101

priate. That means saying no and remaining calm and dispassionate even in the face of a tantrum, and not responding to a child's request until he asks in an appropriate tone of voice. A child who receives whatever he wants just because he whines is going to be slow to give up that behavior because it works. He also won't learn patience or better, more sophisticated methods of asking. He will essentially be stuck developmentally. (See *Whining*, *Temper Tantrums*, *Oppositional Behavior*, and *Immature Behavior*.)

Preverbal children are likely to be more demanding because they are frustrated by their lack of communication capabilities. Preschoolers want immediate action and have to be taught to delay their gratification. By the time a child is in school, you should be able to reason more with him. Tell him your reasons for denying or granting his request. (See *Impatience* and *Interrupting*.)

For children who have regressed from being generally cooperative and patient to more demanding, volatile, "babyish" behavior, think about recent family circumstances. A move, birth of a sibling, death of a grandparent, serious illness in the family, or parental conflict are all events that may make a child feel more vulnerable and needy. Handle those regressions with some empathy and lots of positive attention when a child is *not* misbehaving. (See *Regression*, *Reaction to Loss*, *Reaction to Parental Conflict*, and *School*.)

(For more specific tips on managing demanding behavior, see *Attention-Seeking*.)

Dependency

Dependency is a trait best judged along several lines: by a child's age and developmental stage, by his temperament, by his behavior in a variety of settings, and by recent life events. A three-year-old clinging to his mother on his first day of nursery school is developmentally normal and acceptable. So, too, is a four-year-old dogging his mother around the house. (See "Separation Anxiety" under *Anxiety* and the Developmental Tasks Appendix.)

Conversely, a ten-year-old sobbing as he waits for the school bus, or an eight-year-old who isn't interested in playing with his peers, is atypical. Such inappropriate dependency is understandable, however, if that child has recently suffered a major stress: a move, the death of a relative, the hospitalization of a parent for a serious illness, or divorce. (See *Reaction to Loss* and *Reaction to Parental Conflict.*) Regression to toddler-like dependency is also to be expected in a preschooler when a new sibling is born. (See *Regression.*)

The key question is the duration or severity of the dependency, or if a child's clinging seems tinged with intense anxiety about the welfare of his family. Is it coupled with nightmares? (See *Anxiety, Anxiety Disorders,* and *Post-Traumatic Stress Disorder.*)

Some children are just innately more hesitant, restrained, and slow to warm to new situations. If your child has always been more dependent than his peers, you shouldn't worry unless his dependency hampers normal social progress. (See *Temperament, Adaptability, Clinging,* and *Immature Behavior.*)

Depression

At some point in our lives, we all feel depressed or sad. Children are no different. They have roughly the same basic range of emotions as adults, sadness included. The death of a grandparent, a geographic move, divorce, a pet that dies or runs away, or doing poorly on a test can all be crises that cause a child to grieve or to be unusually pensive. It is natural to want to protect your child and make him happy, but not letting him feel or talk about strong emotions can be detrimental. It may teach a child to suppress or deny his feelings of sadness or discontent, or, worse, not to discuss them with you.

That means not replacing the family hamster the same day in which it dies; not dismissing former friend Bobbie as a nasty kid if he excludes your child from his birthday party; not saying soccer is a stupid sport if your son is left off the team.

Feeling sad usually has to do with loss. It indicates your child

103

placed a value on the thing or the relationship that is now missing. Even though they may eventually cause him pain, it's important that a child be able to form such attachments. Without them, he will be a very lonely person. (See *Sadness, Reaction to Loss,* and *Making Friends.*)

After experiencing a loss, most children gradually feel better and return to their usual energy and activities within a few weeks. A supportive talk (in which you listen to everything a child has to say and normalize his feelings by admitting, "When I was your age I remember feeling the same way when . . .") should help a child work through his feelings. Try to view it as an opportunity to discuss emotions and give him better perspective. Remind him that tomorrow does offer new opportunities and chances to try again. Avoid saying, "You're being silly; this should be the happiest time of your life." (See also *Self-Esteem* and *Perfectionism.*)

The key is to lovingly teach a child how to work through emotions *himself.* "Fixing it" with a new bike won't help him in the long run. One of the goals of parenting, after all, is to produce a healthy, self-assured, self-sufficient adult. Being able to cope with sadness (or other powerful human emotions) is an important element of gaining independence from parents. (See also *Anger.*)

If there are persistent problems in the home, such as parental conflict, alcoholism, or chronic depression, try to change your child's environment for both his and your own sakes. Children frequently respond to such protracted stress by becoming depressed themselves. (See *Reaction to Parental Conflict.*)

While it is still relatively unusual under the age of twelve, some children can also experience an adult-like form of clinical depression. This is not just feeling sad following a trauma, loss, or life-style change, but feeling worthless and hopeless. This kind of depression impedes daily functioning. A child is so sad he cannot go about his business. He shows no interest in things that previously gave him pleasure. He may also have physical symptoms such as headaches and stomachaches, loss of appetite, and an inability to sleep.

As with adults, depressed children may feel listless, irritable, fatigued, or unable to concentrate. On the other hand, because they lack sophisticated vocabulary to describe their feelings, some children may show their depression by "externalizing" or "acting out" behaviors that run counter to the popular concept of depression. They may become hostile, defiant, aggressive, fidgety, or hyperactive, or, in the worst-case scenarios, they may vandalize, steal, or abuse drugs.

In short, any abrupt change in a child's usual personality is a warning sign that something may be wrong. A sudden drop in school performance or a shift in friends are also red flags for children six years and older. In preschool children, a marked slowdown in normal developmental tasks may be a sign of depression.

Infants to Preschoolers

A depressed infant won't eat well and may not become engaged with an adult or make eye contact. He doesn't light up when he sees a familiar face or a brightly colored object.

A depressed toddler won't display the curiosity that is the hallmark of her age. She won't separate from her parents to explore the environment. Or, paradoxically, the toddler may seem hyperactive, showing no sense of structure. Such a child may also be experiencing uncomfortable emotions that she chooses to discharge with frenzied activity. Constant head-banging and other inappropriate self-stimulation, such as picking at hair or masturbating, may also indicate that a child is depressed and trying to find a way to comfort or invigorate himself. Compulsive overeating may be an obese child's way of coping with depression. (See also *Head-Banging*, *Masturbation*, and *Obesity*.)

School-Aged Children

Once in school, a child should learn at a rate consistent with her intellectual capabilities and begin to socialize with her peers. If she doesn't do so and the pattern is persistent, find out why.

Remember to keep your child's temperament in mind. An innately shy child may have only one close friend at a time. But if she was previously gregarious and social and suddenly becomes withdrawn, she may have undergone an embarrassment and is trying to avoid being teased or repeating the situation. Continued withdrawal may result in true social isolation, a lonely state that can perpetuate depression. Friends and community involvement are powerful buffers for depression at all ages.

A child aged six to nine is typically intrigued by learning and is developing a strong sense of right and wrong. This is the time children most enjoy board games with clear-cut rules. If a child this age is cheating, bullying, lying, or stealing, she may be depressed. Instead of being sad or withdrawn, she is provocative. This child may be testing you to see if you really *do* care, if she really is as bad as her low self-esteem is telling her she is. (See also *Lying, Cheating, Stealing,* and *Bullying.*)

Also, a school-aged child who suddenly becomes disinterested in a hobby he once enjoyed is unusual at this age. Erikson characterized the main task of this developmental stage as being a struggle between a feeling of "industry versus inferiority." It is a time in which a child is absorbed in perfecting his skills. His self-esteem is largely determined by his definition of himself according to his abilities. He calls himself a swimmer, a piano player, a budding scientist. If he is not embroiled somehow in this kind of self-exploration, he is atypical of children his age. (See the Developmental Tasks Appendix.)

Excessive impulsivity, risk-taking, or being unusually accident-prone are also reasons for concern. A child who is constantly covered with bruises (not as a result of abuse but from his own play) may be just a rambunctious, active, hardy child. However, he may also be troubled. A child who is truly reckless, who cannot learn to be careful and to keep his body safe, may have poor self-esteem and not think himself worthy of care. In extreme cases, this activity may even suggest unconscious self-destructive or suicidal intent. (See *Self-Injurious Behavior.*)

Preteens

For preadolescents—children in the sixth and seventh grades—peer groups are becoming terribly important. It is a time when the opinion of friends seems critical to a child's self-worth. Exclusion from a party, rejection by a friend, criticism or ostracism by clique are weighty crises at this age. (See also *Popularity.*)

Given the importance of peer acceptance, then, behavior that suggests a complete disinterest in garnering it should be suspect. Primping in front of the mirror has aggravated many a parent, but a complete disregard for physical appearance is unusual in a preteen. On the other hand, premature sexual activity may be a warning sign of a child seeking comfort. At this age "romances" tend to be conducted over the telephone and in the safety of groups.

As we all know, emotional ups and downs at this age are commonplace, as are conflicts with parents, but any extreme mood swings or expressions of hopelessness and low self-esteem should be heeded. Also, be alert for a persistent, fatalistic attitude. If a preteen thinks all situations are hopeless, that he is never going to accomplish anything, or that he is incapable of succeeding no matter the circumstances, he is beginning to display black-or-white thinking. This fatalistic behavior is associated with suicide, the third leading cause of death among adolescents.

In preteens, hormonal changes may contribute heavily to depression. Clinical depression results not only from a reaction to loss, change, or environmental stress, but from biochemical imbalances and heredity. Moods are influenced by chemicals, or neurotransmitters, that carry messages within the brain. Any abnormality in their regulation may lead to dysfunctional behavior, feelings, or thoughts.

The three neurotransmitters most commonly linked to depression are serotonin (which helps regulate sleep and memory functions); norepinephrine (which influences alertness and energy); and dopamine (which helps regulate movement and emotion). Hormonal imbalances or medical conditions may also present themselves as depression. These include thyroid problems, hypoglycemia, diabetes, cancer, or even vitamin deficiencies.

Like a diabetic, a depressed child has inherited a susceptibility to his disorder. Many studies have shown that children of depressed parents have a greater risk of developing depressive symptoms. This vulnerability may need only an environmental nudge to manifest itself in a full-blown depression, typically during adolescence or adulthood.

What to Do

If your child displays both the physical and emotional symptoms of depression, he should be given a complete medical workup to ensure there is no physical condition displaying itself as depression. Then seek the aid of a mental-health professional experienced in treating children your child's age.

Treatment may include antidepressant medication to stabilize biochemical imbalances and ease physical symptoms such as sleeplessness or concentration problems. Be aware that all drugs have potential side effects, psychotropic drugs included. Discuss medication carefully with a child psychiatrist, then make sure your child takes it properly.

Psychotherapy, the "talking cure," will help a depressed child learn new ways of thinking about himself and the world, as well as new ways of coping with the inevitable hurdles life will present. Families' participation in therapy as a group is also effective. This will help you learn how to help.

Plus, a child's family is his context. Excessive perfectionism, for instance, is a common component of depression and is often learned at home. In that case, your own attitudes need to be addressed as well. If a child tries to change his outlook but the family doesn't, it's likely he'll relapse in some way.

Learn to be flexible in your own thinking and what you consider acceptable, since you are your child's strongest model for beliefs and behavior. Give yourself some leeway for mistakes or faltering and tell yourself that tomorrow offers another chance. Your child is more likely to do the same for himself. Encourage him to make friends and join clubs, which help build a sense of purpose, social status, and self-definition. With a foundation of healthy attitudes and associations, one loss or failure is just that, an isolated incident within a context of generally positive life experiences and relationships.

If a child seems clinically depressed, act quickly. Prolonged depression affects a child's self-esteem, motivation, schoolwork, and ability to interact with others. The first signs of mental illness often occur in childhood, and early prevention can avert more ingrained and devastating problems. With proper treatment, the NIMH says 90 percent of depressed people improve within a month.

For more information, contact the National Institute of Mental Health's Public Inquiries Branch, 5600 Fishers Lane, Rockville, MD 20857 (301-443-4513); or the American Academy of Child and Adolescent Psychiatry, 3615 Wisconsin Avenue, NW, Washington, D.C. 20016 (202-966-7300). Recommended reading: *When Your Child Needs Help: A Parent's Guide to Therapy for Children*, by Norma Doft, Ph.D., with Barbara Aria (Harmony Books); *Coping with Teenage Depression: A Parent's Guide*, by Kathleen McCoy (Penguin Books).

Destructiveness

(See *Aggression, Temper Tantrums,* and *Oppositional-Defiant Disorder*)

Dieting

(See *Eating Disorders, Obesity,* and *Food Refusal*)

Difficult

(See *Temperament, Oppositional Behavior,* and *Adaptability*)

Disobedience

(See *Oppositional Behavior*)

Disorganized

Children are generally less organized than adults. They need to *learn* systems of organization: how to prioritize tasks and schedule themselves, how to arrange their school notes for productive study, how to

109

organize their clothes for easy retrieval. They will require your help to learn that kind of categorizing.

A major pitfall of disorganization is that a child may feel so overwhelmed that he is discouraged from even attempting a task. And that can have a negative impact on a wide range of things. If a child has too many toys, all jumbled together in piles or buried in a toy box, they'll be less inviting, even daunting, to him. If there is no storage system, he certainly won't be motivated to pick them up. If his closet is in chaos, his clothes strewn about the floor, he'll have difficulty getting himself ready in time to catch the school bus. (See *Play*, *Chores and Cleaning Room*, and *Dressing*.)

One of the major challenges of growing up and attending school is to begin to organize one's thoughts, so that information can be processed and applied to a variety of problems. Many children need help structuring themselves to study. It's important to schedule uninterrupted homework time for your child and then reinforce his efforts with praise. That is very different from doing homework for him. (See *Self-Esteem*, *School*, *Procrastination*.)

Most children will become more organized as they mature cognitively and learn how they study best. Some children, however, seem to have disorganized thinking or great difficulty processing information in a way that allows them to succeed in school. These children may have learning disabilities. If a child is highly impulsive and active as well as disorganized, he may have Attention-Deficit Hyperactivity Disorder (ADHD). (See *Learning Disabilities* and *Attention-Deficit Hyperactivity Disorder*.)

Also, a child who seemed organized previously but now seems to be forgetful, distracted, or listless may be preoccupied or troubled by something. If he has recently suffered what he views as a loss, watch for other signs of depression. (See *Reaction to Loss*, *Reaction to Parental Conflict*, *Depression*, and *Post-Traumatic Stress Disorder*.)

Distractibility

Distractibility has to do with a child's ability to pay attention and concentrate, abilities that naturally increase as a child matures. A book that a two-year-old couldn't possibly sit through from beginning to end will probably be absorbing entertainment for him when he's three.

Highly distractible children have *persistent* trouble focusing their attention, concentrating, and completing tasks. They often forget instructions, lose things, and appear not to listen to parents or teachers. They may daydream in class or seem restless and fidgety.

Such behavior is obviously frustrating to parents and teachers alike, but keep in mind that it may just be part of his innate personality. In that case, make eye contact and your requests or instructions in simple, succinct language. Build in break times during homework, household tasks, or games to help a child regain his energy for concentration. (See also *Listening.*)

Inattention may also result from a specific situation or worry. A child can seem distracted for all sorts of reasons: his parents have been arguing a lot recently; his dog has run away; or he's sitting next to the class bully, who pesters him each day during recess. He may even be having some trouble adjusting to being in school in the first place.

If a child who once had no difficulty concentrating now seems restless and "tuned out," it's pretty likely there is a specific cause of his distraction. Talk to him in a sympathetic, nonaccusatory fashion to see what's bothering him. (See *Reaction to Loss, Reaction to Parental Conflict*, and *School.*)

If he insists that nothing is wrong, consult your pediatrician. There may be a physiological underpinning. Something as simple as a chronic low-grade viral infection can cause fatigue and hamper a child's ability to concentrate. Alternatively, a child may have an undetected hearing loss or language disability that makes listening frustrating for him. (See *Hearing* and *Language and Speech.*)

Another possibility is that a very distractible child may have a true attention deficit. Couple his inattention with an unusually high level of activity and poor impulse control and you may have a child who dashes from one toy to another, interrupts constantly, and seems incapable of following directions. His schoolwork and peer relationships are likely to suffer. That child may have Attention-Deficit Hyperactivity Disorder. (See *Attention-Deficit Hyperactivity Disorder.*)

Divorce

(See *Reaction to Parental Conflict*)

Dressing

If you have an active, spirited child, dressing can be a challenge from the first year on. The first year may actually seem easy by comparison. Pinning down a squirming baby to pull a T-shirt on her seems simple after chasing a three-year-old who absolutely refuses to wear anything other than her ballerina costume. You may think she's misbehaving on purpose just to make you late. Well, maybe she is. One of the most effective ways for a child to stop parents rushing about and leaving for work is to sit down, scream, and refuse to put on clothes.

Like eating, dressing can become an activity that evolves into a battle for control between you and your child. But it doesn't have to be so bad, if you think about why children fight getting dressed or reject certain clothing. Mostly it has to do with autonomy, especially during the "terrible twos." A child grows tired of being told when and what to do, and the daily rituals of meals and dressing are perfect opportunities for expressing her opinion with extreme clout. (See *Oppositional Behavior, Food Refusal*, and *Temper Tantrums.*)

For many children, dressing in the morning also means parents will soon leave for work or that they have to go to school. For children with age-appropriate separation anxiety or who are tense about going into a

112

different environment, procrastinating about dressing is a perfect way to avoid what they don't want to do. (See *Anxiety* and *Procrastination.*)

Other children have trouble with dressing because of temperamental traits. They may have a supersensitivity to certain textures and literally cannot stand wearing scratchy fabrics. Others may have poor adaptability so that dressing in a hurry throws them into a tantrum, especially if it interrupts their play. (See *Temperament* and *Adaptability.*)

Many children may become fixated on wearing certain outfits for the same reason they may demand hot dogs for lunch every day. Favorite clothes are comfortable, familiar, a way of creating rituals and soothing predictability in a world that children recognize is controlled largely by outside forces. School-aged children usually want to wear what their friends are wearing. It's a way of blending in. Finally, older children may have trouble getting themselves dressed because their clothes are not organized in a clearly accessible manner for them. (See *Chores and Cleaning Room.*)

Recognizing these reasons should help defuse your frustration over clothing battles. It also helps if you can view dressing as an opportunity for a younger child to have a little independence (in choice of outfits), which should lower her overall frustration level. It's also a chance to build her self-esteem. "I dressed myself" can be a very proud claim for a preschooler.

What to Do

The first thing is to allow plenty of time for dressing. The more you rush, the more unnerving it is to a child and the more she'll protest. Also, the younger she is, the less developed her concept of time may be. Try getting up fifteen minutes earlier to provide a comfortable cushion of time to complete dressing.

Make dressing a means to a pleasant end. Say, "Guess what? We've got to get dressed so we can go out and play." Or, "If we get dressed before eight o'clock, Mommy will have enough time to read you a book before she leaves." If that doesn't work, make further activity contingent upon her dressing. For instance, many children watch *Sesame Street* as their parents prepare breakfast. It's all right to use that as positive reinforcement: "Guess what? The television doesn't come on until everyone is dressed." Stick to that limit once you've set it, even if she protests.

With younger children, distraction often makes dressing easier. Tell

113

a toddler a story or sing a song together while you dress her. Put her shoes on while she's in her high chair enjoying breakfast. Also, make her feel part of a process. Even a one-year-old can push her arms through her sleeves or help pull a shirt down. Then, take advantage of a two- or three-year-old's drive for accomplishment. Say, "Look what you did. You're such a big helper." When they do pull their pants on themselves, praise their achievement: "You did it yourself!" Have clothes that pull on and off and fasten easily to fuel their desire to try dressing themselves.

Allow preschoolers to choose clothes themselves; start by giving them an either-or choice between two outfits you've selected. Perhaps progress to allowing them to pick anything that is suited to the weather. Try not to cringe at their mix of colors or patterns or to correct them unless it's *truly* important.

If a favored dress or shirt is really too dirty to wear again, say so and stand firm. It helps if you include children in the laundry process, so that they know when clothes are washed and when that beloved item will again be available to wear. Have them help you put it into the washer.

For children who are old enough to dress themselves, make the process as simple as possible. Arrange clothes where they can reach them and in a logical fashion. Separate underwear from outerwear, playclothes from school clothes. Have coats, boots, mittens, and hats in one place. Many children benefit from choosing and laying out clothes the night before. Keep checking on a slow dresser to make sure she hasn't stopped to do a puzzle or play with her hamster.

Reward prompt dressing with time together. Enjoy cups of hot cocoa together or read a favorite book before the school bus arrives or you have to leave for work.

Ear-Pulling

(See *Habits*)

Eating Disorders

Eating disorders are very different from the common and typically benign feeding difficulties that beset almost all families as children learn to eat solid foods, feed themselves, and express opinions about what they like. (See *Food Refusal, Fads, and Feeding Problems.*) Eating disorders are serious problems in which food is used as a method of expressing and perhaps meeting emotional needs. Body size and food have become obsessions, whether a person compulsively diets, refuses food, binges, or purges. Underneath these behaviors lurk disquieting feelings: low self-esteem, a need for control, fear of budding sexuality and growing up, or a need for immediate gratification.

Although instances of anorexia (excessive dieting) and bulimia (eating large quantities of food to achieve a high or to relieve emotion and then purging by self-induced vomiting) have been recorded as early as biblical times, the disorders have had widespread prominence only in the past few decades. Eating disorders occur almost exclusively in upper-middle-class, white, Western society. At the turn of the century and today in underdeveloped nations, robust, even chubby children were and are the talismans of economic success. It is only recently, and in the wealthiest nations, that being thin, showing restraint in the face of abundance, is a sign of self-control, admirable willpower, and attractiveness.

Ninety percent of all anorexics and bulimics are female. Statistics for prevalence vary, but a good estimate is that one percent of American girls are anorexic and 4 percent are bulimic. Some studies of bulimia have suggested that as many as 19 percent of college women have experimented or actively engage in binging and purging.

Both disorders involve an intense fear of being fat. Why? Certainly our society places a heavy emphasis on slender figures, from the pages of fashion magazines to television advertising. Yet while we publicly prize bone-thin figures, our society promotes eating nonnutritious, sweet, fattening foods. Given such contradictory messages, it's no surprise that preteen girls, just establishing their self-image and unsure of themselves, show anxiety over their figures. Still, eating disorders can hardly be blamed entirely on societal pressures or definitions of beauty or all women would be bulimic or anorexic.

Instead, eating disorders probably result from a complex intermingling of many factors. Family environment; a genetic predisposition to addictive behaviors, such as alcoholism or depression; and the changing hormones of puberty all help push a young woman to focus obsessively on her weight. And although eating disorders are more common in teenagers and college-age women, they are showing up at earlier ages. There are reports of girls dieting in the fourth and fifth grades. Entering seventh grade (junior high school) is a particularly risky time for children vulnerable to anorexia.

Caught early, eating disorders respond well to treatment. Allowed to develop into chronic patterns, however, anorexia and bulimia can necessitate hospitalization. In some extreme cases, girls may also have incurred serious, irreversible medical complications.

Anorexia

Anorexics often claim to feel superior because they can control their food intake. Their self-esteem is largely based on the fact that they believe they have more discipline than the average person. To a certain extent they're right; they do have unusually strong willpower. As the American Psychiatric Association's diagnostic manual points out, anorexia, meaning loss of appetite, is a misnomer, since most anorexics do in fact suffer extreme hunger pangs. They also love food and often read cookbooks and prepare lavish meals for others so they can touch and smell the food they refuse to eat.

With that in mind, anorexia seems a particularly brutal self-punishment. Anorexics typically are rigid, perfectionist high achievers who take pride in those personality traits. When confronted with a plate of food, they may ritualistically push food around, consuming only a tiny morsel here and there. They usually exercise strenuously with the deliberate purpose of burning up calories.

But as they drop pound after pound, anorexics still see themselves as fat. And rather than displaying their hard-won thinness, many dress in layers of clothes to conceal their figures. Such discomfort with their bodies is a hallmark of anorexia.

In fact, most anorexics may be trying to keep their appearance childlike. They seem terrified of growing up, separating from parents, or developing breasts and hips. Entering junior high school, experiencing a loss, or early menstruation and breast development all seem to increase the risk for emotionally vulnerable girls.

There may be biological as well as psychological factors involved. During puberty, the level of hormones such as estrogen and progesterone surge. Since hormones have an influence on brain function and play a role in depression and anxiety disorders, it is probable that they might influence the development of eating disorders as well. There also seems to be a correlation between eating disorders and the age at which puberty begins: American girls are maturing (developing breasts and menstruating) earlier than in the past. At the same time the average age of the onset of anorexia is decreasing. It is rare but not unheard-of for children as young as ten years old to be diagnosed with the disorder now.

Other warning signs include: a drive to excel in all endeavors, particularly school; unhappiness; social isolation; wanting to eat alone; complaints of looking fat even when bone-thin; cessation of menstruation; and increased irritability. The anorexic is typically introverted, unusually dependent on and involved with parents, and slow to show interest in socializing with boys. For them the rites of teenage years are overwhelming and frightening, not happy or exciting.

Their parents may be obsessive exercisers and calorie-counters themselves. Typically they avoid conflict and expressing anger, taking pride in self-control. They may be loving to a fault. Ironically, an anorexic's refusal to eat is a method of finally exerting independence, all the while creating a physical appearance that ensures she remains visually, at least, her parents' little girl.

Anorexia can result in serious medical complications, similar to those

brought on by starvation. It is particularly damaging for preadolescents, who have not yet undergone the growth spurt brought by
puberty. For them, the effects of malnutrition are often irreversible—
for example, their growth may be permanently stunted, they may be
infertile, or they may become prone to brittle bones, a condition
called osteoporosis. There is also research indicating that chronic
anorexics have higher rates of psychiatric problems and even suicidal
risk later in life.

Bulimia

Bulimics are similar to anorexics in their intense fear of weight gain,
high self-expectations coupled with low self-esteem, and dependence
on other people's opinions for self-definition. They, too, may obsessively
diet and exercise, but they lack the anorexic's fanatical self-control.
Typically, they cannot stick to their diets and resort to self-induced
vomiting to rid themselves of food. They may also use laxatives. Purging
typically follows a binge, during which bulimics rapidly consume large
quantities of sweets or carbohydrates. Initially, these binges are meant
to achieve a kind of euphoria or to alleviate loneliness, anxiety, or anger.
Eventually, the behavior becomes an addiction.

Because they have poor impulse control, bulimics often engage in
other addictive behaviors. Many abuse drugs or alcohol. Some shoplift
(for the thrill and to sustain their "habit," since binges are often expensive ventures). Some are sexually promiscuous; others suffer from
clinical depression; some have been sexually abused. Typically, bulimics are extroverted, impetuous, or self-deprecating. Like anorexics,
bulimics can emerge from completely functional, healthy families.
When there are family difficulties, however, they tend to involve
problem-solving and communication styles. There may be intense conflict between parents and little support or involvement with their
children. Quite often there is a family history of addictive disorders,
substance abuse, depression, and obesity.

To be diagnosed as a bulimic, according to the APA's diagnostic
manual, a girl must binge twice a week for at least three months. It is
frightening but not unusual for adolescents to hear about purging as a
method of weight control and to experiment with it during a time of
stress or when they need to meet weight limits for sports. Don't panic if
you discover your child has tried purging, but don't ignore it either.
Discuss the dangers of bulimia in a calm, matter-of-fact manner. Then

try to encourage a child to discuss what's going on in her life, to identify the emotional motivators for her behavior.

Warning signs that bulimic purges are becoming a cycle include: evidence of unexplained vomiting (most children inform parents loudly when they've been sick); a stash of Ipecac, laxatives, or food in a child's room; cuts on their knuckles from sticking their fingers down their throat; or eroded tooth enamel, caused by the acids in regurgitated food. Excusing oneself from the table and disappearing into the bathroom immediately following a meal is a tip-off to trouble, as well as dizziness or unexplained complaints of sore throats. So, too, are extreme weight fluctuations.

Just as with anorexia, the medical complications of bulimia are serious. Constant vomiting can produce tears in the esophagus, electrolyte imbalances, and irregular heartbeats.

What to Do

In the case of anorexia and bulimia, get help from professionals who specialize in treating eating disorders. (Many hospitals have specific eating-disorders units and programs.) The untrained general therapist or pediatrician may not have the experience to recognize eating disorders, which are often masked by other symptoms. Patients may also benefit from the help of nutritionists and support groups of other anorexics and bulimics.

If a child is displaying a proclivity for the disorders without yet practicing their behaviors, or is dieting at a young age, examine your own attitudes about food and body image. Don't engage in extreme dieting, exercise, or self-criticism. Downplay the importance of physical appearance. If your child complains that she is fat, don't immediately say, "You're being ridiculous," even if she is terribly thin. Such a comment provides parents an excellent opportunity to talk with a child about how she views herself. Ask her why she thinks she's fat and how it makes her feel. Find out how school is going, what her friends are up to, and if, in short, something has happened to cause such low self-esteem and misinformed self-image. Then, talk about her positive, preferably nonphysical attributes: her accomplishments, talents, or personality.

Treat food and eating in a neutral fashion, as part of nutrition and health, not as proof of affection and obedience. Eat regular meals together as a family. As opportunities present themselves (when a child looks at a thin model in a magazine, for instance), challenge society's idealization of slenderness. Exercise regularly but not compulsively as a method of remaining fit, not solely as a method of weight control.

Don't criticize your child for weight gain or nag her if she takes a second helping at dinnertime. Just make sure that nutritious food is offered in moderate amounts. It will be easier to stay calm if she exhibits a slight roundness during preadolesence if you remember that this is the time nature designed for her to put on a little weight.

For further information, contact the American Anorexia / Bulimia Association, 418 East 76th Street, New York, NY 10021 (212-734-1114); National Anorexic Aid Society, 1925 East Dublin Granville Road, Columbus, OH 43229 (Hotline: 614-436-1112, or 614-846-2833); the National Association of Anorexia Nervosa and Associated Disorders, PO Box 7, Highland Park, IL 60035 (Hotline: 708-831-3438); or the National Institute of Mental Health Eating Disorders Program, 9000 Rockville Pike, Building 10, Rm. 3N228, Bethesda, MD 20892 (301-496-1891).

Recommended reading: *The Golden Cage: The Enigma of Anorexia Nervosa*, by Hilde Bruch, M.D. (Vintage Books); *A Parent's Guide to Eating Disorders and Obesity*, by Martha M. Jablow for the Children's Hospital of Philadelphia (a Delta Book / Dell Publishing); *New Hope for Binge Eaters*, by H. Pope and J. Hudson (Harper & Row); *A Parent's Guide to Anorexia and Bulimia*, by Katherine Byrne (Henry Holt); and *A Parent's Guide to Eating Disorders*, by Brett Valette (Avon Books).

Eating Nonfood Objects

(See *Pica*)

Elective Mutism

(See *Refusing to Speak*)

Embarrassment

(See *Self-Consciousness*)

Empathy

(See *Insensitivity*)

Enuresis

(See *Bed-Wetting, Day-Wetting*)

Eye Contact

Newborns come into this world equipped with a group of behaviors called innate releasers. These are biological mechanisms designed to elicit a caregiver's nurturing response. They include sucking, clinging,

121

crying, and the ability to wake up and momentarily make eye contact. As your baby grows, his ability to focus strengthens and the time span of his loving gaze lengthens. It's probably his strongest method of reaching out, of engaging you socially.

Eye contact remains an important element of communication as humans age. Making eye contact remains the best way to ensure your child hears you or, on the other hand, to show him that you're listening attentively to him. (See "Active Listening" in the Parenting Skills Introduction.)

Some children are particularly active and may not be able to sit and look directly into someone's eyes for long talks. Most reach a developmental stage around eleven or twelve years of age when they are far less interested in sitting down and chatting with parents. Children who are usually very open and direct in their gaze, who suddenly become secretive or avoidant may be afraid of revealing something or of being caught in a fib. (See *Lying* and *Refusing to Speak.*)

These are normal responses and behaviors. What's abnormal and very rare is for a child ardently to avoid eye contact or social interaction. If he does so from infancy, he may have a more serious developmental delay. Talk to your pediatrician.

Fatigue

Fatigue is expected after a hard day's work or play, or when a child is sick and his body tries to fight off a cold, flu, or infection. Stress also causes fatigue. Some people, perhaps by temperament, just seem to have less energy than others. In severe instances individuals may suffer chronic fatigue syndrome, a condition in which they are so tired they are often unable to get out of bed at all.

Usually, fatigue in children is not serious and passes. But you should always take a child to a pediatrician when he complains of fatigue for more than a week, to make sure he has no underlying medical condition. If nothing physical is found, a child may be unhappy or worried about something that is manifesting itself in fatigue. Acting tired and listless, having no motivation, and showing disinterest in once-pleasurable hobbies are features of depression and low self-esteem.

Ask yourself: Is his fatigue out of character and sudden? Is there an event or a situation that seems associated with it? Has there been a change of circumstances with his friends, or at school or at home? Does he seem unusually afraid of failure or of trying new things? Has he isolated himself from friends, or shown a change in his eating and sleeping habits?

It is not uncommon for children to go through phases in which they lose interest in people and hobbies or claim they are bored by something. However, if you answered yes to several of the above questions, your child is probably emotionally troubled by something and the issue bears exploring. (See also *Depression, Self-Esteem, Perfectionism, Reaction to Loss, Reaction to Parental Conflict, Popularity*, and *School*.)

Fears and Phobias

We all have fears. They are our instinctive way of protecting ourselves from possible danger. As a species, we become less afraid of things as we grow up and learn from experience what is harmful and what is not.

It makes sense, therefore, that a baby hearing a thunderclap for the first time is going to be afraid. She has no idea what it is or if it can hurt her. Once she is old enough to comprehend an explanation of what produces thunder and how to take precautions against lightning to keep her safe, her fear will most likely disappear.

She will develop different fears at each developmental stage, as she changes cognitively and emotionally. A three- to five-year-old, for instance, who once loved going to the pediatrician may suddenly become anxious in the doctor's office. She has become private about her body and aware of how small she is next to an adult. Consequently, she may feel vulnerable when examined. A preteen is going to be particularly susceptible to social fears ("Am I pretty enough, smart enough?") because peer acceptance is so very important to her.

Infants

Infants are often afraid of loud, unexplained noises: dropped pans, sirens, thunder, or yelling. Around nine months of age, when a baby really recognizes her parents as being distinct from other people, she will develop fears about strangers and being separated from her mother or father. She hasn't yet learned that objects and people still exist outside her view. She doesn't know, then, that when Mommy leaves the room, she can and will predictably return. (See *Anxiety*.)

Toddlers and Preschoolers

Toddlers are skittish around large, loud machines such as vacuum cleaners. Some may develop a fear of bathtubs. All these concerns have to do with a toddler's concept of size and self. If the vacuum cleaner sucks up dirt, if the bathtub drain sucks down water, why couldn't they easily do the same to him? He may also develop a similar fear of toilets, since they flush loudly and make objects disappear. Toilets are enormous contraptions to a two-foot-tall toddler. (See *Toilet Training*.)

Preschoolers fear animals, losing their parents in some way, and

124

imaginary creatures such as ghosts and monsters. Their imaginations are developing, and they are very aware of the fact that they are small and not very powerful. They also engage in "magical thinking" and believe what they think or feel becomes real. Similarly, they become afraid of the dark and what might be lurking there. (See the Developmental Tasks Appendix.)

School-Aged Children

Between five and six years of age, a child may dread natural disasters, accidents, and crime. She hears about earthquakes and plane crashes on television and may worry that they will occur in her own town or to people she loves. As soon as she enters first grade, social and performance fears begin. "I might make a mistake on my test"; "she's prettier than I am"; "my dress is dumb-looking and everyone will laugh at me" are common anxieties that often grow stronger as a child grows older.

Although "phobia" is a word our culture uses synonymously with "fear," these words have very different meanings medically. A phobia is an intense, chronic, irrational fear of a specific situation or object. A phobia interferes with a person's day-to-day life. An adult with a bridge phobia may become so paralyzed by his anticipatory fear of crossing that he is unable to do so. A person who has a phobia of dogs might avoid parks, shopping malls, or, in extreme agoraphobic cases, may never leave her house.

While true phobias are not common in children, the foundations for full-blown adult phobias and panic attacks are probably laid in childhood. Early attention to these problems may well decrease the risk of anxiety disorders later in life.

What to Do

Anxiety disorders tend to run in families, suggesting a genetic, physical link as well as learned behavior. Using new imaging technology, people who suffer from panic attacks have been shown to have biochemical abnormalities in specific brain centers. But keep in mind that children can pick up on a parent's hesitation. A mother who hovers around the edge of the swimming pool may unintentionally transmit her fear of water to a child through her own behavior.

On the other hand, a parent who trivializes a child's fears, teases her

125

for having them, or insensitively forces her to confront them in a kind of "sink-or-swim" showdown will probably only fuel her fright as well as humiliate her. It will also teach her to ignore instinctive feelings that tell her to get out of dangerous situations—to go inside during a thunderstorm, to find you when she's approached by a stranger whose intent is questionable.

So, acknowledge what she's feeling. Avoid saying, "Oh, there's nothing to be afraid of, you're being silly." Fears are very real in a child's mind, whether they are over a bathtub drain, a dog, or imagined monsters in the pool.

Instead, try to "desensitize" the child by gently bringing her into controlled contact with the object of her fears. Take the toddler out of the bathtub before letting the water out, and let her watch the process from a safe distance. Then let her pull the plug herself, if she wants to, so that she's the one in charge.

Look at dogs through the window of a pet shop, then play with a small puppy. Finally, work your way up to her petting a large friendly dog while an adult keeps a firm hand on him. Or let her "play" out her fears. Giving a child a make-believe doctor's kit and stethoscope so she can pretend to be a physician often lowers her anxiety level during checkups.

Help her develop rituals or self-soothing techniques that empower her. Fears are often about not being in control. So, if a child is afraid of monsters in the closet, leave a night-light on and give her a stuffed animal to hug that has been endowed by you with magic powers. Promise her you're right down the hall and will come when she calls and keep her safe. Perhaps curtail her viewing of scary movies until she's feeling more secure.

With natural disasters, acknowledge that they happen rarely. If you live in an area where there has never been an earthquake, say so. If your area is prone to them, admit that, too, and reassure the child that adults have made plans to keep people as safe as possible. Children need to know that adults are responsible and make plans to guard their well-being. During the Persian Gulf War, for instance, many children worried the fighting would come to their front door. Teachers and parents needed to explain how far away, geographically, Kuwait is. And in cities like Washington, D.C., where there were heightened concerns about bomb threats, teachers told students they had made contingency plans for their safety in case something unusual happened.

If a child who fears flying must get on a plane, explain that crashes don't happen very often. Introduce her to the pilot and flight attendants and let them tell her what they do to keep her safe. Then, during the flight have lots of toys and activities to keep her preoccupied.

Let a first-grader anxious about school tuck a picture of you in her knapsack to look at when she's nervous. Put in her pocket a soft piece of fabric sprayed with your familiar perfume, which she can hold or smell. Tell her to take deep breaths or think about something she does enjoy doing at school if something bothers her while she's there.

Helping a child learn ways to make herself feel better when worried will make her a strong, self-reliant adult. No need to resort to alcohol, drugs, or domineering relationships if she can recognize, confront, and cope with her emotions on her own.

Children who are truly afraid of school may claim to have headaches or stomachaches to keep from getting on that bus. (See *School.*) Anytime a child seems anxious about a social situation, try to find out exactly what it is she fears. Ask: "What's the worst that can happen?" Children often make a situation seem far more catastrophic than it is. If she says, "I'll fail the test, flunk math, and never get into college," you can respond, "Missing one question or failing one test will not mean you'll flunk." Maybe add, "When I was in fourth grade I was terrible at spelling. I thought I'd be a failure." Clearly you're not and your child will be reassured. She will also learn not to think in self-defeating, black-and-white terms. Plus, your admission of a weakness proves that successful, functioning people can have and admit flaws.

Parents can also put fears in context and make them seem more normal to a child by telling her many people have had similar feelings. Try saying, "I know a lot of children are worried about going to school because they don't know the teacher or are afraid of a mean kid. Are you worried about something like that?"

Books are also a wonderful tool in dealing with fears and proving to children that they're not alone. Would someone write a book about feeling this way if a lot of people didn't experience the same fear? Also, reading about spiders or snakes and their habits is a good way of discussing feared creatures at arm's length.

Recommended reading for parents: *The Magic Years*, by Selma Fraiberg (Charles Scribner's Sons). For children: *There's a Nightmare in My Closet*, by Mercer Mayer (Dial Books for Young Readers); *My Mama Says There Aren't Any: Zombies, Ghosts, Vampires, Creatures, Demons, Monsters, Fiends, Goblins, or Things*, by Judith Viorst (Aladdin Books); *All by Myself*, by Anna Grossnickle Hines (Clarion); and *The Something*, by Natalie Babbitt (Farrar, Straus & Giroux).

Fidgety

(See *Hyperactivity, Distractibility, Habits, Anxiety*)

Fighting

(See *Aggression, Bullying*)

Fingernail-Biting

(See *Habits*)

Fire-Setting

Most young children are fascinated by fire, its origins and properties, much as they are by water. The interest seems to intensify around the age of five or six, especially in boys.

It is extremely important at this stage for parents to keep matches, lighters, and cigarettes hidden and out of reach, or better yet locked up. A child should always be supervised around fires. When he's older, you may decide to satisfy his curiosity by letting him feed sticks into a fire in a fireplace or a camp fire, but you must watch him closely.

He should also be taught about burns, safety precautions, and escape routes. Many fire departments are happy to talk with young children about prevention and dangers. Identifying with fire fighters and understanding the life-and-death situations into which they put themselves can be powerful deterrents to a child playing with matches.

Pyromania—the inability to resist an impulse to set a fire—is a serious and life-threatening disorder. Arson is one of the fastest-growing crimes committed by children in the United States.

A pattern of fire-setting suggests that a child is emotionally disturbed and is not supervised closely enough by adults. His family may be dysfunctional or disrupted by stress. Fire-setting is one way a child can cry for help and attention. However, it is rarely an isolated behavior. Usually a fire-setter engages in other antisocial or destructive behaviors as well: lying, stealing, vandalism, truancy.

Fire-setting in childhood is considered a major psychological and practical crisis by experts and can be a compelling reason to admit a child to a psychiatric hospital or unit.

Food Refusal, Fads, and Feeding Problems

At some point during early childhood, meals are likely to become battlegrounds. That fact has much to do with the symbolism and emotions we attach to eating and food preparation. You may feel rejected when a child refuses to eat an appetizing, nutritionally balanced meal you have lovingly prepared. You might worry that the child will starve or that you are somehow inadequate as a parent and a cook. You shouldn't. Your child probably just doesn't like that particular food, or has come to learn that food is a perfect way to exert control. The more you change menus to please, the more you cajole or threaten, the more the child may balk at what you serve.

Such emotional matters should be stricken from the mealtime menu. Eating together is a social, nurturing, pleasurable event, but it is also about fueling a body. Children must learn to eat when they are hungry and stop when they are full, not to please or annoy someone, or to assuage boredom or sadness.

Infants and Toddlers

Often, mealtime trouble occurs first between nine and eighteen months of age, as a baby moves to solid foods and self-feeding. Some children have a hypersensitivity to textures and consequently do not tolerate certain foods. These picky eaters may genuinely fear trying anything new, since it could be something they might vehemently dislike.

Other picky eaters may simply be strong-willed. Refusing food becomes one of the few ways infants and toddlers can speak their mind and have their opinion completely understood. Developmentally, all children between the ages of two and three try to separate and individuate. They are still very dependent on parents, but want to have more autonomy. They cling one moment and shout "Let me do it" the next. Some toddlers recognize that mealtime is the perfect stage for exerting power. You may shovel food into a toddler's mouth, but you can't make him swallow.

In very extreme cases, babies who refuse to eat may become "infantile anorexics" and exhibit "nonorganic failure to thrive." These babies can suffer malnutrition and stunted growth. They may have depressed caregivers or chaotic homes, and some have been classified as experiencing "environmental deprivation syndrome." Another uncommon reason for food refusal involves posttraumatic stress. If a child choked, or underwent intrusive medical treatment that required a tube to be put down his throat, he may come to associate feeding with pain and refuse to eat. In both of these highly unusual instances, trained experts are probably needed to help a child begin to eat again.

School-Aged Children

Don't be surprised if the power struggle around eating continues well into elementary school, when children often go through "food fads." Peanut butter and jelly may be all your son wants to eat. Not only that, the sandwich may have to be cut in a prescribed way, and the portions had better not touch one another on the plate. Such rigidity is less a matter of defiance than his way of creating rituals and routines, a predictable sameness that provides a sense of security in an ever-changing world.

* * *

It is often a mother with the best intentions who falls into the trap of food battles. Perhaps her own mother was punitive or strict about eating, and she doesn't want to behave in a similar fashion. So she carefully plans and arranges food, provides endless alternatives if meals don't please, and pleads with her child to eat. That child may run the risk of growing up with a false sense of power or experiencing separation anxiety later, since he and his mother may be too enmeshed with each other emotionally.

Endless tugs-of-war over food may also lay the foundation for more serious eating disorders—obesity, bulimia, and anorexia—later in life. Bulimia and anorexia stem from an intense fear of being fat and lead to either excessive dieting or binging and purging of food. All three conditions result in part from a person being unable to regulate his diet according to hunger and fullness, and can sometimes cause serious medical conditions.

What to Do

Begin by trying to adopt a neutral attitude about your child's food intake. Parents may control three things: what is offered to eat and where and when it is offered. The child should control how much he eats.

The goal is to make a child want to eat because he is hungry when he sits down at the table. Keep to a schedule of three meals and only planned snacks. If he is hungry an hour after lunch because he didn't eat, he has to wait until dinner or until a planned snack at three o'clock.

Don't allow a child to graze throughout the day; he'll never learn to recognize an internal feeling of hunger. Say, "I know you didn't have much for lunch, so you're hungry. But you must wait for our snacktime or for dinner." They may drink water but not glass after glass of juice or milk. Prepare yourself for a child's irritation when you first begin sticking to this schedule.

At meals, solids should be offered first, fluids last if a child tends to fill up on milk. Put small, nonintimidating portions on the plate. He can ask for more if he finishes what you've given him. Include something you know your child likes to eat. (In the case of a food fad, offer something in addition to it.) No games, TV watching, reading, or other distractions during meals. He should be allowed about thirty minutes to finish, no more. Remove his plate at that time, especially if he's just playing with his food.

An infant just learning to feed himself should be allowed to make a mess. Typically, conflict at this stage is over who is going to put food into the baby's mouth. Prepare finger foods to make eating easy. Praise him for self-feeding skills, not intake: "I see you got the spoon all the way into your mouth. Good job." Sit down and eat your meal. You are modeling proper self-feeding as well as keeping yourself from concentrating too much on what he puts in his mouth.

Respect a child's true aversion to certain foods if he seems to have a consistent sensitivity to them. If you think back to your own youth, you'll probably remember you too disliked particular foods. The sensitivity seems to run in families. It may also have something to do with temperament. Some children are just naturally hesitant about trying new things. They should be gently introduced to unfamiliar foods. (See *Temperament* and *Adaptability*.)

Put a tiny dab on the plate and say, "You may taste it if you want to." Most toddlers are so curious they will want to taste whatever you're eating. Sometimes the best way to pique interest is not to offer him a food you're eating until he's asked you for it.

Children whose likes seem completely dictated by whim are probably testing their control over you. Satisfy his desire for autonomy by giving him the choice of two things: eggs or Cheerios, for instance (either of which you are happy for him to have). Breakfast is the best meal to give options (because it's one of the easiest and quickest meals to fix). Once he's chosen and it's set before him, do not get up from the table again to fetch new demands. Tell him what's on his plate is what is available.

Finally, try to see such a child's assertiveness as an asset rather than a liability. Being strong-willed and persistent can be a valuable trait in adults. A child waging battle over food is often intelligent, perceptive, and very aware of interpersonal cues. He can see your reaction and knows that his finickiness may be rewarded with more attention. This child is a challenge. Try to keep a sense of humor. Be tolerant without succumbing to his demands for different food. Never call him a "bad boy" for not eating. (See also *Oppositional Behavior* and *Attention-Seeking*.)

* * *

132

Parents should correct a child, however, for engaging in inappropriate table behavior: *purposefully* throwing food, utensils, or temper tantrums. Your response should be dictated by a child's age. With a twelve- to eighteen-month-old, say, "No!" firmly and remove your attention (look away from him) until he behaves properly.

For a toddler, give him one clear warning before acting, but only one. If he continues to misbehave, turn his chair away from the table, perhaps to the wall, so that he can't interact with you. As in the case of a regular time-out (See "Time-Outs" in the Parenting Skills Introduction), tell him it will be over when a timer sounds. Time-outs should last no more than one minute per year of a child's age and sometimes less to ensure that it's you who starts and ends a time-out. Then return him to the table to correct his behavior. If he repeats the scenario, you should repeat the consequence. Give him lots of love and attention after dinner, during playtime.

Explain the time-out procedure to him before the occasion arises— that if he engages in certain inappropriate behavior he will receive a time-out. An angry child won't understand what is going on without prior explanation. He'll just be surprised. Be consistent in your limit-setting. Don't tolerate something tomorrow that you didn't today.

If the child insists on the same food day in and day out, take heart that he'll probably adopt another favorite within a week or two, typically something his friends like. It is also appropriate to encourage some variety in his consumption by setting the rule "No sweets or crackers until you've eaten some nutritious food first." Actively involving him in grocery shopping may stimulate his curiosity about different menus. Try reading him the Dr. Seuss classic *Green Eggs and Ham*, in which the main character discovers that he really does like a new dish once he agrees to taste it.

Lastly, model proper eating habits. Sitting in front of the television consuming junk food teaches a child to eat out of boredom. Avoid giving food as a reward for success or as an antidote to sadness, particularly for a child with a tendency to chubbiness. Take him to the park to play, instead.

It's hard not to be hurt when your child dislikes food over which you've labored, but remember by allowing him to control his intake you're teaching him self-discipline and self-control, in the form of heeding his own internal cues of hunger and fullness.

* * *

Recommended cookbooks: *365 Foods Kids Love to Eat*, by Sheila Ellison and Judith Gray (Forward March Press, Redwood City, CA); *Feed Me! I'm Yours*, by Vicki Lansky (Meadowbrook); *Once Upon a Recipe*, by Karen Greene (Perigee Books).

Forgetfulness

Most of us have occasional lapses in our memory, especially when we're tired or overstressed. We can forget where our keys are when we're in a hurry, or leave our umbrella in the subway because we're thinking about the meeting to which we're heading. Children are no different.

Memory is achieved through several steps, the first being attention, the next concentration. A child can't remember an instruction, for instance, if he hasn't heard it or focused on it while it was given. (See *Listening.*)

There are also many neuronal connections that must be made within the brain for an instruction to be processed and stored adequately. In some cases, the root of forgetfulness is not really the act of losing previously held knowledge; it may have to do instead with the brain having difficulty in processing or retrieving information. It doesn't necessarily mean a child lacks motivation or intelligence. (See *Memory Development* and *Learning Disabilities.*)

Usually, occasional forgetfulness is nothing serious. Children may just need more help organizing themselves so they can find things more easily. There are also techniques for improving a person's ability to remember things, such as associating a letter with an animal (an S looks like a snake), or finding a rhyme ("In 1492 Columbus sailed the ocean blue"). (See *Memory Development* and *Concentration.*)

But sometimes a faulty memory may be an indicator of brain dysfunction. If a child seems uncharacteristically forgetful following an injury or a high fever, he should be taken to a doctor immediately. He could also seem forgetful if he has seizure disorders, which temporarily make him lose full awareness of his surroundings. (See *Staring Episodes.*)

Gender Identity Disorder

A child who suffers from gender identity disorder is discomforted by his or her sex and truly appears to want to be what he physically is not. This is very different from a child who worries that he cannot adequately fill society's expectations of his gender role, or who dabbles in cross-gender behavior (see *Playing with Dolls*), both of which are common and normal. The disorder itself is rare.

In the beginning, a little boy might not only play with dolls, but he will also dress like a girl, want to play strictly female games, or have no interest in traditional male activities. In extreme cases, he may refuse to acknowledge the presence of his penis or testes. A girl may refuse to sit to urinate.

The disorder becomes most noticeable in preteens, when children developmentally tend to gravitate to cliques of their own sex. A boy that age who says that all his best friends are girls, or that he wants to be a girl, may well be diagnosed as having gender identity disorder.

According to the American Psychiatric Association's diagnostic manual, as many as one-third to two-thirds of boys who really meet the criteria of this disorder may become homosexuals as adults. Fewer girls do.

What to Do

A parent overreacting to a boy asking for a doll is jumping the gun and running the risk of making his child ashamed of his curiosity. If a child consistently displays several characteristics of gender identity disorder, however, a parent should seek professional help. Children who truly are unhappy with their gender and are unable to play with both sexes will have trouble fitting into their peer groups. Gay adolescents have more psychological problems and as a group have a higher rate of suicide and depression.

Growth Problems

One of the primary goals of school-aged children is to be as much like everyone else as possible yet still be special. But not too special. One of the most significant ways of being different is to be much taller, or much shorter, than your peers.

Boys are particularly sensitive to being short, and girls to being tall. Extreme height differences tend to run in families and there is little a child can do if he or she is genetically slated to be short or tall. Children may feel betrayed by their bodies as their friends either shoot up or remain the average height. The peak time of trouble generally comes around age twelve, as most children begin their adolescent growth spurt. Short boys in particular may try to overcompensate for their size with either aggressive or clownish behavior.

The good news is that their efforts may pay off and make them special in sports in an unusual way. Many a team has had a smaller-than-average star basketball player who was particularly agile and speedy. Children also tend to befriend peers who are like them. All it takes is another statuesque girl to make a tall girl feel more comfortable.

Acknowledge your child's uneasiness but at the same time help her accept her body as is and find the advantages therein. For instance, a very tall child is likely to do well in some sports. (See *Making Friends* and *Self-Esteem*.)

Keep in mind that some growth problems have medical causes. Exceedingly short children should be evaluated by a pediatrician.

Guilty Feelings

Guilt is an uncomfortable feeling that a person experiences when he believes he has violated a code of ethics, his own or society's. Over the ages, philosophers, religious leaders, and social scientists have felt that guilt is one force that acts to keep people in line morally. In fact, until a

136

person has become cognitively able to define right and wrong in a more abstract fashion, it is respect for authority and desire for approval that help steer and modify his behavior.

Feeling too much guilt, however, can have detrimental, inhibiting effects. Parents need to remember that conscience and empathy are things a child acquires as he matures. Suggesting to a preschooler that he should feel bad about snatching a toy away from a playmate is really inappropriate. He isn't yet capable intellectually of standing in another person's shoes and considering his emotions. You will only confuse him. That kind of empathy doesn't begin until around age six. Then, it is reasonable to *ask* (not tell): "How would you feel if Johnny did that to you?" (See *Insensitivity, Aggression, Making Friends*, and *Rudeness and Developing Manners*.)

Instead, provide young children with structure and external consequences for inappropriate behaviors. You are the authority defining what's right and wrong, but stay flexible and forgiving. A young child who frequently feels guilty is probably overcontrolled and required to comply to too many rules. (See *Compliance* and *Perfectionism*.)

On the other hand, feeling absolutely no guilt or remorse can be a serious problem. Children with conduct disorders, who bully or engage in antisocial acts, clearly are unable to consider the rights and feelings of others. By the time a child is a preteen, he should demonstrate an understanding of the terms "right" and "wrong."

Like so much about behavior and your response to it, taking a stance somewhere in the middle is probably the best course on guilt. And before trying to construct a value system for children, be clear in your own mind what you really believe in and think important.

Habits

Habits such as fingernail-biting, hair-twirling, nose-picking, ear-pulling, and thumb-sucking usually serve two emotional functions: to relieve anxiety or to provide stimulation. Rhythmic, repetitive motions soothe and release tension. Such habits are common, particularly among school-aged children as they do their homework or are under stress.

The problem is that most children's habits annoy or embarrass parents because they are socially unacceptable. No one wants to watch Johnny pick his nose at the dinner table. But before you reprimand a child too harshly, consider your own habits and don't demand more of a child than you do of yourself. We may like to think we've outgrown the need for such tension releasers, but doodling, foot-tapping, biting pencils, and jiggling change provide similar relief.

Most kids outgrow their habits, given some time, but you might wish to nudge that process along, especially if a child suffers peer harassment or causes herself physical discomfort or changes her appearance with the activity. (Excessive nail-biting can make fingertips sore; hair-pulling can produce bald spots; nose-picking can leave painful scabs.) Also of concern is a child who uses her habit obsessively, as a method of social avoidance.

Try to notice a pattern. Is the habit compounded by nervousness or boredom? If a child uses it unrelentingly during school, while separated from you, or in social situations there is probably an underlying anxiety that you need to help her address. Sometimes such habits become more pronounced when change occurs, such as a move, beginning school, or the birth of a sibling.

What to Do

Most habits can be eliminated or at least reduced through behavior modification. Keep in mind that it will be easier to break a habit when it's done for pleasure than when it's done out of nervousness. The latter will take more patience and reassurance.

First, talk to your child about it. She may not even realize that she does it. To heighten her awareness, gently and quietly remind her (without embarrassing her in front of people) when you see her repeating the behavior. Together, try to figure out when she's most prone to do it and then discuss alternative ways to relax or calm herself. (See *Fears and Phobias*, *Anxiety*, and *School*.)

Of course, she may legitimately wonder why her habits are your business. Explain that you're concerned her friends may tease her. But grant her that behaviors that are not socially acceptable may be permissible in private. (Genital stimulation is one such habit. See *Masturbation*.) Try saying, "Honey, that's inappropriate to do in front of people. If you want to do that, you need to go to your room," or "Please don't do that in front of me. I don't like it."

Often children engage in habits while sitting, mesmerized, in front of the television. Perhaps say, "I notice when you watch TV that you pull your hair [or pick your nose]. We've talked about how I don't like that. Since I think the two are connected, I'm going to turn it off." That's often enough to stop a child.

Be sure to praise her effort and improvements, plus give her positive attention when she's not engaging in her habit.

If these techniques fail, try a more systematic approach. Set up rewards and incentives for abstaining. Work first on limiting the frequency of the behavior—that's a more realistic and obtainable goal than wiping it out entirely. For instance, when a child typically engages in the habit during TV-watching, say, "I want you to go for half an hour without doing it, then I'll turn the television back on."

Once she can go an entire day, keep track of those successes and reward her with a predetermined activity or treat at the end of a week. Maybe the reward should be something related to giving up the habit— a pretty pair of gloves or nail polish for the reformed nail-biter.

Don't place *too* much emphasis on success, as that kind of pressure may only exacerbate her anxiety level. Don't criticize her when she slips. Instead, try saying, "We'll try again tomorrow."

(See also *Thumb-Sucking* and *Masturbation*.)

Hair-Pulling

(See *Habits*)

Headaches

Headaches are a common malady caused by the flu, ear infections, toothaches, anxiety, or even stuffy rooms. Generally headaches are not serious unless a child has had a recent head injury, or if the headache is accompanied by a fever over 100 degrees, neck stiffness, confusion, and intolerance of bright light, which may indicate he has meningitis or encephalitis. If your child has these symptoms, it is a medical emergency. Contact a physician immediately.

Some children seem to have chronic headaches. If they are accompanied by nausea, they may be migraine headaches, which tend to run in families. Chronic headaches should be brought to the attention of a child's pediatrician to rule out the possibility of an underlying medical condition.

If a child complains about headaches only during weekdays and seemingly as a way of avoiding school, he may have school reluctance or phobia. (See *School* and *Anxiety*.) These headaches are usually not accompanied by fever or stomach cramps. Still, the pain may be very real to children. We all know that anxiety can make our heads pound. The link between emotional distress and physical aches is becoming increasingly clear.

If stress seems to be the cause of a string of headaches, find out what is worrying your child and try to help him deal with that anxiety. In the case of school phobia, the most effective medicine is to send him to school, making arrangements for him to lie down in the clinic if his head hurts. Keeping him at home day after day will only increase his phobia and provide unanticipated benefits to the child such as parental attention, avoiding schoolwork, or controlling family schedules. (See School Phobia under *School* for other advice.)

141

If a child has headaches coupled with a sudden shift in his eating, sleeping, or social habits, he may be depressed. (See *Reaction to Loss*, *Reaction to Parental Conflict*, and *Depression*.)

Head-Banging

During the first year of life, it's fairly common for babies to bang their heads. Once they've mastered sitting up, they tend to rhythmically rock back and forth and sometimes bang their head in the process, either by accident or on purpose. Head-banging also seems to occur as a child moves from crawling to standing. Again, this probably has to do with the rhythmic motion involved in the process. (See *Rocking*.)

If head-banging persists or seems severe in its intensity, consult a pediatrician. The behavior may suggest a neurological or developmental problem and, in rare cases, can be a sign of autism.

Another time head-banging is relatively common is during the "terrible twos" stage. Some children bang their heads during a temper tantrum. When a child is that out of control, he doesn't realize the danger of his actions. Banging his head will hurt and probably only serve to fuel his fury and thrashing. Try to contain a child for his safety, in a style that is protective without being rewarding. Of course, that is easier said than done. Try holding the child at arm's length and saying, "I love you, but I don't like this behavior and I cannot let you hurt yourself." Or perhaps give him an alternative behavior, such as ripping up paper or hitting a pillow. (See *Temper Tantrums*.)

Hearing

Good hearing brings the sounds of the world to a baby—her mother's humming, birds warbling, the wind sweeping trees against her bedroom window. It also helps keep her out of danger.

But most important, it lets her communicate. Without hearing, a child cannot understand what is being said to her. Nor can she learn to speak. She must first hear *precisely* the sounds of language before she can attempt to imitate them. The longer an infant or toddler's hearing is obstructed or muffled, the harder it will be for her to talk and learn words.

Hearing is achieved through a complicated and delicate physical process. The outer ear gathers sound waves as they move through the air. Those waves travel down the ear canal and then strike the eardrum. Behind the eardrum is a space filled with air and containing two muscles, the eustachian tube, and three tiny bones called the ossicles.

As the eardrum vibrates, so, too, do the ossicles. They pass the message on to the inner ear. Inside the inner ear are millions of tiny hair cells that receive and decode sound. That action causes the auditory nerve to fire and to transmit the message to the brain.

Any impediment along the way can cause hearing loss. These losses can be permanent or temporary (caused by ear infections or wax buildup, for instance) and range from serious to subtle. The majority of hearing-impaired people are not deaf. Many hearing-impaired children, for instance, may hear low-frequency sounds (vowels) well but have difficulty distinguishing high-frequency ones (consonants). Or words may sound different from day to day depending on whether or not a child has fluid buildup from a middle-ear infection.

In any case, such difficulties may bring delays in speech and language acquisition, which in turn may cause all sorts of social, behavioral, and academic troubles.

There are basically three types of hearing loss: conductive (problems in the outer or middle ear that are generally transient or medically treatable); sensorineural (nerve deafness in the inner ear that is permanent but often can be improved with the use of hearing aids); and mixed (a combination of the two).

Hearing loss may be present at birth if the mother contracted German measles or another dangerous viral infection during pregnancy; if there were complications during a child's birth; if the baby was premature or had a blood problem; or if hearing problems run in either parent's family.

Hearing loss may be caused after birth by childhood illnesses such as mumps, measles, or meningitis; a significant head injury;

repeated, undetected middle-ear infections or allergic reactions; exposure to loud noises, either once (such as a gunshot or firecrackers) or chronically (listening to a Walkman at a high volume); or wax buildup. Most wax works its way out naturally. Parents should *not* try to clean a child's ears as they probably will only push the wax down the ear canal, impacting it further. Take a child to her pediatrician or use drops to soften the wax so that it comes out on its own.

Parents should note that middle-ear infections are the second most common health problem for preschoolers. (Colds are number one.) According to the American Speech-Language-Hearing Association, 50 percent of all children have at least one episode before they are a year old, and 35 percent of children aged one to three have repeated bouts.

When children are young, the middle ear is particularly susceptible to infection because of the flat angle of the eustachian tube, which connects it to the throat. Infections can range in severity from a mild buildup of clear fluid behind the eardrum to nasty glue-like blockages, which can cause permanent hearing damage if undetected.

Even when a child's condition is mild and she is on antibiotics, the eardrum's ability to vibrate and transmit sound is dampened. Sounds are likely to be muffled and perhaps hard to understand. It's vital, then, that a child receive treatment as soon as possible. Symptoms include fever, irritability, pulling on ears, listlessness, misunderstanding directions, or requesting that the radio or TV volume be turned higher than normal.

Watch your baby for signs that she's hearing well. The following guidelines are a few listed by the Alexander Graham Bell Association for the Deaf and the American Speech-Language-Hearing Association.

Between birth and six months she should be startled by loud sounds and turn to look for their location; be soothed by her mother's voice; and make noises such as "ooh" and "ba-ba-ba." (A hearing-impaired baby will make these noises at first because of the physical stimulation of her tongue against her mouth, but if she lacks her own auditory reinforcement she will eventually stop babbling.)

Between seven months and a year of age, she should look up when you call her name and become quiet and listen when you speak to her. Her babbling should have many different sounds to it, such as *p*, *b*, and *m*. She should be starting to combine them in long and short sequences, much like speech.

By fourteen to eighteen months of age, she should have ten or more single words, and by twenty-four months be able to speak in two-word phrases. By two and a half, she should be constructing short sentences. (See *Language and Speech*.)

It is often difficult to detect subtle hearing problems, particularly if the child is smart and learns to compensate for auditory deficits by being especially attentive to visual cues. Warning signs that a toddler or preschooler is experiencing some hearing problems include speaking in a nasal or flat tone with no inflection and in a very loud volume. She may be unusually aggressive, easily frustrated, and prone to tantrums because she has difficulty comprehending people or making herself understood. She may seem to hear properly only when watching your face. She'll probably say "What?" a lot.

If one ear is affected, she may *always* put the telephone up to the other, working ear. She may also have trouble pronouncing certain sounds, such as *r*, *l*, *th*, and *s*. (Such speech problems are fairly common developmentally, but may be a sign of trouble if combined with other indicators of hearing loss.)

(See also *Language and Speech*.)

What to Do

If you suspect your child has a hearing problem, take her for an evaluation sooner rather than later. The longer she experiences the difficulty, the more delayed her speech and language acquisition may be. The hearing of babies as young as six months can be evaluated by watching behavioral responses. Children do not have to be talking to be tested. Surgery can correct many serious problems and even newborns can be fitted for hearing aids. And the younger a child, the more easily she adjusts to wearing hearing aids.

For further information contact the American Speech-Language-Hearing Association, 10801 Rockville Pike, Rockville, MD 20852 (1-800-638-TALK); or the Alexander Graham Bell Association for the Deaf, 3417 Volta Place, NW, Washington, D.C. 20007 (202-337-5220).

Hitting and Kicking

There is a big difference between a child who hits and kicks offhandedly during play and one who purposefully punches someone. There are plenty of television shows that feature martial arts or daredevil heroics that children may replicate in playacting. Try to gauge the intensity and intent of a child's actions before interceding. A pattern of extreme roughness with others probably deserves your intervention. So, too, does a child who picks up an object with which to hit a playmate. That child has learned that using something other than his hand is more efficient and painful to the recipient, and less hurtful to himself.

It is also valuable to determine if your child's aggression is situational: Is he attacking or defending himself? Socially acceptable, alternative behaviors can be taught to both types of aggressive children.

(See *Aggression.*)

Hoarding

Many children like to collect treasures from vacations or to proudly save their artwork. That is different from hoarding, a behavior that has more to do with building up inconsequential stores of objects. Generally, children are secretive about hoarding, and parents discover these collections only by accident.

Hoarding in and of itself does not mean a child has a problem and often is merely a passing phase. But it may also be an activity that accompanies other conditions, such as depression, conduct disorders, or eating disorders. Obese and bulimic children may hoard food for private binges. Anorexics may actually be hiding the food parents thought they ate. (See *Eating Disorders.*) Children who shoplift also tend to take nonsensical items and keep them as trophies. (See *Stealing.*)

146

Ask a child in a nonaccusatory way, "What's this?" if you discover a stash of unrelated items. Listen carefully to the answer and monitor his behavior closely in the coming weeks or months.

Hyperactivity

"Hyperactive" is a word much like "depression" and "anxiety," which have come to general use but can have very different meanings in the vernacular than in clinical terms. During the 1970s, hyperactivity was the formal medical diagnosis for a common condition now called Attention-Deficit Hyperactivity Disorder (ADHD).

Today, some parents use the term "hyperactive" to describe their highly energetic child. Many children are exuberant, boisterous bundles of energy. It's part of their innate personality—they just came into the world squirmy and curious. They may be hard to keep up with, but there is probably nothing wrong with them. In fact, if parents of active children think back to their own childhood, they were probably the same way. The trait seems to have some inheritability. (See *Temperament*.)

In the best-case scenarios, these children may grow up to be athletes, performing artists, scientists, social leaders, adventurers. Parents who learn how to accept and cope with a child's rambunctiousness make everyone happier, and build on his natural courage and inquisitiveness. (See *Risk-Taking*.)

An intense level of activity can be a problem, however, if it is accompanied by a high degree of distractibility and impulsivity. Such a personality mix may lead a child to take foolish risks, to develop behavior problems, or to have trouble fitting in with peers. It may also make it very difficult for him to sit still and listen in class, to concentrate on and complete tasks, or to tolerate frustration. This cluster of behaviors suggests that a child may have ADHD. (See *Attention-Deficit Hyperactivity Disorder* and *Risk-Taking*.)

147

Hyperventilation

It is not unusual for a young child who breathes rapidly and gulps large amounts of air during a temper tantrum to cause himself to hyperventilate. In extreme cases, he may even faint.

If hyperventilation recurs frequently, he's probably triggering it for attention, much as he might hold his breath. At first, it probably happened by accident because he was violently crying. But if parents respond to an episode of hyperventilation with alarm and lots of coddling, a child will quickly learn that working himself into a frenzy brings a desired result. Try to respond as nonchalantly as possible when he tries it, or place consequences on the behavior. ("If you do that, this will happen.")

(See also *Breath-Holding*, *Temper Tantrums*, and "Time-Outs" under the Parenting Skills Introduction.)

In a few cases, hyperventilation is beyond a child's control, and probably the result of intense anxiety or serious neurological problems. It may also occur when a child is school phobic. If a child seems to hyperventilate without any intention of manipulating you—there is no tantrum or power struggle involved—have him evaluated either by a mental-health professional or a neurologist. Talk first to your pediatrician. (See also *Anxiety* and School Phobia under *School.*)

Imaginary Friends

Creating an imaginary friend is a common and often delightful flight of fancy for preschoolers, particularly girls. Even though you might be slightly unnerved by being warned not to sit on an invisible being, you should try to "see" that make-believe friend as the product of a creative and healthy mind.

Imaginary friends serve many purposes for a child. Besides being fun, these fantasy playmates can help children feel safe in the dark; express feelings such as anger that they might be afraid of voicing otherwise; or take the blame for bad acts that they wish they hadn't done. (For more on the latter, see *Lying*.) They can also be a source of comfort and companionship when a new sibling is born or when a best (real-life) friend moves away.

If you are wise, you can learn a lot about what your child is feeling by listening to her imaginary friend. The mother in the cartoon strip "Calvin and Hobbes," about a little boy and his stuffed tiger, certainly does.

Follow a child's lead about how involved to become in her fantasy. There's nothing wrong with setting an extra plate at the table if a child requests it. But don't you suggest it. Let your child set the tone of your mutual playacting if she does include you. Much of what she loves about her make-believe scenarios is that they belong to her. She controls their outcome, which is a large reason why they can be such effective outlets for anxiety. (See *Play*.)

Most children give up their imaginary friends once those creations have served their purpose (after a child has more or less accepted the arrival of a new baby, for instance) or before the age of seven. Parents shouldn't be concerned unless that imaginary playmate takes up so much of a child's attention that it impedes her relationships with other children. If a child with an invisible buddy seems lonely or terribly shy, you may need to ask if you are providing enough opportunities for her to play with real-life peers.

In a few, very rare cases, a child may be having delusions, in which case she would have other symptoms and lapses in reality. If this occurs, seek professional counseling.

Immature Behavior

The important thing to remember about development is that what is considered "normal" spans a wide range. Each individual is different and has his own course of evolution. Some children walk at ten months of age, others at sixteen. Some may have one hundred words at eighteen months, others only a handful. Some children achieve a capacity for happily separating from parents during preschool while others continue to struggle with more mature behaviors until they enter first grade.

Immature behavior suggests that a child is different, less "sophisticated" than his peers. The question to ask yourself is whether or not that behavior is causing a child trouble. Is it hampering his ability to befriend peers? Is it bringing him embarrassment or into conflict with teachers at school? Does the behavior cut across situations, or is it isolated to one environment? (Actually, if your child acts immaturely only at home, that's good news. It suggests there is something about your relationship or family circumstances that can be changed to improve his behavior, and that he is capable of some self-control in public places.)

For the most part, immature behavior such as whining, clinging, temper tantrums, and aggressive play habits should have disappeared by the time a child is five or six years of age. Of course, you will need to help children shed those behaviors and adopt more socially acceptable ones. A child's temperament may slow the process if he is innately more anxious, hesitant, or slow to warm. (See *Attention-Seeking*, *Demanding*, *Whining*, *Clinging*, *Aggression*, and *Temper Tantrums*.)

Keep in mind that children often regress into less mature behavior when a new sibling is born, or when they have experienced a change such as a move, parents separating, or the death of a relative. (See *Regression*, *Reaction to Loss*, *Reaction to Parental Conflict*, and *Sib-*

ling Rivalry.) Handle these regressions with empathy and lots of positive attention when a child is *not* misbehaving. Continue reminding him what behavior is inappropriate and unacceptable. But try not to shame him by calling him "a baby." Sometimes a *gently* put "You know better, honey, you're my big boy" can help inspire him to retrieve his more mature demeanor.

Impatience

Children do not come into this world armed with patience. In fact, it probably runs against instinct, since a baby's survival in the wild would depend on speedy response to his needs. The ability to wait for gratification, to tolerate frustration, is probably something that must be learned. You will need to teach patience, model it yourselves, and reinforce it with praise when children practice it. Life is full of situations that keep us from immediately realizing our goals and desires. Without some degree of patience, children may become anxious, frustrated, and unhappy with themselves.

Patience does evolve as children mature intellectually and learn that they really can wait a few minutes to get something and that those minutes do, in fact, pass. (That working knowledge comes at around age six or seven.) To encourage the process, set consistent limits to help a child modify his demands. If a child immediately receives whatever he wants as soon as he whines, he'll be very reluctant to give up whining. (See *Attention-Seeking*, *Whining*, and *Demanding*.)

Some children are just temperamentally more impatient, impulsive, and quick to be upset. (See *Temperament*, *Adaptability*, and *Impulsivity*.) This is probably also true of firstborns, who haven't had to compete yet with siblings. You might need to work a little harder with these types of children.

Start with helping toddlers tolerate frustration in learning and playing. If he kicks away blocks after his tower has toppled, say, "Oh well. It doesn't matter, we can build it again." Then help him do so. Or, if he seems overwhelmed by the complexity of a puzzle, for instance, acknowledge that it might be hard. Say, "Gee, this is complicated. But I bet if I put in this one piece, you can do the rest." Introduce new puzzles or challenges when a child is ready for them and when he's in a good mood—not when he's hungry or tired and more prone to frustration and annoyance.

Impatience is even more pronounced in children who are perfectionists and who expect themselves to be able to do everything right on their first try. Learning is best done by a series of failed attempts that eventually lead to success. That sequence will enhance a child's sense of accomplishment and ability to problem-solve far more than will instant success. (See *Self-Esteem* and *Perfectionism.*)

Don't forget to praise a child when he does wait patiently for you in the grocery store checkout, or when you've had to answer the phone just as the two of you were leaving for the playground.

Finally, practice what you preach. If you have low frustration tolerance, he is likely to follow your lead. Hold your own tongue when trapped in a traffic snarl and don't become impatient as he struggles to button his coat on his own.

Impulsivity

An impulsive person acts before he thinks. Until children get a little experience behind them and mature cognitively, most act in a way that we might call impulsive. They head for an electrical socket because it's intriguing. Even after we've told them no, they still crawl for it because they just can't quite contain their curiosity. They must learn, through repeated warnings, that a socket poses danger and should be avoided. You'll have to condition toddlers and preschoolers this way about a variety of safety issues. (See *Risk-Taking* and *Accident-Prone.*)

You'll also have to help children learn to control playtime aggression, which is often impulsive. Toddlers hit or shove playmates who have a toy they want. Such aggression is "goal-directed," a method of obtaining something from someone immediately. Usually it is not premeditated or even personal to the offended playmate. Such impulsivity will eventually be modified as children learn what is acceptable and what is not, mostly by being censored by their own peers. (See *Aggression.*)

Most children do learn to control their impulses with some thought-out caution or empathy around the time they enter school. They've been socialized by parents and preschool playmates. And around seven years of age, a significant developmental change in their thinking takes place. Psychologist Jean Piaget called it "concrete operations." Children are suddenly capable of understanding that there are logical connections, causes and effects, rules and procedures for determining certain outcomes. That means they can consider before they act: "If I do this, what might result?" (See the Developmental Tasks Appendix.)

Unfortunately, some children seem to have impulsive personality styles. Many are rambunctious, adventuresome individuals who will get themselves into scrapes and scare their mothers but come out just fine. Others may have Attention-Deficit Hyperactivity Disorder (ADHD). A few will put themselves into real physical danger with their antics, their impulsivity clearly going well beyond joyful spontaneity.

Impulsivity is a problem when a child shows poor judgment, when his impetuousness constantly puts him at physical risk or impedes his ability to function in social groups and stay within societal rules of conduct. An impulsive child might interrupt teachers, blurt out answers when he's not being asked, take a peer's turn at a game. He might run out into the street. He might have trouble stopping inappropriate impulses such as stealing or hitting another child. He just can't seem to stop, think about the consequences or impropriety of an act, and then stop himself. He acts in what we might call a knee-jerk fashion.

Parents need to take extra time to help impulsive children learn to think out situations themselves. Don't lecture; try asking, "What do you think will happen if you do this?" "How do you think [hitting or interrupting] made your friend feel?" (See also *Insensitivity.*) Rehearse difficult situations in advance with the impulsive child.

If your child's impulsivity frequently gets him into trouble with his teachers or friends and seems coupled with an inability to concentrate, hyperactivity, and distractibility, you should ask his pediatrician about ADHD. (See *Attention-Deficit Hyperactivity Disorder.*)

Insensitivity

Preschoolers and toddlers often act in ways we adults consider insensitive. They snatch toys away from playmates, shout "I hate you" when you refuse to hand over a cookie, or smack a dog who has accidentally knocked them down. Often these actions stem from a lack of impulse control and knowledge of what is acceptable. Such internal checks on behavior come with time and socialization. They also come with empathy, a trait some human beings may have naturally, but one that usually needs nurturing.

Social sensitivity, as Selma Fraiberg calls it in *The Magic Years*, requires a child to be able to put himself in another person's shoes, to think about how another person might feel as a consequence of his actions. Such "identification" and imaginative thinking is nearly impossible for a three-year-old, who is struggling to recognize and express his own feelings. But it should come, usually around the age of six, after some careful guidance and role-modeling by parents. Tell a toddler to "be nice." Ask a five- or six-year-old how he'd feel if his friend acted unkindly toward him. Peer pressure and group censorship should also help instill a respect for the feelings and rights of others since an insensitive child will not have playmates for long. (See *Aggression* and *Guilty Feelings*.)

If a school-aged child seems incapable of considering the feelings of others, he may be witnessing insensitivity or brutality at home and following suit. He may be emotionally troubled and physically displaying his sadness or anger about a situation (see *Reaction to Parental Conflict*), or he may have a more general behavior problem (see *Aggression*, *Bullying*, *Oppositional Defiant Disorder*); he might also have a problem with impulsivity. (See *Impulsivity* and *Attention-Deficit Hyperactivity Disorder*.) In some cases, insensitive children are reacting to undetected hearing, language, or learning problems that are frustrating or embarrassing, thereby exacerbating aggressive tendencies. (See *Hearing*, *Language and Speech*, and *Learning Disabilities*.)

Finally, older children seem to go through a developmental stage around ten to twelve years of age, when cliques are vitally important. Hostility and verbal aggression between rival groups may not be desirable or admirable but are common to the age-group.

Indifference to the feelings of others is also an autistic quality, but autism is a serious disorder with many other severe symptoms that usually manifest themselves before a child is three years old. (See *Autism.*)

Insomnia

(See *Sleep*, *School*, *Anxiety*, and *Depression*)

Interrupting

Interrupting is a common problem faced by parents of young children. In certain situations, it should probably be tolerated. Children are children. They become excited and want to share news with you and it's hard for them to wait.

Frequent interrupting, however, can be another attention-seeking device, much like whining, clinging, or tantrums. Children will typically interrupt at the most inconvenient times: while a parent is on the phone with his employer, for instance. Because such interruptions may be a power play on a child's part, you need to respond calmly and in a way that doesn't reinforce the behavior.

Don't yell. Don't immediately give him whatever he's demanding to make him quiet. Set limits. Try saying, "Go over there and count to ten. Then you may come back and ask Daddy." (See also *Attention-Seeking*, *Whining*, and *Temper Tantrums*.)

Keep in mind that certain situations test the limits of a child's patience and set him up to interrupt. Long telephone calls and having your office at home are prime examples. Office equipment and computers look like so much fun to play with. It's just too tempting sometimes. Children want your stimulation and interaction. Try to remember how you felt when you wanted your own parents' attention and didn't receive it.

Make sure your child has something or someone fun to occupy him during the times that you *must* work or conduct business on the phone. Be prepared to be flexible and to let the answering machine pick up calls when you two are playing or sharing a meal. Return the calls during his nap or after he's gone to bed for the night.

Finally, model the behavior you want your child to exhibit. Don't interrupt him when he's speaking. Say, "Excuse me," when you must interrupt his play to talk with his baby-sitter or friend. Give him full attention during normal conversations. It will be much easier for a child to wait to tell you something if he knows that he will *really* be heard when you stop to listen. (See also *Listening* and *Refusing to Speak*.)

Older, school-aged children can also be taught about manners, and that interrupting someone as they speak is disrespectful and may hurt their feelings. (See *Rudeness and Developing Manners* and *Insensitivity*.)

Irritability

Children, like grown-ups, can be irritable for a host of reasons. They may be tired, hungry, or cutting teeth, or they may have an ear infection, a cold, or the flu. Irritability can be a first warning sign that they're not feeling well. In preschoolers, chronic crossness may stem from an undetected hearing loss that makes it difficult for children to understand and acquire new vocabulary. (See *Hearing*.)

However, irritability can also be an element of temperament. Some children come into this world being fussy, hard to soothe, or easily upset by loud noises, bright lights, or general hubbub. When there is not a medical reason for it, watch for a predictable pattern of irritability. Does it happen at the same time of day or in certain situations? If so, try to work around those factors so that you don't put too many unachievable demands on a child during his most irritable moments. (See *Temperament*, *Adaptability*, *Colic*, and *Temper Tantrums*.)

If a child's irritability is sudden and in marked contrast to his typical moods, think about whether he's just experienced a drastic life change. Has your family recently moved, divorced, experienced the death of a relative, or had a new baby? When a child's irritability is linked to such an event, it should subside after a few weeks and some careful reassurance and empathetic discussions with you. (See *Reaction to Loss, Reaction to Parental Conflict, Anxiety, Attention-Seeking, Regression,* and *School.*) If his irritability doesn't go away after a reasonable time and is coupled with changes in sleep and eating patterns and social withdrawal, seek the advice of a professional. (See *Sadness* and *Depression.*)

Finally, don't confuse irritability with argumentativeness or defiance, which usually are more about a child's growing intellect or quest for autonomy than about mood. (See *Argumentative* and *Oppositional Behavior.*)

Language and Speech

Language is the use of symbols (letters, words, or gestures) in a system determined by rules (grammar) for communication with others. Speech is the spoken version of language, the motor and oral act of talking.

Language and speech allow us to convey our needs, wants, and ideas to each other. It is perhaps our most human characteristic, since that capability differentiates us from most other animals. It's the basis for our socialization and mutual cooperation, perhaps even the prerequisite for civilization. If a child's ability to learn language and speech is impaired or delayed, he will find it difficult to learn, to befriend his peers, to understand instructions, or to describe what he's thinking or feeling.

Think of a toddler, whose tantrums usually subside as he becomes more verbal. Once a child is able to use words, he's far less frustrated by his environment. He may even ask for a toy instead of grabbing it from a playmate.

Sometimes, however, that development doesn't occur properly. Such faltering has far-reaching impact on a child. Think of yourself when you can't remember a word or a name you want. You're probably embarrassed and annoyed. Perhaps you withdraw from the conversation altogether. Or think of what it's like when you're in a foreign country and you can't tell where the words of the natives stop or start, let alone what they mean. Will you ask for directions, or just blunder ahead, anxious and defiant?

That's what it's like for children with language and speech problems. Many of them will have correlating learning disabilities and eventually develop behavior problems.

A child learns language and speech by listening and imitating. Babies' brains are beautifully prepared to learn it. There is evidence that infants

159

breathe in rhythm to language and shape their mouths to mimic the sounds their caretakers make.

Talk to them from day one. It's the interplay, with eye-to-eye contact, that helps them watch, hear, and understand that language is for communication, and then try to imitate it themselves. "Listen" to a baby's cooing and babbling as if she's talking, because, in truth, she is. Respond to her. Use simple words and clear, short sentences. Avoid talking only in nonsensical baby talk.

Remember that it is vital that children hear well for them to be able to differentiate the subtle shades of sounds in any given language. Physical hearing impairments or a series of middle-ear infections affect the way a child takes in language, which may hinder her language acquisition and delay talking. The sooner such problems are diagnosed, the better. (See *Hearing*.)

Between six months and a year of age, a baby will begin to pick out some of the words she hears ("bottle," for instance) and understand what they mean. She's starting to achieve what researchers call passive, or receptive, language. She's absorbing and comprehending. By the end of her first year, she should be able to follow simple commands such as: "No" or "Hand me your bottle, please" or questions such as: "Are you hungry?"

This is the time for parents to begin "labeling" things for a baby to acquire their names. Say things like: "Here is your ball. Catch the ball." If she gestures to something she seems to want, give her its name. Ask: "Do you want the flower? The red flower? Let me pick the flower for you. Here's the flower." Point out the eyes, mouth, ears, and nose on a beloved doll. Read to your child and label objects in a book's pictures. Ask her to find the horse, the dog, the star.

Usually around the time a child is a year old, she begins to speak simple words: "Mama, Dada, dog, hot, bye-bye." After that, her vocabulary may proliferate at an amazing speed. She should probably add a few words each month and by the end of the second year be combining words into very short phrases. Help her learn by expanding her single words into more complete thoughts. If she points to a dog and says, "Doggie," for instance, respond with: "I see the dog. He's by the tree."

Remember there is a wide variation in what's considered normal. Many children are slower to start talking. This is particularly true of boys; younger siblings, who have less individual time with adults; and very active toddlers, who are concentrating on perfecting their motor skills. Some have only a dozen words by eighteen months of age and that's fine. However, language and speech specialists say the outside parameters of normal are for a child to have five words at eighteen months and to be combining two words—"More juice," for instance—by twenty-four months.

The following language milestones are a few listed by the American Speech-Language-Hearing Association and the National Institutes of Health: Between the ages of two and three, a child may develop a 200- to 400-word vocabulary. By the end of that year, she should have a word for every familiar object; be constructing two- or three-word sentences using verbs; understand the difference between "in" and "under"; and be able to complete a two-step oral instruction ("Get your teddy and come into your bedroom," for example).

From three to four years of age, a child's vocabulary expands enormously. By the time she's four, she can correctly use "*is*" at the beginning of a question; express the concept of future events: "We're going to go to the park"; use some irregular plurals, such as "feet"; and tell stories that relate accurately the sequence of two events.

By five, she'll be able to tell when words rhyme and that one thing doesn't belong in a group (a circle in squares, for instance); relate several details ("I saw a brown dog run after the ball"); and use contractions such as "don't." By six, she should use all irregular verbs ("be," "go," "do," "have"), articles ("a," "an," and "the"), and prepositions ("to," "of," "in") correctly; be able to stay on a topic in order to tell a long story; and answer *why* questions with her own explanation.

During these preschool years, it is not uncommon for a child to experience some articulation problems. She's still practicing and mastering her skills. Help her by not becoming impatient while she searches for a word or stammers over part of it. Don't correct her, instead use a word correctly when she mispronounces it. ("Yes, sweetheart, I see the *r*abbit," when she says "wabbit.") Some sounds take longer to learn, but children should have mastered all English language sounds by the time they're eight years of age, according to the American Speech-Language-Hearing Association. (See *Articulation Problems*, *Stuttering*, and the Developmental Tasks Appendix.)

There are many, many problems children can have with language and speech. Some children may not hear properly, some may have difficulty distinguishing closely related or similar sounds, and some may have an auditory processing problem, which means that the brain is not deciphering or storing sounds and words properly.

Other children may understand oral language but have an expressive, word-finding problem. They have the vocabulary, but can't retrieve a specific word, say it, or construct a sentence. (Such children might be able to point to a picture of a house, for instance, but be unable to say the word.) Or they may have trouble producing the sounds of language, so that their speech is difficult to understand.

Having such pronounced difficulty in comprehending conversation or making themselves understood can make children self-conscious and socially withdrawn, or more aggressive and frustrated. After age four, language becomes crucial to peer activity and to learning. Most play involves verbal exchange and most school instruction is delivered orally.

Language and speech impairments are probably the result of a combination and an interaction of physical, genetic, and environmental factors. Problems tend to run in families and affect more boys than girls. Physical handicaps such as a cleft palate, neurological inefficiencies in the brain, and environmental stress or neglect can all contribute to language and speech difficulties.

Warning signs that a child is not acquiring language and speech at a normal pace include:

- an inability to follow directions;
- frequent grammatical mistakes;
- heightened frustration, aggression, and tantrums past the age of three;
- a very short attention span for listening to a book being read;
- not developing a larger vocabulary;
- continuing to mispronounce words and not sounding as intelligible as his peers;
- difficulty learning to read;
- anxiety when called on in class.

Take a child for an evaluation sooner rather than later if you suspect he has a language or speech problem. Language pathologists can help correct or compensate for difficulties before they have embarrassed or isolated a child, hobbled his academic learning, or affected his self-esteem.

For more information, contact the American Speech-Language-Hearing Association, 10801 Rockville Pike, Rockville, MD 20852 (301-897-8682) (1-800-638-TALK); the Council for Exceptional Children, division of Children with Communication Disorders, 1920 Association Drive, Reston, VA 22091 (703-620-3660).

Recommended reading: *The First Twelve Months of Life* and *The Second Twelve Months of Life*, by Frank and Theresa Caplan (Perigee Books/Putnam Publishing).

Latchkey Children

(See *Self-Sufficiency*)

Laziness

(See *Motivation, Procrastination, Achievement Issues, Sloppiness*)

Learned Helplessness

Learned helplessness is a condition first described in the 1960s by psychologist Martin Seligman. Through lab experiments, he found that rats subjected to inescapable shock and then later placed into situations where they could, in fact, escape, failed to try to do so. The rats had become conditioned to believe they were powerless to do anything to help themselves.

Learned helplessness is a term more typically applied to adults than to children. These people seem to believe they cannot succeed no matter what they do, no matter what the circumstances. Such an attitude obviously has detrimental impact on self-esteem and motivation. Why bother if one is preordained to fail? Such people are at risk for depression, anxiety, and suicidal thoughts.

If a child begins to be extremely negative about himself, saying and beginning to believe: "I never do anything right," parents should help him find activities or studies he enjoys, in which he can do well. Praise his achievements. Start with small, clearly accessible accomplishments and move up. Avoid pressuring him to succeed or demeaning him when he fails. Try to find out if there is someone of importance in his life—a teacher, a coach, or a mentor—who is being overly critical with him. If there is, talk with that person. (See *Self-Esteem*.)

When a child makes a lot of self-derogatory remarks, has such low self-esteem that he doesn't try to make friends or participate in school, and shows other signs of depression or anxiety disorders, he may need some professional counseling. Keep in mind that when worrisome behavior is just beginning, parents can seek out one or two consultations with a child therapist for advice in dealing with the problem. (See *Depression*.)

Learning Disabilities

The term "learning disabilities" arose out of the frustration educators and parents felt with children who seemed at least average in ability but did poorly in school, despite their hard work. It applies to children who can't seem to learn at a normal rate, for whom there is a distinct discrepancy between their measured IQ and their academic performance. Learning disabilities do not refer to significant sensory handicaps; severe emotional problems such as depression; brain damage; mental retardation; or lack of adequate school instruction. Instead, learning-disabled children should, by all appearances, be normal, successful students.

The difficulties of learning-disabled children seem to stem from some sort of neurological processing problem. That doesn't mean that they are deficient intellectually. On the contrary, many learning-disabled children are of above-average intelligence. Instead, it has to do with a flaw in the way neurons, which carry information within the brain, communicate with one another. In other words, there is something faulty in the way the brain is physiologically structured. The fact that these disabilities tend to run in families and affect more boys than girls supports that concept.

Anywhere from 2 to 10 percent of all children have a learning disability. The vast majority of these disorders are related to reading and language and how verbal information is processed within the brain. People will most often think of *dyslexia*, a disorder that causes a child to reverse letters. Actually, dyslexia accounts for only about 10 percent of learning disabilities.

Parents shouldn't panic if their preschooler arranges letters backwards. Until a child is six or seven years old, the idea that it's important to go from left to right, that directionality even matters, doesn't occur to him. If, however, he continues to confuse *b* and *d* or *p* and *q* or reverse letters in words after he's been in school a bit, there may be a problem.

Many learning-disabled children have a language and/or central auditory processing problem that interferes with how they perceive sounds. Their hearing may be fine, but there is a problem in the way in which the sound is internally transmitted to or translated by the brain. What that means is that a child will have difficulty in phonetic analysis and recognizing the relationship between sound and symbol (a letter of the alphabet).

These children often start off doing well in school because they have what's called sight vocabulary. They can identify small words such as "cat" because they've memorized what they look like. Longer words throw them, however, since they can't "sound them out" correctly. They may, for instance, confuse "ta" with "ca." Consequently, they'll quickly start to fall behind their classmates.

Other learning-disabled children have language-related problems that involve understanding the structure of language. They don't have

165

an automatic sense of grammar or syntax, and perhaps read one word at a time. Most of us read in phrases, not word to word. Such a dysfunction represents an inability to perceive or efficiently process sequential information, which is really what language is all about. (See also *Language and Speech*.)

What to Do

If you suspect your child has a learning disability, have him evaluated. Learning disabilities do not go away. Often, children will have to learn to compensate by finding other ways they do learn easily and capitalizing on those functional talents.

Many parents worry that classifying a child as having a disability will harm his self-esteem. In fact, it is more likely that not recognizing or acknowledging the reasons for his problems will be detrimental. Undetected learning disabilities often lead to a belief that these problems result from laziness or inferior intellect, perhaps setting up a self-fulfilling prophecy. It should help a child (and his teachers) to know that his is a physiologically based problem, not one having to do with his personality.

With the help of a trained tutor, a child comes to recognize and use the ways in which he works best. He'll learn how to compensate for his disabilities in ways that should make learning more successful, efficient, and fun. It's when a child works hard but continues to lag behind, and is then criticized as an underachiever, that he may lose confidence and motivation. Make sure to find a tutor who is experienced in working with children with learning disabilities, who is flexible and a good observer, so that he can discover how a child works best and help him apply that to other areas.

Classroom teachers can also help learning-disabled children once they're identified to them. A teacher can face a child when talking, write down as well as present an instruction orally, or rephrase it to make sure a child comprehends all its nuances.

For more information, contact the Learning Disabilities Association (LDA), 4156 Library Road, Pittsburgh, PA 15234 (412-341-1515); and the National Center for Learning Disabilities (NCLD), 99 Park Avenue, New York, NY 10016 (212-687-7211).

* * *

Recommended reading: *The Misunderstood Child: A Guide for Parents of Learning Disabled Children*, by Larry B. Silver (McGraw-Hill).

Listening

It's important to remember that children often have different agendas, and different ideas of what is and isn't important, than you do. A child who's in the middle of stacking a tower of blocks or playing in the backyard may not be ready to stop and listen while you are trying to discuss something with him. Although you may feel he's being defiant, he's probably just busy. It can be hard for a child to break his focus and change gears in response to a single cue from a parent.

Help him do so. Listening requires attention. Make sure you have a child's attention *before* beginning to talk. Adopt some classroom techniques. Before making an announcement, teachers say, "Let me have your attention." They're priming children, alerting them to concentrate on what's about to be said.

Make sure you're in the same room as the child. Try to make eye contact. Say his name first and add, "I need to talk with you." Some children need a tactile cue. Put your hand on his shoulder, for instance, as you say his name.

Try to encourage active listening. Good lecturers will tell students as they begin, "There are three major points to remember . . ." Students will listen for those three elements as the lecturer speaks. Teachers will also help orient children by saying, "I want you to watch for these important themes as you view the film."

As you talk, be precise, don't talk too long, and use words a child understands. Then, ask if he has questions. If he can essentially repeat what you've said, you know he's heard you. (See also *Motivation* and *Chores and Cleaning Room*.)

Finally, model the behavior you want children to exhibit. Pay close attention when *they're* trying to tell *you* something. Turn and look at a child, and acknowledge what he says by reframing or labeling his

167

emotions: "That must have made you angry when Frank took your puzzle."

Recommended reading: *How to Talk So Kids Will Listen & Listen So Kids Will Talk*, by Adele Faber and Elaine Mazlish (Avon Books).

Loneliness

Some children are perfectly happy with only a handful of friends, and enjoy playing by themselves or reading books in their room. Parents need to be careful not to project their own childhood insecurities or concepts of social success on their offspring. A rule of thumb is that all a child needs is one or two good friends. It's quality, not quantity, that really matters.

If a child says he feels isolated, however, and is unhappy, you should heed his request for help and try to find ways to facilitate his making friends. (See *Shyness, Adaptability, Making Friends*, and *Social Isolation*.) Prolonged loneliness and discomfort with peers can eventually lead to low self-esteem or depression. (See *Depression* and *School*.)

Loudness

It is perfectly natural and appropriate for a child enjoying a boisterous game of tag to become excited and loud. Even though his shrill shrieks of pleasure may hurt your ears, it would be a shame to stifle his enthusiasm in that context. If, however, a child is being loud to get attention, you may want to ignore the outburst at first (so as not to reward inappropriate behavior) and then ask the child to repeat his request in a calmer or lower tone of voice.

Usually, the time that parents are most worried about a child's decibel level is when they are visiting another person's house. Children can learn that there are different rules in different houses, and that politeness requires some self-discipline and containment; but to some extent Grandma needs to accept the fact that children are likely to be rambunctious. The younger the child, the less capable he is of self-control and the more adults need to adapt to him.

If Grandma truly is offended by a child's exuberance, perhaps a visit with her should be postponed until that child is older. You can then use reinforcement techniques to foster the behavior you desire—in other words, you can say to a preschooler or older child, "If you play quietly at Grandma's we can do [whatever a child really likes] afterwards" and expect positive results.

Remember that children model their communication styles on what they see within their own family. If parents yell, speak loudly, or interrupt one another, a child is likely to do the same. (See also *Interrupting*.)

Finally, if a child speaks loudly all the time, plus shows signs of not hearing you when you talk to him, have his hearing checked. (See *Hearing* and *Language and Speech*.)

Lying

"Lord, Lord, how this world is given to lying!" laments Falstaff in Shakespeare's *Henry IV, Part I*. And so it is. It seems to be part of human nature. And like most elements of human nature, lying comes in degrees. Social "white lies" ("Gee, Aunt Gertrude, I think your hair looks great!") are far different from criminal lies (forging checks).

Although we like to think of children as uncorrupt innocents, they, too, are completely capable of fibbing. Think of the fourteen-month-old baby who's just made a bowel movement in his diapers but shakes his head No when asked if he's dirty. In all likelihood, he'll smile, knowing it's not true. It might even be cause for worry if a child seems completely *unable* to fib. He'd lack a certain social tact or maybe even get into danger. If a child is alone, for instance, and a potential thief comes to the door asking if anyone else is home, most parents would prefer their child to fabricate the presence of an adult, perhaps napping upstairs.

Lying is different from fantasy. It is a deliberate deception, meant to manipulate or mislead others. According to Paul Ekman in *Why Kids Lie*, children lie to avoid punishment or an awkward situation; out of embarrassment; to protect their privacy or their friends; to obtain something they can't have otherwise; or to garner the admiration of their peers.

Toddlers and Preschoolers

Trying to avoid punishment or disapproval is the major motivation for lying in young children. Asked if they colored on the wall, for instance, many will deny it or blame it on someone else, usually an imaginary friend. The lie is not made maliciously (although some parents react as though the child is insulting them), it's simply a spur-of-the-moment way of avoiding blame and consequences. (See also *Imaginary Friends*.)

Part of the reason young children lie has to do with the way they think. Preschoolers view people as either good or bad; therefore, it is impossible for a good person to do something bad. To remain good, a preschooler has to disclaim responsibility for a bad act. Nothing is more important to him than your believing he is good.

Preschoolers also engage in magical thinking: They believe that what they wish to be true—that they didn't *really* color on the wall—can be true. To them, telling a tall tale fabricated by their imagination is not a lie. At this stage, there is no clear line between fantasy and reality. They believe in Santa Claus and that stuffed animals can talk. A preschooler who swears there is a monster under his bed probably really believes it to be true or possible. He's not *just* trying to keep you in his room.

Lying can also be a way of avoiding embarrassment about immature behavior. A little girl who's been potty-trained for some time might claim she sat in a puddle to avoid admitting she wet herself. (See also *Regression*.)

Frequent lying at this age, however, is unusual. It suggests that parents might be setting too many expectations or restrictions so that a child is afraid of making mistakes.

School-Aged Children

The ability to preconceive a lie and totally understand its consequences as fully as an adult begins around the time a child is seven or
eight years of age. This has more to do with children's new cognitive
abilities than with a lack of moral development. Jean Piaget dubbed this
stage "concrete operations." Children at this age begin to understand
cause and effect, and can logically think through methods of getting
what they want. "If I'm good, maybe they'll get me that bike I want" is a
typical reasoning. (See the Developmental Tasks Appendix.)

Lies, then, are planned shortcuts. Rather than show parents a bad
report card and have to deal with the consequences, a child this age
might throw it away and claim it was lost.

Preteens

Older children may lie because they feel parents' questions intrude on
their privacy. Peer loyalty is also very strong at this point, and they may
fib to protect their friends or to have opportunities to see friends
parents disapprove of. (See also *Secrecy* and *Self-Sufficiency*.)

Lying is a problem when it's a habit, when it cuts across contexts
(school, home, playground), and when it looks as if it's becoming a
fixed personality trait. Studies have shown that frequent lying is often
associated with more serious antisocial behavior such as stealing, substance abuse, or conduct disorder.

What to Do

Try to view your child's first lie not as a major moral or criminal offense
but as an opportunity to build on your relationship. Remember that
yelling and self-righteous indignation will make it harder for him to
admit his mistakes to you in the future. Appropriate handling of the
small, relatively innocent lie of a seven-year-old is an investment in
your child's future, when as a teenager he'll be tempted with all kinds of
illicit behaviors, including drinking and driving, taking drugs, or having
unprotected sex.

You want your child to feel that he or she can come and tell you
anything, no matter how reprehensible it may be. This is how parents
can help children learn and grow from their initial mistakes in life.

Remain calm. If that means you have to wait an hour to discuss an incident rationally, do so. Keep in mind the nature of the "crime" that precipitated the lie and react accordingly. Accidentally knocking down a vase during roughhousing is different from using it to bash a sibling. With the former, all you probably need to do by way of "discipline" is have him help you clean it up or repair it.

With young children, who are so afraid of losing your approval, be sure to say it was the behavior, not the child, that is bad. "You're better than that" conveys the idea that you do think he is a good person. But be sure to say it in a way that will not shame him.

Try to help a child explore *why* he lied, as a way of coming to understand himself. Instead of yelling at him for lying about the whereabouts of his report card, try, "Tell me about the report card. Was it bad? How bad?" Explain that you are disappointed, that lying breaks trust. Perhaps help him build a sense of consequences by asking, "What do you think I should do about this?" Children often come up with far more dire disciplinary actions than you would ever impose. The answer probably lies somewhere in the middle.

Praise a child for his honesty, for "fessing up." A child who grows up in a home where it's safe to admit mistakes is more likely to be an honest, morally sound adult.

Watch your own behavior. If a child hears you constantly making up phony excuses for lateness or turning down social engagements, he'll follow suit. The social lie generally involves a dilemma of some kind: You don't like a person or you have a schedule conflict that might hurt that person's feelings. Help a child develop a code of ethics by discussing that dilemma, the pros and cons of certain actions, and asking, "Would that be right?"

Finally, don't lie to your child. Don't replace a dead hamster and claim it was the original. Err on the side of believing your child. Why bother telling the truth if no one listens? Admit your mistake and apologize when you thought he was lying and wasn't.

Recommended reading: For children, a good version of *The Boy Who Cried Wolf* and *Pinocchio*. For adults, *Why Kids Lie*, by Paul Ekman (Charles Scribner's Sons); and *The Magic Years*, by Selma Fraiberg (Charles Scribner's Sons).

172

Making Friends

In today's competitive world, parents are always worrying about putting away enough money for their child's college, about giving him an intellectual leg up with educational toys, about helping him maximize his potential. With so much emphasis on intellectual growth, parents sometimes forget to help a child focus on another, equally important aspect of his development: making friends.

We humans are social creatures. That's how we originally survived as a species and it's largely how we survive today emotionally. One of the most important buffers against depression, for instance, is a strong, supportive network of family and friends, a feeling of belonging to a community. Studies show that children can overcome great obstacles if they have the ability to form at least one intimate friendship with a peer or an adult. The capacity to connect means a child has empathy and the belief that he is worthy of someone's attention and affection. It translates into healthy self-esteem.

Also, all the intellectual and material successes in the world boil down to very little if a person has no one with whom to share them.

Of course, you shouldn't go overboard and push your child to be the most popular kid in school, particularly if he is shy or reticent by nature. What's important is that he has one or two very good friends. That's all he needs.

You can't make friends for your children, but you can be helpful by facilitating playtime: Set up playgroups for toddlers; encourage children to bring classmates home from school; agree to host a slumber party. You can also help by modeling good friendships and the art of conversation, or by assisting a hesitant child in finding ways to join in playground games. (See *Shyness*, *Self-Esteem*, *Adaptability*, and *Boasting*.)

What to Do

Toddlers and Preschoolers

The first psychosocial task a child faces, according to Erik Erikson, is developing trust—a confidence that his parents are there for him and that he can influence the world. He should accomplish this task as a baby. After that, he must fight to establish some independence from parents, some self-determination and self-sufficiency. An important element of that evolving autonomy is learning how to relate to his peers, to travel in a world of his and his little friends' making. (See also the Developmental Tasks Appendix.)

The ability to make friends, then, has its roots in the second year of life. Even though children this age engage in "parallel play" (alongside but not *with* one another), it's important for them to spend some time together. They must learn to negotiate a social contract, to share toys and the attention of an accompanying adult, to be a little less self-centered. (See *Play*.)

It's best if some of this learning occurs *before* a child is enrolled in a nursery school, where he has to interact with a larger group of peers. Taking a child from being with only Mommy or a baby-sitter all day and then putting him into a classroom can be akin to throwing a child into water without his having had any swimming lessons.

The best thing to do is to take a toddler to the local playground or, better yet, identify one well-matched playmate. Look for a child who seems to have a similar or complementary personality. It's hard for working mothers to arrange such encounters, but try to set up some brief Saturday-morning playtimes. Usually an hour of play in the morning, followed by a quick lunch and departure, is best. Any longer and children will become tired and are more likely to fight over toys. Put away your child's most treasured possessions before his playmate arrives to avoid really emotional tugs-of-war.

Don't expect these playtimes to go smoothly every time. Children are just as clumsy learning how to play as they are when they learn to eat. They may be aggressive, do the wrong things, or upset the other child. As they get older and acquire more language, they'll be able to tell each other what they like and don't like. Intercede if a child is physically threatening another, but if they are simply arguing over a toy, try to let children resolve the conflict on their own. They'll learn much more about debate and compromise. (See *Aggression*.) In any event, hang in there with your early attempts at helping to socialize even an aggressive or inordinately shy child.

Model playing in your own games with a child. Demonstrate give and take; don't let him boss you around too much, since his playmates certainly aren't going to like that kind of behavior. Say please and thank you. (See *Bossiness*.)

Parents who are old friends may also find that sometimes if they get together with their children (two mothers with two two-and-a-half-year-olds, for instance), the children will spend their time vying for the adults' attention rather than playing with each other. That's probably because the adults are happily chatting. If the goal is to have the children play together more, one adult might want to leave for a while so that the other can instigate a game of catch more successfully.

Recommended reading: *The Playgroup Handbook*, by Laura Peabody Broad and Nancy Towner Butterworth (St. Martin's Press).

Preschoolers

Between the ages of three and four, children will really begin "cooperative play," in which they can follow group-determined rules or create social dramas together. Playing house, for instance, means each child assumes a role and reacts to another child's character and dialogue. Facilitate such play by providing a box full of dress-up clothes and old kitchen utensils. (See *Play*.) Stay on the sidelines and let them play on their own.

This is when a child may begin to ask specifically to play with another friend. Don't be worried if these early friendships seem fleeting and fickle. Children have yet to develop a sense of future, that friendships are things that can endure and should be nurtured. Right now, they gravitate to peers who play in the same manner and with the same toys: Billy likes to play with Johnny because they both love to pretend to be Batman. If tomorrow and the next day Johnny wants to play with marbles instead, Billy will probably seek out another super-hero aficionado.

Always keep your child's temperament in mind when you take her to the playground to look for friends. Some children are just innately "slow to warm" and need time on the sidelines watching before they join a group game in the neighborhood or playground. They're soaking up important information while standing beside you—who the leader of the children is, what they are playing, what the game's rules are— that will make it easier for them to blend in once they've decided to take the plunge. Continue taking such a child to the park or to school soccer games, even if all she does is watch, so that she can get a feel for the environment. (See *Adaptability* and *Shyness.*)

School-Aged Children

Children in school will have plenty of opportunity to see one another during class, but they still need some unstructured time together, when they (not adults) decide what they want to do. That should be separate from after-school sports, clubs, and lessons, in which they have less opportunity for conversing, sharing, or using their own creativity. Continue to host after-school or weekend playtime and sleep-overs.

Some tips on sleep-overs: Don't push your child to sleep over until he's emotionally ready for nighttime separation from home. If he still has trouble adjusting to baby-sitters, he's probably not ready. It's best for that first sleep-over to be in a home he's already very familiar with. Prepare him for what to expect; talk about how he'll spend the evening. Tell his hosts about anything that your child needs. If he sleeps better with a night-light on, for instance, or is allergic to a particular food, say so. Then, if he calls at the last minute and wants to come home, go and get him, without any teasing. When you're the host, do something special that evening, such as going to the movies. Show your guest where everything is, where he'll sleep, etc., when he arrives. Find out what he likes to eat beforehand. Be prepared to calmly call his parents in the middle of the night if he wakes up and really is inconsolable.

If a child is particularly shy or self-conscious, help him find ways of inserting himself into group situations that carry the likelihood of some success. For instance, a boy who likes basketball but isn't particularly adept at dribbling or passing may be able to become proficient enough at free throws that peers will want to include him in pickup games. Or help him develop a hobby he can share with a like-minded child as a base for friendship. (See *Shyness* and *Self-Esteem.*)

If he is habitually excluded or ignored by his classmates, try to assess if he's actively doing something to alienate them. Ask him what he thinks he might be doing, or talk to his teacher if it is a real problem and your child can't seem to pinpoint the cause. Talk about better conversation techniques, about the importance of taking turns. (See *Clowning* and *Boasting*.)

Remember that one or two close friends is all a child really needs to be happy and well adjusted.

Preteens

Friendships are of increasing significance to children as they get older. Girls will tend to have fewer but more intense friendships than boys, but peer exclusion carries the same sting for both sexes. Unfortunately, this is the time children really begin to separate themselves into groups, a process that starts around the fourth grade.

When snubs happen, it is vital for you to help your child sort out what's important, what her values are. Working on such issues when a child is nine or ten years old will pay off mightily when she's twelve and peers have become all-important. (Of course, parents underestimate their influence during preadolescence. No matter what they might say in defiance, preteens still worry about what their parents think. It is especially important during these roller-coaster years, when peer relationships are so unstable that a child feels more secure in her family.)

Materialism and physical looks are questionable but common reasons for ostracizing a child. If a child is excluded from the "in group" because she doesn't have the right kind of shoes, for instance, parents can gently challenge that kind of thinking. Acknowledge her hurt, but consider asking, "Would you reject someone because of her shoes? Do you really want to hang out with people who like or dislike someone just because of her shoes?"

If she still wants to associate with them, ask her why. What does she expect to gain? If it is so very important to her, help her think about ways to befriend the group. But also ask if there is another person or group she might like to spend some time with. Help her begin to see the importance of developing her own internal sense of values, of what is right and wrong for her as an individual. Finally, try to recall some similar snub in your own youth to show her that such hurts do pass and become relatively unimportant in the context of a longer life.

Recommended reading for children: *Best Friends*, by Steven Kellogg (Dial); *Little Bear's Friend*, by Else Holmelund Minarik, illustrated by

Maurice Sendak (HarperCollins); *Amos & Boris*, by William Steig (Farrar, Straus, & Giroux); *The Hating Book*, by Charlotte Zolotow, illustrated by Ben Shecter (Harper Trophy); *The Secret Garden*, by Frances Hodgson Burnett, illustrated by Tasha Tudor (Lippincott / HarperCollins); *The Hundred Dresses*, by Eleanor Estes, illustrated by Louis Slobodkin (HBJ); and *Charlotte's Web*, by E. B. White, illustrated by Garth Williams (Harper & Row).

Masturbation

Children engaging in self-stimulation of their genitals is a common and normal practice, particularly among adolescents. Probably half of all preschoolers try it at some point as well. Young children touch their genitals at first because the body parts exist and, therefore, pique curiosity. Repetition is reinforced because of the associated pleasurable sensation.

Parents are often squeamish about confronting a child's sexuality and bodily exploration. Typically, they are uncomfortable witnessing it but are afraid they'll adversely inhibit or shame a child by asking him to stop. Avoid such discomfort by handling masturbation as being more a matter of socially appropriate manners than of morality. It is not something to be done in front of people. But it really is a child's business if he does it in private. Explain that genitals are "private parts." Perhaps add, "It's not nice to do in front of people. If you want to do that, you need to go to your room."

It is unusual for older, school-aged children to masturbate in public because they have generally learned by then what behavior is accepted by society. Children who masturbate in public may be insecure or trying to shock you. Examine what might be causing those kinds of motives. (See *Habits*, *Anxiety*, *Reaction to Parental Conflict*, *Oppositional-Defiant Disorder*, and *Depression*.)

If a child masturbates excessively, uses sexual language that someone his age shouldn't know, or seems to engage in sexualized behavior for the purpose of stimulating others, he may have been sexually abused. Typically, there will be other troubling behaviors accompanying the masturbation that should alert parents that something is wrong. (See *Sexual Abuse*.)

Materialism

"Mommy, Mommy, there's that sweatshirt Jessica has. I want one, too." "I want that new computer game; the old ones are boring." "I want sneakers just like the ones I saw on television." "I need a new bike. All the kids have better ones than I do."

Sound familiar? Advertising, peer pressure, a recent cultural emphasis on designer names and status symbols all converge to influence children, who don't have the capacity to discriminate between what they truly need and what they merely want. They also believe the message that having this one particular thing will make them popular, stronger, prettier. Then again, adults can fall into that trap, too.

But there is a distinct danger in being preoccupied with material possessions. A child who defines her self-worth by what she wears or owns or how she looks is at risk of being overly influenced by external forces, and of judging people for what they have, not who they are. The danger increases as children reach puberty, when being and having the same thing as everyone else seems almost a life-or-death issue.

Succumbing to materialism may also convince a child that growing intellectually and working hard to accomplish things are of little importance. Are you a good parent solely because you own an expensive, status-symbol station wagon? Is your child automatically a better basketball player because he's wearing sneakers a famous ball player promotes on TV? Of course not. You as an adult understand this, one hopes, but you must help your child learn this lesson in today's increasingly materialistic world.

What to Do

You will be doing your child a big favor by trying to curb excessive consumerism early. This is particularly true during the elementary school years. During this stage children naturally determine their self-worth by what they can do. "I'm a swimmer, a ballerina, I like to read," they say, by way of defining themselves. A critical part of growing up will be lost if a child thinks he's a good person because he owns a pair of designer high-tops rather than because he has practiced hard and mastered the skill of free throws. (See Erikson's "industry versus inferiority" in the Developmental Tasks Appendix.)

Another part of growing up is learning to tolerate frustration. If you've just bought sneakers and a week later your child demands a new, designer pair, it makes sense to say, "The sneakers you have are fine. Next time you need a new pair, we'll think about the ones you're asking for. Or maybe we can get those for your birthday." Of course, the child may protest. But think of it as an opportunity to instill some values and the idea that possessions and special treats are more a privilege than a right. The next time you say no it will be easier.

With older children, discuss the expense of the item. If they really want something desperately, help them find a way to help pay for it. Maybe they can save their allowance or do extra chores for pay. This will teach them about finances and money management, about how to go about achieving what they want.

Remember that your own behavior is probably the most important influence. If you insist on designer labels yourself, or feel inferior because you don't own something a neighbor does, don't be surprised when your child thinks the same way. Also, try not to buy gifts to make up for not spending enough time with your child.

Ask your child who "everyone else" is, when he uses that argument for leverage on you. It may just be one child. Rampant materialism is probably a good discussion for PTA meetings, so that parents can determine some common ground for possessions. It makes it easier for everyone concerned to show some buying restraint when the argument of "everyone else does" simply isn't true.

Meanness

(See *Aggression, Bullying, Insensitivity, Cruelty to Animals, Sibling Rivalry*, and *Teasing*)

Memory Development

Memory is one of the aspects of the human condition in which the poetic and the purely physical meet, almost in mystery. Memory houses our lifetime. It holds our most treasured experiences from childhood, the feeling of the first day of school, of holding our newborn, the names of our loved ones. Yet this emotional phenomenon is achieved through electrical firings and connections within the brain's tissues. The brain contains actual memory traces, pathways of knowledge as intricate as a spiderweb's latticework. But beyond that, we know very little about how the act of remembering really works.

Parents need to remember the physical realities of memory if their child seems to have difficulty with it. Memory requires attention and concentration, both of which can be affected by temperament or marred by faulty gathering or processing of information within the brain. The latter is less a function of personality than of physiology. (See *Learning Disabilities*.)

It's not poetic, but think of the brain as a computer: the mechanical, neuronal tissue is the hardware; memories, experiences, schooling are the software. Memory requires encoding.

There are three major types of memory: immediate, short-term, and long-term. Immediate means that you can look up a phone number, make it to the telephone, and dial it. Short-term means that with some "rehearsal"—repeating it to yourself—you can probably retain that phone number for a while, say twenty minutes, and still be able to dial it from memory. Long-term involves storage of knowledge. It requires the brain to consolidate things in short-term memory and then move them somewhere else to store for later retrieval. A person can have a breakdown anywhere along this complicated process, and these problems can be compounded by anxiety.

As long as there is no learning disability involved, memory can be enhanced through word associations and visual cues. For example, try teaching a child that the letter "s" is shaped like a snake; repeat a rhyme such as "In 1492, Columbus sailed the ocean blue"; or think of acronyms such as SUN to remind a child to carry her sweater, umbrella, and notebook to school. Play games that require the act of memorizing, such as "concentration," a card game in which players turn over cards and try to remember where their matches are. Make sure, too, that school-aged children have studying environments that are suited to their personalities and ability to focus on tasks. (See *Concentration*, *Motivation*, and *Procrastination*.)

Memory is important to learning, but try not to place too much emphasis on this skill. Memory doesn't guarantee a great thinker. In fact there are many people expert in rote memorization who can't think abstractly or conceptualize. If your child really seems to be struggling to retrieve knowledge for school, hire a tutor experienced in assessing a child's learning abilities, who will teach him how to capitalize on his strengths and compensate for his weaknesses. An objective third party, not a parent, typically makes the best and most productive tutor.

Sudden, uncharacteristic forgetfulness may be the sign of brain damage. If a child develops lapses in his memory following an accident or a high fever, seek out a medical evaluation. He could also seem forgetful if he experiences petit mal seizures, brief staring episodes in which a child momentarily loses awareness of his surroundings. (See *Staring Episodes*.)

Moodiness

(See *Irritability*, *Temperament*, and *Sadness*)

Motivation

Generally speaking, children aren't as motivated or as disciplined as adults. And because of that, it's important to define whose goals you're really pursuing when you try to motivate children—yours or your child's. Most goals in which motivation becomes an issue involve school, sports, or making friends. Some children may be naturally more achievement-oriented. Others take a more relaxed approach. For the latter, becoming motivated will often require buying into their parents' value systems and attitudes. The danger, of course, is that you might push them beyond their natural abilities.

Children can be intrinsically or extrinsically motivated. Intrinsic motivation means a child has an internal desire or drive to do something. Extrinsic refers to external motivators such as praise and reward systems that parents set up to help prompt and then positively reinforce a child's efforts. Children's internal motivation, especially for tasks that are laborious or low in pleasure, often comes only after parents have put external motivators into place.

Take piano lessons, for instance. The goal of being able to play the piano typically originates with parents. They hire a teacher and may have to set up rewards (stickers, higher allowances, or special events) to encourage a child to practice. But then something changes. If a child is diligent (and has some innate musical talent) his playing will inevitably improve. His accomplishment bolsters his self-esteem. With the experience of competence and mastery comes intrinsic motivation.

A child now practices because *he* wants to. He can see his skills developing and that spurs him on. He's working to please himself, not others. Enjoyment is the best motivator of all.

Helping a child find hobbies and activities that he enjoys and does well is important to his self-esteem. It's equally important to recognize when a child really isn't interested or adept in a particular area. No amount of external motivators will be able to change that reality. (See *Self-Esteem*, *Perfectionism*, and *Competitiveness*.)

On the other hand, you can and probably should continue to use reward systems for behavior you deem truly necessary or when children ask for help, when studying, for instance. (See *Procrastination* and *Chores and Cleaning Room*.)

A sudden drop in a child's motivation may suggest that he is under a lot of stress at home or at school. In some cases it may be a symptom of depression if the change is accompanied by shifts in a child's sleep and eating habits and circle of friends. (See *School*, *Reaction to Loss*, *Reaction to Parental Conflict*, and *Depression*.)

Moving

(See *Reaction to Loss* and *Making Friends*)

Nagging

(See *Whining*, *Temperament*, *Attention-Seeking*, and *Complaining*)

Napping

The average newborn sleeps sixteen hours a day; the average eighteen-month-old, thirteen hours. Much of that sleep is acquired through naps. They are a much-needed time of rest and emotional replenishment for both a baby and her primary caregiver.

Generally speaking, a baby will have one morning and one afternoon nap, and a toddler one long afternoon siesta. Often between the ages of two and three many children start to resist naps altogether. If a child is not fussy on the days she skips her nap and sleeps longer at night as a result, she is probably ready to give up naptime. If, on the other hand, she hits 5 P.M. and is irritable or even uncharacteristically excited (which can occur when a child is overly tired), she probably still needs her nap.

A good solution to help ease this transition time is to require daily "quiet times," during which a child may sleep or simply spend some tranquil time in her room. Pull down shades and dress her comfortably. Set clear limits, saying, "It's okay if you don't sleep, but I want you to stay in your room and read books or do puzzles."

You'll still have some time to yourself and she's less likely to throw temper tantrums from being overtired.

Negativism

Negativism is a term used to describe a child who resists parental requests. It can be passive (procrastinating or pretending not to hear) or active (doing the exact opposite of what was asked of him). Usually, negativism is perfectly normal and occurs when a child tries to establish some independence from his parents during certain developmental stages. Negativism is a problem only if it becomes pervasive and creates obstacles to good interpersonal relations with family members and friends. (See *Oppositional Behavior.*)

Nightmares and Night Terrors

It's important for parents to know the difference between nightmares and night terrors. Nightmares are bad dreams that awaken a child and stay in his memory. They are common, especially among preschoolers, who engage in magical thinking and are developing some predictable fears. They tend to be exacerbated by stress or specific worries, by reading scary books or watching frightening TV shows or movies. (See also the Developmental Tasks Appendix and *Fears and Phobias.*)

Night terrors are a less frequent but a more serious problem if they persist. Children are less likely to remember night terrors, even if you wake them. Usually, they scream out suddenly and may be in a cold sweat when you reach them. They seem awake but are actually in a state of semiconsciousness, perhaps staring off into space. A child can become even more agitated if you try to comfort him.

What to Do

Nightmares generally start around age three or four. These dreams are just as genuine to children as daytime reality. To them monsters, witches, and dragons can and do exist. Don't dismiss a child's fears as silly by saying, "It's just a dream." Instead, hug and gently reassure him that there are no monsters in his room, or if there were, you would make them go away. Add: "That's my job as your mommy [or daddy]." Most bad dreams are about being attacked or abandoned, so children need to see and hear their parents after a nightmare has awakened them and know they will protect them if need be. Leave a night-light or a low-level lamp on in a child's room so that she can see for herself that there is nothing lurking in the corners. Let her hold onto her teddy or a blanket, or any safe, transitional object that soothes her when you're not there. Keep her bedroom door open, but encourage her to go back to sleep on her own, in her own bed.

The morning following a nightmare, ask her about it to see if she describes an obvious theme. Sometimes moving, the death of a relative, or the beginning of school can spark bad dreams. So, too, can violent and inappropriate TV shows or movies. Try limiting what she is allowed to watch or read. (See also *Fears and Phobias*, *Reaction to Loss*, and *Reaction to Parental Conflict*.)

Nightmares are a frequent cause of subsequent sleep problems. Often children are afraid to go back to sleep by themselves. Many parents take a shaken child back to their own bed for security and comfort. Be forewarned that such a strategy can produce sleep-association problems. A child may not want to go to sleep except in your arms or in your bedroom. (See *Sleep*.)

Night terrors may be aggravated by trying to hug or soothe your child. Stand beside his bed without touching him until the episode passes. Night terrors can be alarming, but try to be calm and reassuring if he does wake up.

During a night terror, part of a child's brain is still working while the remainder rests. Typically, children outgrow them as they mature neurologically. But if your child has night terrors that persist, talk to your pediatrician, especially if he also sleepwalks or has body tremors.

Nose-Picking

(See *Habits*)

Obesity

As many as one in five American children are at risk of becoming obese, a rate that has doubled over the past twenty years. This seems unlikely given the nation's idealization of thinness and increased knowledge of the benefits of exercise and a healthy diet, but, ironically, improved nutrition and a bountiful food supply are part of the problem. According to a 1988 report on nutrition and health by the Surgeon General, Americans have greatly reduced their physical activity since 1900 while also increasing the amount of fats in their diet.

Obesity is defined as weighing 20 percent more than the ideal weight for a person's gender, height, and age. Parents will probably notice when a child begins to need chubby sizes at the clothes store. Your pediatrician should be able to detect unusual weight gain by keeping track of your child's weight progression in growth charts. Still, remember that the growth spurt brought on by puberty can cause dramatic fluctuations in body size. Babies, too, are usually quite plump before they are able to crawl or walk, physical activities that burn off calories.

Obesity can be a difficult condition to endure. Overweight children are often subjected to ridicule by their peers, and are at increased risk for medical complications such as diabetes, heart disease, strokes, high blood pressure, and joint and respiratory problems. Taunts of "Hey, fatso," never being chosen for a team, or losing friends because of appearances can take a terrible toll on a child's fledgling self-esteem. Teachers or coaches who assume a plump child is lazy or has no willpower may instigate a self-fulfilling prophecy.

Obesity tends to run in families, suggesting children can inherit a physiological propensity to being overweight. However, environment plays an important role as well. Obese adults often have poor eating and exercise habits, which can fuel their own weight problems. Unfortunately, a child usually adopts his parents' habits as his own.

What to Do

The good news about obesity is that parents can help children trim down and avoid extreme problems. Early attention is vital, since it's much more difficult to change eating habits and a sedentary life-style once they are entrenched.

To help children avoid obesity, set up structured eating: regular meals and set snack times. Offer healthy foods at snack time: raw vegetables instead of sweets, fruit juices rather than sodas. Never force a toddler to finish a meal; allow his intake to be regulated by his own internal feelings of hunger and fullness. It is your job to determine what food is offered, the child's to decide how much to consume. (See *Food Refusal, Fads, and Feeding Problems*.) Sit down to eat. It's hard to feel satisfied when eating on the run.

Don't use food as a reward for accomplishment or solace for failure or peer rejection. This type of emotional association with food sets up a child for the more extreme behavior that leads to obesity or addictive/compulsive eating. Instead, take a child on a favorite outing, preferably one requiring physical exertion. Play tennis or go camping. Don't permit him to sit in front of the television for hours or to consume limitless amounts of food as he watches. Then, practice what you preach. (See *Eating Disorders*.)

Preschoolers and school-aged children enjoy grocery shopping and watching you cook. Take advantage of these opportunities to talk about the nutritious properties of food. Find sports that a child can excel at and enjoy. (See also *Self-Esteem*.)

Finally, remember that preadolescence is a time nature designed for children to gain some weight in an intense growth spurt similar to that in infancy. Girls, in particular, are *supposed* to become rounder, to gain some fat at their hips and breasts in preparation for childbearing. Avoid sounding the alarm when these changes occur, as it may increase a child's self-consciousness or cause secrecy regarding eating.

Recommended reading: *Childhood Obesity*, by Platon J. Collipp, M.D. (Warner Books); and *How to Get Your Kid to Eat . . . But Not Too Much*, by Ellyn Satter (Bull Publishing).

Obsessions

(See *Compulsions*)

Oppositional Behavior

One of the first words a baby learns is no, since it's easy to say and also helps him establish some independence and control. It's a forceful method a child can use to test limits and find out what is acceptable and what is not.

In some cases, it may seem that "NO!" is the *only* word a child will ever use and that he delights in doing the exact opposite of what his parents ask. In the early years, this may in fact be true. Young children have really been exposed only to their parents' way of doing things and their only alternative is to go to the opposite extreme. Try to view such willfulness as a necessary and beneficial part of growing up. It's not just sheer contrariness; rather it's a way for your child to establish independence. Children (and parents) will eventually find some middle ground through trial and error.

Toddlerhood through preschool and adolescence are the two periods when children most actively defy and oppose parents. It's not uncommon to hear a parent describe a child's age as "three going on thirteen," and, indeed, there are many similarities in the intensity and the combativeness of those two stages. (See also the Developmental Tasks Appendix.)

Toddlers and Preschoolers

No matter how annoying it is, constantly shouting "no" can be developmentally appropriate behavior for many two- to three-year-olds. They are at a particularly volatile age when they fiercely want autonomy but are still emotionally dependent on parents. They also want to be able to do things alone but may be physically incapable of completing tasks unassisted. Their first instinct is to defy, to shout, "Let me do it," while the next moment they will run and hug their parent's knees for reassurance. It can be a turbulent, confusing time for everyone concerned. Try to keep in mind what two- and three-year-olds are trying to accomplish. They are beginning to want some control over the events in their lives and to establish their own rhythm, tastes, and style. They don't want to be interrupted with dinner when they're in the sandbox. They may want to choose their own clothes or food. (See *Food Refusal, Fads,* and *Feeding Problems* and *Dressing.*) They refuse to go to bed if they're not sleepy. This kind of defiance represents a natural resistance to your authority and control.

Children may also behave defiantly when they're frightened. A child who refuses a bath may have developed some fear about taking one. Perhaps she slipped one night, or is afraid that she might go down the noisy drain with the bathwater. (See *Fears and Phobias.*) Reassure her of the bath's safety.

School-Aged Children

Children can be oppositional at any age, but excessive defiance in children over the age of four and under the age of eleven or twelve is fairly uncommon. By the age of four most children have established a better sense of who they are and shouldn't automatically reject outside suggestions. By elementary school, they become absorbed in a developmental task Erik Erikson described as "industry versus inferiority." Children are most concerned with perfecting their talents and with defining themselves according to what they like or are able to do—e.g., soccer player, piano player, good student. (See "industry versus inferiority" in the Developmental Tasks Appendix.)

They are also developing a very firm idea of right and wrong, what is fair, and what is acceptable behavior. They now understand and believe in the rules of games. They have been fairly well "socialized," meaning they've learned through parental and peer disapproval what behavior will be tolerated. That's why fighting or other aggressive acts are unusual at this age. Bullying and repeated defiance of authority figures are warning signs that a child might be in trouble emotionally or have some kind of developmental delay. (See *Aggression, Bullying.*)

Highly oppositional children at this age might also have Attention-

Deficit Hyperactivity Disorder (ADHD). ADHD children are extremely impulsive and physically active and have difficulty paying attention. It's very hard for them to sit still in class or to keep themselves from sticking their fingers into an intriguing science project. Consequently, they're often in trouble with teachers and may fall into a cycle of annoying people and receiving punishment, only to repeat the aggravating behavior. (See *Attention-Deficit Hyperactivity Disorder.*)

Preteens

Talking back becomes increasingly common at this age as children travel more and more in a world of their own making, outside their home. They will compare the attitudes and beliefs of their peers and mentors with yours. Negativism, resisting external suggestions or expectations, will appear in the form of rejecting ideas and life-styles. They may also want to debate you purely for the intellectual stimulation it provides. They're proud of their new knowledge, and ideas. (See *Argumentative.*)

What to Do

Keep a sense of humor about you. Remember that being assertive and persistent will actually serve your child well as an adult. You don't want her to grow up compliant and submissive, unable to think or stand up for herself.

Allow children to make decisions whenever possible to satisfy that thirst for autonomy. Present a preschooler with two choices you can live with, such as the red dress or the green dress. Or permit her to choose any clothes as long as they suit the season. When she really can't have a choice (you must get to nursery school by 9 A.M.), say, "It's time to go now," not "Are you ready to . . . ?" which sets her up to say no, purely for the sake of resisting. Prepare her for the departure by talking about it beforehand. (See *Adaptability*, *Temperament*, *Dressing*, and *Motivation.*)

While allowing some choices, it is very important to establish strong limits where they matter (no running across the street; get off the swing and come indoors during a thunderstorm). Be consistent about setting limits. Decide the consequences for certain behaviors before

193

they happen and stick to them. Don't let a child play one parent against the other. Finally, keep some daily routines set, such as dinnertime and bedtime.

Limits actually make a child feel secure. She knows what is expected of her and what is not acceptable. Within those boundaries she can safely defy, question, oppose, learn, and grow. Limits, lovingly and reasonably imposed, tell a child that her parents care about her and that she doesn't have to be responsible for always knowing what is right and wrong. Deep down, children don't want that kind of power. (See *Temper Tantrums* and "Consistent Limits" in the Parenting Skills Introduction.)

Be sure to explain that while feeling negative emotions is normal, they must be expressed appropriately. Children in the throes of an oppositional outburst are likely to scream that they hate you or that you're stupid. Give yourself a moment to calm down and say something like, "I understand you're angry at me and that's okay. But it's not okay for you to be disrespectful [rude or mean]." It's important for children to learn that disagreements occur, but that they must be handled in a civil fashion. Accord your child the same respect you demand from him. (See *Anger.*)

Keeping yourself from feeling hurt and angered by a child's defiance will help avoid a vicious cycle. The more you overreact, the more she'll dig in her heels and repeat the behavior. A child can't feel good about herself if she's locked into a constant battle with her parents. Try to stay calm, firm but kind.

In *The Magic Years*, a classic volume of child psychology, Selma Fraiberg wisely wrote that defiance is "a political gesture, a matter of maintaining party differences while voting with the opposition on certain issues. . . . It's a kind of declaration of independence but there is no intention to unseat the government. . . . If we err and regard this negativistic phase as a revolution that imperils the government instead of a passing developmental phase we may find ourselves engaged in a struggle which can be prolonged for years, one that frequently produces a child who behaves as though his integrity as a person is in danger if he submits to the smallest demands of his parents."

Recommended reading: *The Magic Years: Understanding and Handling the Problems of Early Childhood*, by Selma Fraiberg (Charles

Scribner's Sons); *Toddlers and Parents: A Declaration of Independence*, by T. Berry Brazelton, M.D. (a Delta book / Dell Publishing); *Your Two-Year-Old* and *Your Three-Year-Old*, two books in the series by Louise Bates Ames, Ph.D., and Frances L. Ilg, M.D. (Delta books/ Dell Publishing); *The Second Twelve Months of Life*, by Frank and Theresa Caplan (Perigee Books/ Putnam Publishing); and *Your Baby & Child: From Birth to Age Five*, by Penelope Leach, Ph.D. (Alfred A. Knopf).

Oppositional-Defiant Disorder

Oppositional-defiant disorder is a diagnosis in the American Psychiatric Association's diagnostic manual and is believed by many researchers to be the precursor to a more serious problem called conduct disorder. It occurs when a child's defiance starts to become a consistent pattern of behavior, stopping just shy of the violation of the basic rights of others that defines conduct disorder.

These children constantly test the rules, irritating adults and peers alike. They haven't learned normal self-control, and according to the APA's diagnostic manual, they can be negative, hostile, aggressive, argumentative, and verbal or physical bullies. If a teacher tells them to stop talking, they might laugh and keep on misbehaving. Swearing, lying, and cheating are often part of their behavioral style. They may deliberately annoy someone and deny responsibility for their acts.

These children have probably managed to alienate almost all their friends and teachers so that their behavior can often have a self-perpetuating quality to it. They risk being seen by everyone around them, and eventually by themselves, as bad. (See *Bullying.*) Typically, their school performance is poor and their self-esteem low.

Such children are at risk of developing a conduct disorder, substance dependence, or depression. They may also have other, undiagnosed problems such as learning disabilities or Attention-Deficit Hyperactivity Disorder (ADHD) that have caused them to get into self-defeating, oppositional patterns of behavior. As many as half of ADHD children eventually develop oppositional-defiant or conduct disorder. Children who have both ADHD *and* oppositional-defiant disorder probably don't set out to annoy people, but they do so because of their inability to sit still. When corrected, they have trouble containing themselves and often a relentless cycle emerges of misbehavior and subsequent punishment from teachers and parents. (See *Attention-Deficit Hyperactivity Disorder.*)

If a child has several overlapping features of this disorder, seek professional guidance. Studies have shown that without intervention these children continue to do poorly in school, have difficulty holding jobs as adults, and have higher rates of divorce and substance abuse. The best treatment approach for the young child with this pattern of behavior may be basic behavior modification, under the supervision of a qualified mental-health professional.

Overactivity

(See *Hyperactivity*)

Overanxious Disorder

(See *Anxiety*)

Panic and Panic Attacks

Some adults suffer phobias that evolve into panic attacks. During these attacks their bodies respond as if they are in a life-or-death situation: their hearts race, they tremble, they sweat, they feel faint. Often they look as if they're having a heart attack. Panic attacks are biologically based, stemming from an abnormality in one of the brain's emotional centers. This chemical overreaction in the brain is typically brought on by exposure to or thoughts about a specific (seemingly irrational) phobia. People with panic disorder are most often afraid of things such as bridges, airplanes, elevators, or other high-technology environments where they feel out of control.

No one knows for sure whether or not children have panic attacks. However, there is a great deal of clinical observation to suggest that very anxious children do experience rapid heartbeats, stomachaches, and hyperventilation when in situations that frighten them. It also makes sense that children who are fearful and anxious and who don't learn ways of coping with their discomfort could grow up to be adults with phobias or other anxiety disorders. (See *Fears and Phobias*, *Anxiety*, *Anxiety Disorders*, and school phobia under *School*.)

Passivity

(See *Compliance*)

Peer Problems

(See *Aggression*, *Making Friends*, *Bossiness*, *Popularity*, *Bullying*, *Clowning*, *Competitiveness*, *Boasting*, and *Materialism*)

Perfectionism

Perfectionism is anxiety about neatness, order, doing something exactly right on the very first try, and being the best. It often begins as a personality trait that seems to run in families, especially those with gifted individuals. Firstborns seem particularly prone to perfectionism (possibly because they spend so much time with adults and consequently place unreasonable demands on themselves to be adult-like). Environment probably fuels this inclination: either by teachers, peers, and parents demanding that children excel, or by high-achieving parents who model pressure for perfectionism in their own behavior.

In an achievement-based society such as our own, it is very difficult for parents not to push their children to succeed. However, the most critical question parents must ask about their child is: "Is he doing *his* best?" not "Is he *the* best?" If the answer to the first question is yes, he really is working hard and achieving the highest level he can, given his natural talents and interests, then parents must learn to reinforce those efforts with praise and acceptance. If he really could be doing a little better, try to encourage and motivate him to find ways of honing his strengths. (See *Motivation* and *Achievement Issues*.) This is a very fine line to walk. Pushing a child beyond what he realistically can accomplish may damage his self-esteem or increase his anxiety level. (See *Self-Esteem*.)

Of course, there are children who are intensely self-critical, meticulous, and overwrought about succeeding even if parents aren't demanding. These children can be unjustly intolerant of what they perceive as their own inadequacies, and may resist trying anything new because they're afraid that they won't be any good at it. These children

198

have little staying power and are quick to quit a new activity after a few inconclusive tries.

It's important to continue to help a self-critical child achieve some flexibility and patience. Perfectionism may be a sign of insecurity, low frustration tolerance, and a rigid, black-or-white thinking that places a child at risk for depression if he does fail at something that is terribly important to him.

What to Do

You can help curb perfectionism early on. A perfectionist child will often display that tendency in toddlerhood, when he's first beginning to build a block tower, for instance. He may kick the blocks away in frustration and anger or throw a tantrum when his tower falls.

Help him cope with failure and frustration by modeling an even temper. Perhaps say, "Let's try again. Building a tower can be hard sometimes." Build one and knock it down, adding, "Oh well, it fell. Let's try it again." In fact, instilling the idea that momentary failures or mistakes are to be expected and are of no big consequence (just try, try. again) is a critical life lesson. It's making the effort, and then coping well with either success or failure, that is critical. (See *Impatience* and *Play*.)

Keep in mind that dashing in to help a faltering child is not the right approach either. A toddler's self-esteem comes not from your building a beautiful tower for him but from his own persistent trial and error. Think of how many times a child must pull himself up, toddle, and fall before he can walk gracefully across a room.

Offer assistance in ways that allow the child to correct a mistake. When drawing, give him a pencil with a strong eraser instead of a crayon or a pen. Sometimes young children are frustrated by not being able to draw something perfectly. Show them that there are many different, equally good ways of doing things. Better to say of a drawing, "I really like that," than "Oh, you drew the house perfectly." Also, resist the preschooler's tendency to throw away a book when a page is torn. Tape the tear and show how things can be mended and improved—"good as new."

Help a child practice tasks he's struggling with, but in ways that allow him to achieve. That requires you to assess his developing abilities correctly. For instance, a three-year-old might want to play catch but can't possibly toss a softball. Play with a big beach ball that he can see and stop easily. If you constantly correct a child, or run after the ball for him, you will squelch his impulse to try on his own. Let him make mistakes and show him how he can correct them. (See *Self-Esteem*.)

Maintain that philosophy once a child's in school. Let him do his *own* work, even if it's not perfect. If you do his work for him, you're again telling him that his own isn't good enough, it's not the best it could be. You are also showing him it's acceptable to present someone else's work as his own.

If a child is distraught over a grade that is less than an *A*, try to put it in context while acknowledging your child's disappointment. Tell him a B or a C in math is not the end of the world; that he has the next test or next semester to achieve an A if it really matters so much to him and to you. Perhaps help him strengthen his study skills. If math is not his strong suit, support his other talents as being just as valid. Remember, no one is good at *everything*. You can underscore this by telling him about something you have a hard time doing. (See *Anxiety* and *School*.)

Success comes in many forms: in having friends, in involvement with family, in community activities, and in sports or hobbies, as well as in academics. The narrower a child's focus, the more weight is placed on that one area, which may lead to debilitating, perfectionist anxiety. It certainly robs a child of relaxed enjoyment of an interest.

Finally, assess your own reaction to disappointment. If you are terribly critical of yourself, family, and friends, and become upset at minor setbacks, your child will be, too. Let him watch you practice a task or a game until you get it right, so that he sees that adults still have to work at things, too.

Recommended reading: *Perfectionism: What's Bad About Being Too Good*, by Miriam Adderholdt-Elliott, Ph.D. (Free Spirit Publishing).

Pessimism

(See *Perfectionism*, *Self-Esteem*, *Temperament*, *Complaining*, *Depression*, and *Learned Helplessness*)

Phobias

(See *Fears and Phobias*)

Pica

"Pica" comes from the Latin word for a voracious bird commonly known as the magpie. Pica is an eating disorder that can affect very young children, in which they regularly eat nonfood items such as dirt, paper, string, hair, trash, plaster, or animal droppings. Accidental poisoning plus intestinal obstruction are possible and dangerous medical complications.

Pica is not common, affects boys and girls equally, and drops off sharply in frequency after the age of three. Pica can usually be contained by increased supervision of the child's playtime and behavior modification. In all cases, consult your pediatrician.

Play

Play is the joyous, uninhibited, spontaneous occupation of childhood. "It's child's play," we adults say of something that seems effortless and rewarding in and of itself. Children seem to play for the sake of playing—to be instinctively motivated to play out of curiosity, to stimulate their senses, to feel the thrill of moving their bodies about. That's all true. But play can also be the "work" of early childhood.

While it may seem overly analytical to study play, we adults *can* learn a great deal about children from watching their interactions and make-believe scenarios. Play serves serious functions for children, even though they may be blissfully unaware of it.

Through play they *learn*. They learn about shapes and textures, the relationship of objects, cause and effect, problem-solving, and social interaction. Imaginary play can help a child work through emotions such as anger, fear, or helplessness by rehearsing troubling situations or by giving him power to conquer "his monsters." It hones his creativity and imagination, capabilities that will greatly enhance his capacity for abstract thinking later in life. Play helps him make friends.

Play is also an excellent way for you as a parent to befriend your child, to strengthen your relationship and communication. Children are more likely to talk about their emotions and thoughts with parents who've been down on the floor building castles with them. (Child therapists, for instance, often play with children before discussing problems as a way of building rapport and trust.) Play can be a window into your child's most private world and imaginings.

Infants and Toddlers

Babies first play by mimicking. They kick, coo, and smile, mirroring the adults caring for them, mainly as a means of bonding. They are also mastering basic motor skills through their antics.

Play can also teach babies cause and effect. As early as three months of age a baby is becoming aware that his movement—shaking a rattle, for instance—makes something happen. From there, he'll learn about all sorts of object relationships. Between nine and twelve months of age, he'll put that rattle into a container and see how they fit together. (Jean Piaget referred to this first cognitive stage, which lasts until around two years of age, as "sensorimotor." See the Developmental Tasks Appendix.)

Other games teach a baby other lessons. Peekaboo, for instance, shows him that objects exist even when out of sight, a critical bit of information that eventually will help a child allow his parents to leave his sight with less anxiety. (See *Anxiety*.)

Make-believe play begins around eighteen months of age, when children may pretend to feed, bathe, or rock a stuffed animal. They're role-playing, experimenting with activities they see adults doing.

As far as playing with peers, children this age may sit side by side in a sandbox, but still virtually ignore one another. (Until one takes another's toy, of course.) This is called "parallel play." Toddlers engage in similar activity and are aware of one another but have very little interaction.

What to Do

Parents can do several things to help make a baby or a toddler's play more rewarding. First, don't provide too many toys; they will overwhelm him. Organize toys in a way that makes sense and facilitates his exploration and playacting—blocks together in one container; a doll in a little bed with a tea towel cover; a make-believe kitchen with a pot and a few cups.

In fact, the best gift for babies and toddlers is probably a set of blocks. They are so versatile. Playing with blocks builds eye-hand coordination, a sense of spatial relations, numbers, and size. They allow the imagination to work, too. A line of blocks can be a road, a train, or a boat.

Show children how to put one or two blocks together and then let them build on their own. Don't rush in to repair a toppled tower or straighten a teetering one. A child learns to solve problems by doing things himself. Self-esteem comes from a child figuring out how to make something on his own. That takes a series of trial-and-error attempts. (See *Self-Esteem* and *Perfectionism*.)

Even though it seems as if arranging playtime with another toddler is a waste because they don't *really* play together, keep doing it. In fact, these play sessions teach toddlers about sharing toys and adult attention. Parallel play is the precursor to cooperative play, in which a child will become socialized and make his first friends. Sometimes adults are so concerned with the intellectual stimulation of play that they forget about its equally important social aspect. Observing a better-behaved peer in action can also help teach an aggressive toddler more socially appropriate play habits. (See *Making Friends* and *Aggression*.)

To facilitate a child's ability to make friends later, try to act as a peer would. Toddlers are likely to want to direct your play together and can be outright bossy at times. Follow his lead, but when a child is unpleasantly bossy, tell him so, or let him know of your own interests. (You're tired of making the giraffe talk, for instance, and would like to play house, instead.) His peers like playing in a give-and-take exchange. If he has *always* gotten his way, a bossy child will be very surprised when he begins to interact and may alienate playmates. (See *Bossiness.*)

Preschoolers

By the age of three, a child is capable of spinning an amazing fantasy world for herself. She'll want to make her toys talk to each other and to you. She'll make up stories and she may create an imaginary friend who can keep her company or express emotions that she may feel uncomfortable voicing herself. (See *Imaginary Friends.*)

At this age, the line between fantasy and reality is thin indeed, and children can slip back and forth between the two or even blend them together. But what we adults may see as a fib or a wild tall tale, children can view as being completely plausible and desirable. Fantasy, after all, provides wish fulfillment (even adults know and engage in that with their daydreams), and children with magical thinking believe a wish can be true because they want it to be so.

In fact, one of the healthiest uses of a child's make-believe scenarios is to simulate a real-life dilemma or anxiety-producing situation. She may make herself into a witch or a mighty giant to overcome the monsters she believes lurk in the closet. (Preschoolers engage in magical thinking and often develop fears of things in the dark. See *Fears and Phobias.*) Preschoolers may also "rehearse" a difficult situation, such as Mommy or Daddy going to work, by acting it out with their toys.

Around the age of four, children can concoct interactive, cooperative play. They can devise a social drama—play house as a group, for instance, with each child assuming a role, and collectively devise a plot by reacting to one another's dialogue.

What to Do

If asked to participate in a make-believe scenario, follow your child's lead. Resist the temptation to try to correct an emotion she's acting out in play. If she's re-creating your leaving for work, for instance, don't tell the baby bunny to stop crying. Instead ask the bunny what might make him feel better. Let your child work it out and find ways to soothe herself in her play. That's giving her power over a real-life situation in which she feels she has no control.

Try not to be alarmed if your child seems to be terribly aggressive in his make-believe, knocking down his blocks or pretending to slay dragons. Far better for him to be doing it in his play than against his new baby sister. Take the opportunity to ask what's bothering him or what he's thinking about just then. Games may sometimes be symbolic representations. As such they are constructive ways for children to discharge their anger or for parents to discuss emotions. (See also *Anger.*)

If a child continues to play in a very hostile way, however, you may need to talk to a professional to help discover what is so aggravating your child. This also applies if that child seems to be acting in an inappropriately sexualized manner, which may suggest he has been abused. (See *Sexual Abuse* and *Masturbation.*)

Continue to set up playtimes even if your child is in a preschool program. It's in small groups or one-on-one, spontaneous play situations that children learn most about making friends.

Help your child sort and arrange toys in ways that facilitate play. Dumping everything into a toy box is going to create a confusing, uninteresting jumble. Put away toys he's outgrown. Save some for a rainy day. Find toys that have many uses that he can dream up. Computerized games are entertaining but can be rather one-sided and may encourage a passive role. Try filling a box with old clothes and hats for dress-up instead.

Finally, if you want to further encourage a child's fantasy life, be sure to read to him. Make up stories yourself, or prompt him to embellish his tales by asking specific questions, such as, "What did the prince see in the castle?" (It's a fine line, however, between prompting and being intrusive or directive. Your child will probably let you know when you've crossed it.) Limit his TV viewing, which mesmerizes and encases a child within a drama made by television producers, not him.

School-Aged Children

After the age of six, children are being taught in school to sit and listen a great deal, so spontaneous, overt fantasy begins to diminish and eventually will become more private. At home, though, they still like to playact and their dramas will become more and more elaborate. Such imaginative play will probably reach its peak between six and nine years of age.

By age twelve, children are less inclined to play house or knights together. Those games have been replaced by more adult interactions.

What to Do

Continue to read to children. Make up stories with them, which is excellent entertainment during long car trips. Tell them "family legends" about what Granddaddy did during the Depression or about when you traveled abroad. That fosters the tradition of storytelling as a social and cognitive activity.

Continue, too, to allow your child some unstructured time with friends. The danger of overscheduling her with soccer practice, piano fantasize or to interact with her peers spontaneously. lessons, or after-school clubs is that she may lose the ability to fantasize or to interact with her peers spontaneously.

Recommended reading: *The First Twelve Months of Life* and *The Second Twelve Months of Life*, by Frank and Theresa Caplan (both a Perigee Book / Putnam Publishing); *Baby Games: The Joyful Guide to Child's Play from Birth to Three Years*, by Elaine Martin (Running Press, Philadelphia); *365 Days of Creative Play for Children 2–6 Years*, by Sheila Ellison and Judith Gray (Forward March Press, Redwood City, California); and *I'll Tell You a Story, I'll Sing You a Song*, by Christine Allison (Delacorte Press).

Playing with Dolls

Girls and boys are all known to dabble in what experts would term cross-gender behavior. Today, such experimentation carries far less of a stigma than it did in the 1950s and '60s. In fact, it is usually not a problem at all.

Girls who want to play football or soccer with boys are afforded an excellent, natural opportunity to develop athletically and to learn teamwork, something that might have been missing from their mothers' own childhoods. Boys who play with dolls learn future father-ing skills, and parental acceptance of this play can teach sons that displaying tenderness and emotional attachment is not only accept-able, but also fulfilling. Increased interaction between boys and girls at an early age also shows children that friendships between the sexes are just as possible and rewarding as romantic involvement—an important lesson for adults, who will spend their working life in a coed environ-ment.

Boys who play with dolls and girls who are tomboyish, then, are hardly ever a problem unless the child completely rejects traditional play opportunities or voices a distinct desire to *be* the opposite sex and is unhappy with who he or she is. (See *Gender Identity Disorder*.)

Playing with Matches

(See *Fire-Setting*)

Pleasure, Lack of

An inability to enjoy things, and a general disinterest in hobbies and ac-tivities that once gave pleasure, is called "anhedonia." It is a hallmark of depression and should be a warning signal for parents. (See *Fatigue*, *Depression*, *Sadness*, *Reaction to Loss*, and *Reaction to Parental Con-flict*.)

Popularity

Adults and children alike need to remember that it's the quality of friendships, not the quantity, that matters. Parents also need to assess whether popularity is their goal or their child's.

For children, it is natural to want to fit in and be special at the same time—to be liked but still be a leader or renowned for an outstanding talent. Of course, those desires can be contradictory, and anyone whose self-esteem relies solely on the opinion of others may be standing on dangerously unpredictable ground.

That said, there are certain characteristics that tend to make children automatically popular with peers. Athletic boys who excel at sports but never use their strength randomly or cruelly are likely to be perceived as leaders. They are often the team captain. Attractive, verbally witty girls who can come up with a dazzling repartee that neither humiliates nor shames another person are also likely to be popular with their contemporaries.

Being very unusual will generally be an obstacle to peer approval and respect. Children who are too smart, too tall, too small, too fat, too physically mature too early (or the opposite), or not quite smart enough, athletic enough, or socially adept enough often have trouble making friends.

Some children seem natural-born leaders, others followers. Some are gregarious and comfortable in group settings, others are more reserved loners.

Respect a child's innate social style while still creating opportunities for him to make friends. It is very important for a child to be capable of intimate friendships, but nothing is more detrimental to his self-esteem than trying to be something he's not and recognizing that he's disappointing his parents. (See *Making Friends*, *Self-Esteem*, *Shyness*, and *Adaptability*.)

Post-Traumatic Stress Disorder

Post-Traumatic Stress Disorder (PTSD) is a condition originally associated with Vietnam veterans and POWs, but we now know that it may apply to anyone, child or adult, who survives an extremely traumatic event. Children who witness terrible accidents, natural disasters, assaults, or brutal domestic violence may develop PTSD. It also occurs in children who have experienced sexual abuse. These traumas are stressful events that do not occur in the lives of most people. Divorce, a pet running away, or the death of a grandparent are losses that may spark depression or sadness, but are unlikely to bring about PTSD.

In adults, PTSD has been described as shell shock, battle fatigue, and war neurosis. People relive an event in vivid memories, nightmares, or "flashbacks" (recollections that are so strong that a person believes he is truly experiencing the event again). Their anxiety level in general is heightened and they may avoid relationships, situations, or places that are reminiscent of the original traumatic event.

Children with PTSD most typically experience extreme separation anxiety. They do not feel safe, and perhaps even panic, unless they are with a trusted caregiver. They often regress, losing skills such as toilet training or language that they had already mastered. They, too, experience flashbacks in the form of nightmares, thoughts, or even daydreams. They often re-create the incident in their play by acting it out with stuffed animals. They may become generally fearful, perhaps phobic about going to school (and being separated from parents). Older children may use drugs or alcohol in an attempt to wipe out their memories and anxieties.

What to Do

If a child is exhibiting such extreme responses to a traumatic event, he needs professional counseling. In fact, if a family has undergone a life-threatening accident or survived a natural disaster such as a flood, a hurricane, or an earthquake, parents should consider counseling as a precaution and a prevention *before* such symptoms erupt. PTSD is actually the mind's way of trying to deal with trauma. Family discussions are a healthier and much less painful solution.

We all want to believe that our children are too young to remember painful or frightening events. If anything, children are more likely than adults to remember. Just because they don't discuss the event doesn't mean they aren't thinking about it or anxious that it could happen again.

For further information, contact the Public Inquiries Branch of the National Institute of Mental Health, 5600 Fishers Lane, Rockville, MD 20857 (301-443-4513).

Precocious Puberty

One of the goals of youth is to fit in while still seeming special—special but not different. For this reason, precocious puberty can be very stressful for children. They look like adults before their peers, and before they're emotionally ready to be grown up. Among other things, older teenagers may mistake such children as their peers and expect them to be able to make choices for which they are not yet prepared, either by experience or emotional maturity.

The average age of puberty in the United States seems to be decreasing because of improved nutrition. Today, it is not unusual for girls to begin physically maturing in the fifth or sixth grade. But girls who are the first of their friends to develop breasts or to menstruate may become uncomfortable with their bodies. Some might even starve themselves (as anorexics do) in order to halt further physical development. (See *Eating Disorders.*)

Pay attention to a child's evolving self-concept. If a girl complains about being fat, even when she's not, don't tell her she's being ridiculous. Instead, ask her why she feels this way. Gently help her "test the reality" of her statement. Compliment her other attributes, particularly those that *don't* have to do with appearance.

Remember that puberty brings hormonal changes that may make a child moodier, quicker to show anger, and more argumentative. It will also bring some weight gain that is normal. Don't focus your attention on this gain as it may alarm your child. (See *Obesity.*) Consult your family pediatrician about what to expect during your child's puberty.

Finally, the average age that teenagers have their first sexual intercourse is also going down. A child who has experienced precocious puberty may be at higher risk of early sexual encounters. When children display very sexualized behavior or use unusually explicit language before sixth grade, the question of whether or not they have been sexually abused should be raised. (See *Sexual Abuse.*)

Procrastination

Children tend to procrastinate about predictable tasks: homework, household chores, getting ready for school, or going to bed. Like adults, children might dawdle when they are anxious or uncertain about a situation, or when a task just isn't a whole lot of fun or interrupts something that is.

Children also have reasons more particular to them. A toddler or preschooler's sense of time is not the same as an adult's. They may not understand the necessity of doing one thing before another. Children are also typically not well organized. These skills are techniques they must learn with some adult guidance. They are also likely to become very absorbed in one activity and have difficulty breaking away from it for another scheduled event.

You can help children procrastinate less by clearly establishing rituals and times for certain chores or activities such as bedtime. In the case of chores, keep your requests simple and direct. Try setting up reward systems to reinforce timely compliance, and respect small requests such as waiting five minutes until a child's favorite TV show is over to do the dishes (try not to be annoyed when you have to remind him once it's concluded). (See *Chores and Cleaning Room.*)

If a child procrastinates on his homework, help him organize and schedule himself better. Set a specific time for doing homework in a specific, quiet place where he won't be interrupted. Gently remind him about the need to work on long-term projects on a daily basis, not just the night before they're due. Then, fight the temptation to bail him out either by doing his work for him or writing a note to his teacher. A child will never learn the consequences of his procrastination if he never has to face them himself. (See also *Self-Esteem*.)

Sometimes procrastination is part of an overall pattern of stubborn, oppositional behavior. Therapists might call it passive aggression, meaning it's a way to resist parental authority without outwardly challenging or expressing hostility. If a child procrastinates constantly, it's possible that you may be demanding too much of him; perhaps you're not allowing him enough progressive autonomy; perhaps you engage in too many battles of control with him. (See *Oppositional Behavior*.)

Procrastination can also be a symptom of anxiety. If a child really drags his feet about getting ready for school or a soccer game, there may be something about the situation that bothers him. Talk to him about it. (See *Anxiety*.)

Finally, try to remember that some children, by their nature, are simply not as driven as you may be. Children may prefer to linger over projects or activities. We adults, particularly working parents, are so tightly booked that we can sometimes forget the beauty of doing things at a slower, more relaxed pace.

Psychosomatic Disorder

Children respond to stress and crises in a variety of ways: Some cope and show no discernible behavioral upheaval; some are able to talk about it; others may develop behavior problems; some just seem sad; and some may avoid situations that cause them anxiety.

There are times when children may appear to block out stress altogether. Instead of expressing their feelings, they "internalize" them, which often results in physical symptoms. In rare cases, this internalization of problems causes psychosomatic disorders, in which a child's anxiety or anger is manifested in physical maladies that have no detectable physiological cause.

Physical symptoms may be as severe as seizures and limb paralysis or as seemingly commonplace as chronic headaches and stomach pain. The causes of psychosomatic disorders can range from common school problems to fear of domestic violence.

If a child has had a complete medical workup and no physical cause for his symptoms has been found, parents should obtain an evaluation by mental-health professionals.

Reaction to Loss

Loss brings change to a person's life. The death of a grandparent, divorce, a geographic move, switching teachers or baby-sitters, or a pet running away can all represent loss to a child. His reaction can include irritability, anger, guilt, social withdrawal, sadness, change in sleeping or eating patterns, or heightened clinginess—many of the same feelings adults experience.

Accepting the fact that children can be deeply saddened or shaken by a life event is often difficult for parents. We tend to idealize childhood as a time of carefree happiness, and sometimes push children to feel better before it's appropriate to do so. Grieving is normal. It shows that a child is capable of forming strong attachments, which are good and healthy. Life is full of goodbyes, and learning at an early age how to accept them will make the process easier. (See *Sadness*.)

Depending upon the severity of the loss, a child will probably return to his typical mood and activity level within four to six weeks. If he doesn't, seek the advice of a mental-health professional. Your child may be suffering clinical depression or he may need to talk things through more carefully. (See *Depression*.)

What to Do

Listen to, acknowledge, and validate your child's feelings. Address his fears. Be honest. A child who catches you in a lie, even if it's intended to protect his feelings, may not trust you in the future, and consequently may even imagine scenarios that are far scarier than reality. What you *won't* discuss seems far more ominous.

Answer the questions he asks. Use language appropriate to his age. Don't spill over into another aspect of the topic; wait for his next question. Children ask what they need to know. A two-year-old understands far more than he can say, so don't discuss issues around him that you don't want him to hear.

Finally, parents are a child's most powerful model; he'll watch you for cues as to how he should act. If you are distraught or unable to discuss your own emotions following a loss, he will follow suit now and later in life. You may frighten him if you seem inconsolable, out of control, or unreachable. Don't squelch your own emotions, but try to control them in front of a child. And if you find yourself becoming increasingly depressed, seek professional counseling, for the good of your family as well as yourself.

Illness and Death

The illness and death of a grandparent is often the first traumatic loss a child has to face. If a child is advanced enough to ask about an ill grandparent's prognosis, be honest without being alarming. Perhaps say, "We hope Grandpa will get better, but sometimes people can die when they're this sick." If that person truly is terminal, acknowledge it so that a child can have time to say goodbye, if he wants to.

Use caution in taking a child to see someone in a hospital, however. For young children, it may be frightening. If Grandpa is uncomfortable or so sick that he is not aware of his visitors, a visit may not be sensible. Children eight years of age and older can benefit from projects: making cards or presents provides a means for them to express their love in a tangible way.

If the grandparent dies, don't use euphemisms such as "He went to sleep." Children under five years of age are very literal and may be afraid to go to bed at night as a result. Be forthcoming about your religious beliefs regarding death, but be aware that presenting heaven as too wonderful a place can spark suicidal reunion fantasies in a deeply grieving or emotionally disturbed child. And if Grandpa died of an illness, be sure to explain the difference between that disease and a cold. Make sure a child understands the difference between his little heart racing after he's run up a hill and Grandpa's heart attack.

Parents will have helped a child immensely by discussing death as a natural, final, and inevitable part of the life cycle. A preschooler who finds a dead bird presents a perfect, nonthreatening opportunity to define death when the child asks, "What happened?" A child his age will worry about very concrete things: how the bird eats or drinks after

216

death. Explain that it no longer breathes. Its heart and brain have stopped working. It doesn't need to eat anymore.

Children six to eight years old engage in magical thinking. They may conceive of death as an evil spirit that comes and takes a person away. Or they may believe their behavior somehow caused someone's death. Try to dispel those fears by again explaining that death is a natural and expectable part of the life cycle, not a monster or the result of a child's bad behavior or thoughts. Remember to consider positive memories and to help your child to do so also. You can say, "We did have good times with Grandpa when he was alive. Let's look at some pictures of you with him."

As to funerals, remain sensitive to your child and his wishes. If he wants to go, make sure there is someone attending specifically to look after him. Too often parents are so wrapped up in the details of the funeral that they can't be as available emotionally for their children. Other family members can be a big help.

Inevitably, the death of a relative will prompt a child to worry about his own parents' mortality. If asked, be honest. Say something like: "I will die sometime, but probably not for a very long time." You'll need to define "long" in a tangible fashion: "When I'm Grandpa's age. That's after you've finished school, grown up and gotten married and had children of your own."

The most important thing is for you to seem comfortable with whatever method of explanation or comfort you offer. If you seem afraid of death, your child will be, as well.

The death of a beloved pet (or his running away) can sometimes be as traumatic for a child as the loss of a relative. Don't minimize your child's attachment by immediately replacing the animal. Wait until he asks or seems interested.

Recommended reading for children: *The Tenth Good Thing About Barney*, by Judith Viorst (Macmillan); *When a Pet Dies*, by Fred Rogers (Putnam); *Everett Anderson's Goodbye*, by Lucille Clifton (Henry Holt); *Nana Upstairs & Nana Downstairs*, by Tomie dePaola (Putnam); *Lifetimes: The Beautiful Way to Explain Death to Children*, by Byran Mellonie and Robert Ingpen (Bantam Books). For parents: *Tough Questions: Talking Straight with Your Kids About the Real World*, by Sheila Kitzinger and Celia Kitzinger (The Harvard Common Press).

Moving

If a child is facing a move, allow him to mourn the loss of his friends and teachers. Avoid dismissing his sadness or anxiety about your new neighborhood with statements such as, "You'll make just as good friends in our new home." Most children do, but he may not. He may not like his new school, either.

Soften the transition by preparing for it well. Show a child pictures of his new house; get a map of the neighborhood and point out where his new school is. Help him pack a box of favorite possessions that he can open upon arrival. Go with him to school the first day. Give him a chance to say goodbye to his old friends, teachers, and neighbors.

If at all possible, move during summer vacation, so that he doesn't have to make all these changes in the middle of a school year. Try not to move during the final, climactic year of a school. (Sixth or eighth grade can be difficult. The senior year in high school is probably the hardest time.) If you do move then, a child will lose all the status and friends he has worked so hard to accumulate. It's best if a move can occur at a time when most of a school's students are coming into a new environment (seventh grade or freshman year, for instance).

Recommended reading for children: *Annie Bananie*, by Leah Komaiko (HarperCollins); *Gila Monsters Meet You at the Airport*, by Marjorie Weinman Sharmat (Macmillan); and *This Place Has No Atmosphere*, by Paula Danziger (Delacorte).

Switching Baby-Sitters

Saying goodbye is also important when there is a change in baby-sitters. Set up a special event—it may be as simple as milk and cookies—on the sitter's last day. Explain why the sitter is leaving so the child doesn't worry that he or she has done something wrong to make the sitter leave. Introduce her replacement gradually and stick around the first few days. If the child is sad, agree: "You're right, no one will be Mrs. Smith. She was wonderful. But there are other wonderful people in the world, too." If the sitter was dismissed because of a conflict with the parents, it may be wise not to focus on the problem unless the child is eight or older and can understand that those disagreements had nothing to do with his actions.

Reaction to Parental Conflict, Divorce, and Remarriage

All adults disagree on occasion. We get angry and sometimes we argue. This is normal and healthy. It's actually important for children to see that their mother and father can disagree and have strong emotions yet are still good people. No one is perfect.

The trick, however, is to handle disagreements well—to "fight fairly," with no name-calling or black-and-white generalizations about the other person; to listen to the opposing side's opinions and work out a mutually acceptable compromise; and to apologize if you lose your temper or yell. These are good lessons for children. They learn how to communicate, how to negotiate differences, and how to admit their mistakes by watching their parents do so. They also come to accept that people can disagree and still love one another.

Loud, vindictive, bloodcurdling fights, on the other hand, are not productive for anyone, particularly the children witnessing them. Conflict of this nature makes children afraid, anxious, and generally insecure.

Arguing

Children respond differently to parental conflict according to their age and cognitive abilities. But no matter how old they are, all children learn communication styles from their families. If parents yell and demean one another, never resolve their differences, are physically violent, or do the opposite and never discuss their feelings at all, a child is likely to follow suit as an adult. Parents are the most important model for a child's future relationships.

Toddlers and Preschoolers

Young children experience the world almost solely through the context of their family. Parents' arguing destabilizes their universe. While toddlers and preschoolers may not understand what a fight is, really, they will "reflect the feelings" around them. Chronic emotional upheaval can foster aggressive and oppositional behavior. Children may have nightmares or devise scenarios of retaliation or destruction in their play.

At this age, they can't explain what they're feeling, but parental conflict creates insecurity and fear of abandonment. Consequently, children may become more clingy and needy. They may even regress. A child who was able to stay dry through the night might begin to wet again. One who was beginning to form sentences might revert to baby talk. (See *Anxiety* and *Regression*.)

Children under five years of age are egocentric. Cognitively, they believe that the world truly revolves around them. So if parents argue, a child may reason that it's because of some fault in him. This child believes he'll be able to make the fighting stop somehow if he just behaves better.

Preschoolers also engage in magical thinking, which means they firmly believe that their thoughts or fantasies can become reality. For example, let's say little Johnny is angry at his father for making Mommy cry. The next day, Daddy is in a car accident. Johnny may think that he caused the accident with his anger. That's an enormous amount of guilt and responsibility for a child to bear. Make sure a child knows he is not the cause of these arguments.

School-Aged Children

Around the age of seven, children reach a cognitive stage called "concrete operations." (See the Developmental Tasks Appendix.) They are now capable of understanding cause and effect and can speculate about the logical outcome of an event or situation. So if a child has friends whose parents have divorced, he may worry that his own parents are about to separate simply because they're arguing.

Sibling relations may also be affected by continual parental bickering. Brothers and sisters may fight more, mirroring their parents, or they may huddle together, giving each other the emotional nurturance their parents may be too preoccupied to provide.

While a school-aged child can understand intellectually that he didn't really cause his parents' argument, believing this emotionally is another issue altogether. Often his schoolwork suffers because he is preoccupied with his worries about his parents during class, or because he can't concentrate on his homework at night when his parents are fighting. Eventually, he may resort to oppositional behavior to try to grab his parents' attention, and will develop a self-defeating cycle of behavior problems. (See *Oppositional Behavior*.)

Preteens

Children on the cusp of adolescence are more likely to align themselves with one parent against the other. Constant parental conflict may also make them distrustful of the opposite sex or, conversely, throw them into premature romances for emotional comfort. It certainly will make them even less likely to discuss their own lives with parents, who appear to be too caught up in their own intense emotional battles to pay attention to their children.

What to Do

First, if your arguments have become substantial and chronic, seek professional counseling to learn how to better communicate and resolve your differences. That's not admitting weakness; it shows strength and commitment to your family. The emotional and physical demands of raising children, particularly stubborn toddlers, can exacerbate tensions within even the strongest of marriages.

If you have occasional, normal arguments, don't feel you have to hide them from your child. It will, in fact, benefit your child to hear you disagree, debate civilly, and ultimately resolve your differences. If he's worried, try saying, "We don't agree on this point right now, but we'll figure it out. That's our responsibility." If parents still seem to be in charge (and concerned about the welfare of their offspring) during a disturbing situation, children will feel less rattled by conflict and remain more emotionally secure.

However, if your argument is turning into an out-and-out fight, give yourselves a time-out and save further discussion until your child has gone to bed. Perhaps the break will defuse your anger. If not, watch your decibel level. It's very frightening for a child to wake to the sound of his parents yelling at each other.

For older children, explain the argument's outcome and the compromise you made. Or if there was none, say that sometimes people just agree to disagree. A child of any age will have much less anxiety about the potential outcome of your arguments if he knows how you resolve them.

If he seems worried about the possibility of divorce, reassure him. Perhaps say, "We were just having an argument. You argue with

221

your friends sometimes and you still like them. We disagree on this particular point, but we agree on many other important things, including how much we love you. This argument does not mean we'll divorce."

Explain what causes divorce: that a couple is having long-term difficulty *getting along*. Avoid saying, "They were mad at each other," because you don't want children to think that one incidence of anger guarantees divorce or abandonment. Also, avoid using the phrase "stopped loving," because a child may then wonder if a parent can ever stop loving him.

You want to convey the idea that any important relationship takes work, has ups and downs, and is ultimately worth the effort.

Separation and Divorce

The odds are that one out of two of you reading this book has already divorced or will do so in the future. By the time they are teenagers, more than one third of today's children will spend some time in a household headed by a single parent, typically their mother. Most divorcées remarry within three years. Many of these unions create "blended families," mingling children by the couple's previous marriages, and perhaps a few from the new union. Second marriages, unfortunately, have an even higher rate of divorce—probably because of the emotional baggage and complicated configurations of relationships brought to them, according to a review of multiple studies by social scientist Frank Furstenberg in *The Annual Review of Sociology*, 1990.

Those are sobering statistics, which are accompanied by hundreds of changes—economic, emotional, environmental—for children to endure.

It is unclear why the specific long-term impact of divorce on children appears to be so variable. Some studies indicate that many children gradually recover and negotiate the necessary developmental transitions over time. Others point to "sleeper effects" that bring permanent emotional scars and dysfunction in personal relationships. On the other hand, parents who are horribly unhappy in their marriage may not be emotionally stable enough to provide a consistent, nurturing home for their children. For these families, divorce is probably preferable to the continuing upheaval of parents remaining married.

Unfortunately, divorce does disrupt and permanently change a

222

child's world, and parents have to be honest about the impact of the divorce if they want to help make the transition easier on children.

To begin with, a child loses daily contact with one parent. Most of the time that parent is the father. Studies also show that following separation, a man's earning capability goes up, while a woman's economic situation substantially worsens. That reality often requires her to move into more affordable housing or to reenter the work force, which makes her less available. These changes often translate into new schools, new neighborhoods and friends for the children, and perhaps very different day-care arrangements.

So, children of divorce lose not only people, but the intactness of a family as well—the protective, reliable envelope marriage provides them. Furthermore, their economic safety net may be pulled out from under them. In short, writes Judith Wallerstein in *Second Chances: Men, Women, and Children a Decade After Divorce*, "they feel less protected, less cared for, less comforted."

Toddlers and Preschoolers

The worst timing of a divorce for children may be between birth and age three—a stage when predictability and a stable, familiar environment are critical to a child's feelings of security and consequent ability to develop some independence and self-confidence.

Just as they respond to chronic parental conflict (see "Arguing," above), children this age will probably regress developmentally and emotionally following a divorce.

School-Aged Children

School-aged children are at high risk for developing academic problems. Distracted by family concerns, they may be less able to concentrate. They may find it harder to study at night, especially if their single mother has been forced to assign them those household tasks she can no longer manage alone.

Children may also become saddened and lose interest in things they once enjoyed. Such a loss can be detrimental to the self-esteem of school-aged children, who are at a developmental stage of defining themselves according to their skills and interests. (See the Developmental Tasks Appendix.) Other signs of depression include social with-drawal or distinct changes in eating and sleeping patterns.

Often children attempt to hide their troubles from parents. They feel a need to protect Mommy (or Daddy) from any additional pain, and so they deny or minimize their own problems and try to be good little boys and girls. They may even become parents to their parents, patting the adult's hand as she cries, saying, "That's okay, Mommy."

Of course, parents want children to be capable of empathy and compassion, but the danger in this is that a child becomes so absorbed with meeting her parents' needs that she forgets her own or never learns how to ask someone for emotional support. That child is at risk for becoming a perpetual caregiver, possibly marrying an alcoholic or some other needy individual. When she herself becomes a mother, she runs the danger of expecting too much emotional sustenance from her child, repeating the whole cycle in the next generation.

School-aged children are also more likely to fantasize about their parents getting back together. Because of this, one of the most difficult things for them to go through is a series of failed reconciliations.

They may persistently feel that they somehow contributed to their parents' breakup, or hurt that they weren't an important enough reason for their parents to stay together. But once parents separate, children encounter other guilty feelings. They may feel disloyal if they enjoy time with their noncustodial parent. Going back and forth between their parents' two houses also presents a myriad of logistical problems that may compound the emotional ones.

Preteens

Preadolescents are prone to the same responses as school-aged children, but because they are close to the time they'll start having their own romantic interests, their parents' divorce can have an immediate and profound impact. They may avoid or plunge prematurely into dating or romantic entanglements.

Because of their age and relative maturity, preteens can often slide into the role of surrogate spouse or parent, taking on many of the responsibilities and chores once filled by the parent no longer living in the house. Although this can make a child feel important in the short term, he may come to resent being robbed of his childhood. He may also have trouble giving up his adult status if his parent remarries.

The daily absence of a father is particularly hard on preadolescent boys, who benefit from having a role model to emulate (or react against) at this stage in their development.

What to Do

It is crucial to a child's emotional health that parents be as clear and direct as possible about why the divorce is happening. Children have the right to know. There is no need to discuss infidelities, but if there was a basic philosophical difference that could not be reconciled about money management or career, it's sensible to describe that to older children who are capable of understanding. Try to explain the divorce to children together, before one of you has moved out. Take time to discuss and explain how you plan to handle weekend visiting, remarriage, and the merging of stepfamilies. Much research suggests that the continuing and bitter conflict before and after a divorce is even more harmful to children than the breakup itself.

Explain that the divorce had nothing to do with them, and that both of you still and always will love them. Make it clear you view the separation as a way to improve or fix a bad situation, that it will restore calm to the children's household. Don't smear the concept of marriage. Perhaps say, "When we married we fully expected to stay together forever, but we've found that we can't get along. We see that our fighting is making you unhappy as well as us. The divorce will stop the fighting and restore peace and let us have a better, more focused relationship with you."

Use words a child can understand. A three-year-old will not comprehend "divorce," but can grasp "not living together anymore."

Be honest that things will be different and perhaps a little harder for a while. Let them grieve. They have a right to their sadness. If you feel you need to prompt a discussion, begin by normalizing their anger or disappointment with "Sometimes when parents divorce, children worry that . . . Are you feeling something like that?"

When they voice their anger, hear it out, even if it's directed at you. Try to soothe their fears. Many children worry that they, too, will be left or "divorced" by parents.

225

On the other hand, don't let your own guilt about the breakup blind your judgment. Continue to set limits about appropriate methods of voicing emotion. Try saying, for instance, "I understand you're mad at me and that's okay. But it's not okay for you to spit or swear at me. That's inappropriate. Find another way to tell me what you're feeling." (See *Anger.*) Remember that bad behavior or academic trouble is not *always* the result of a divorce. There may be other problems to explore.

Finally, think about some counseling for your children or finding a support group to help them through the transition. Even though about half of all children go through divorce, they think it's happening only to them. It helps them to know they're not alone. Keep other changes to a minimum, especially for children under the age of five. If you must move, try to stay within the same school district or neighborhood. If such changes are unavoidable, try to reassure yourself by remembering that many children of divorce have shown the ability to cope. Being aware of the loss a move represents will help you make it easier for your children. (See "Moving" under *Reaction to Loss.*)

Noncustodial parents need to set up a space in their new home that belongs to their child when he visits. That may be hard at first because of financial limitations, but it's critical to a child's feeling of permanence. Duplicate as many of his favorite possessions as possible so that he doesn't have to carry them back and forth, with the danger of leaving something crucial behind. It will make the environment more familiar, inviting, and secure.

Also, when you go to pick up your child for a weekend visit, be on time. He'll worry where you are and that your lateness will set off a fight between you and his custodial parent. If being pleasant to each other is hard for you and your former spouse, keep the exchange brief and businesslike.

Don't sabotage your former spouse. It's important that a child be allowed a private relationship with both parents. That means not criticizing the other's parenting style or trying to ferret information out of a child about the former spouse's current life. It's not helpful for a child to feel that he is being played by one parent against another or that he is an informer. Also, let him know it's okay for him to have fun with your former spouse.

Develop routine expectations such as having lunch together to begin his visits. Similarly, when he returns to his primary home, sit down to cups of hot chocolate together to discuss the weekend's activities. Similar routines help a child of any age know what to expect, and they ease the transition.

Maintain discipline and limits. Try to keep the two sets of household rules as similar as possible. This is particularly important for preteens. Remember that children feel safest and most loved when their parents care enough to set reasonable, consistent limits. They then know what is expected of them. Divorce makes children feel out of control. Prove to them that you are still the responsible and loving authority looking out for them. Stay the adult in the relationship; don't turn your child into a confidante.

Fathers (and they typically are the ones seeing children on weekends) need to avoid the temptation to engage in nothing but special events when their children visit. Also remember that older children will want to spend more and more of their weekends with peers. If there is an outing with his friends during your visitation weekend, don't insist a child forgo it or make him feel guilty for attending. Try to invite his friends to your house as well.

Never entertain your children's reconciliation fantasies, even if you have them yourself. It's cruel to get their hopes up. Then, be sensitive to their feelings if you begin to date again.

Recommended reading for parents: *Second Chances: Men, Women, and Children a Decade After Divorce*, by Judith Wallerstein and Sandra Blakeslee (Ticknor & Fields); *Divorced Families*, by Constance Ahrons and Roy Rodgers (W. W. Norton); *Growing Up with Divorce*, by Neil Kalter (Fawcett Books); and *Vicki Lansky's Divorce Book for Parents*, by Vicki Lansky (available from the National Council for Children's Rights, PO Box 5568, Friendship Station, Washington, D.C. 20016).

For children: *One More Time*, by Louis Baum (William Morrow); *My Mom and Dad Are Getting a Divorce*, by Florence Bienenfeld (EMC Publishing); *My Mother's House, My Father's House*, by C. B. Christiansen (Macmillan); *What's Going to Happen to Me?: When Parents Separate or Divorce*, by Eda LeShan (Macmillan); *Why Are We Getting a Divorce?*, by Peter Mayle (Harmony Books); *The Kids' Book of Divorce: By, For, and About Kids*, edited by Eric Rofes (Vintage Books);

and *Dear Mr. Henshaw*, by Beverly Cleary, illustrated by Paul O. Zelinsky (Morrow Junior Books).

Remarriage

Remarriage offers adults the happy chance to start over. It also provides children with another adult with whom they may build a special, nurturing bond. Remember, however, that remarriage destroys a child's dream of reconciliation between his parents. It may also throw him into a sea of conflicting loyalties in which he feels guilt for liking a stepparent or great anger if he thinks you're trying to replace his natural parent. Additionally, the rivalry between stepsiblings is far more complicated and potentially explosive than that between natural brothers and sisters.

None of this is insurmountable, as long as parents are sensitive to potential conflicts and don't push to make people like each other before they're ready.

What to Do

Don't ask your child for permission to remarry. It gives him more power than he really wants. But before moving in together, you and your future partner should discuss expectations and methods of parenting. Outline them for the children. Keep them consistent for all sets of children: yours, mine, and ours. Stepsiblings who visit only on the weekends should be treated the same as those in permanent residence.

Set up regular family meetings to air grievances and negotiate settlements. Don't expect an instant family or that stepsiblings will necessarily be friends.

Stepparents might want to say to children, "I hope we can be friends. I don't plan to replace your father [or mother], but we will be living together and I do expect you to treat me with respect." Then live up to that statement. Don't try to be a supermom or a replacement authority figure. Avoid criticizing the natural parent on superficial matters. Try not to feel hurt by a child's natural preference for his own mother or father. Follow a child's lead when it comes to closeness. Children often incorrectly believe that to give one person affection requires taking it away from another and constitutes a treasonous act against a biological parent.

Recognize that preteens in particular might see your presence as a threat or that they have somehow been demoted in the pecking order of the household. They may resent what they view as interfering or reordering their lives. Preteens may constantly test a stepparent to see if he or she will also eventually leave. They understandably don't want to become too attached to someone who may "divorce them" again.

Finally, be aware of the heightened sexuality of a new marriage, especially if there are same-aged stepsiblings of the opposite sex living in your house. Keep your intimacies private. Set up rules about bathroom privacy and being fully clothed around the house.

Recommended reading for parents: *Stepmotherhood: How to Survive Without Feeling Frustrated, Left Out, or Wicked*, by Cherie Burns (Times Books); *The Stepfamily: Living, Loving, and Learning*, by Elizabeth Einstein (Macmillan); and *Making It as a Stepparent: New Roles/New Rules*, by Claire Berman (available from the National Council for Children's Rights, PO Box 5568, Friendship Station, Washington, D.C. 20016).

For children: *Visitors Who Came to Stay*, by Annalena McAfee (Viking) and *Like Jake and Me*, by Mavis Jukes, illustrated by Lloyd Bloom (Knopf).

Recklessness

(See *Risk-Taking*, *Impulsivity*, and *Accident-Prone*)

Refusing to Speak

On any given day, children may choose not to speak for a variety of completely normal and predictable reasons. Some children are "slow to warm" temperamentally and are anxious about talking in social situations (when Grandma arrives for holidays, for instance) until they're comfortable. Few children will talk when they're in the middle of a favorite television program. Other children, preteens in particular, are sophisticated enough to know that monosyllabic responses annoy their parents and they'll use this technique to avoid personal questions. A common and frustrating situation for parents goes something like this: "What did you do in school today, honey?" "Nothing," or shrugged shoulders, is the response.

Children tell parents about their lives when *they* choose to, usually when you're trying to read the Sunday morning newspaper. This method may have something to do with getting your attention, of course, but some of their reluctance to answer direct questions has to do with normal developmental stages.

The typical preschooler is not cognitively equipped to recap her day with you during dinnertime. She's more interested in what's going on right now or in the next few minutes. Five- to seven-year-olds do become a bit more talkative because they recognize that it stimulates parents. But between the ages of nine and twelve they may become quiet again. At this stage, children aren't particularly reflective or interested in what they did and why. They are more concerned with acquiring and perfecting skills. Erikson called this stage "industry versus inferiority." (See also the Developmental Tasks Appendix.)

That doesn't mean a parent should just give up on trying to talk with children. Listen for opportunities and respond when they occur. Put down the newspaper and listen to what a child has to tell you. Try picking her up from school or calling her as soon as she gets home. Sometimes an inquiry that immediately follows an event has more impact.

Try asking specific questions. "What's the best thing that happened today? How did that spelling test go? Did you play with Susie? Did your teacher do anything funny?" For many children and parents, conversation comes more easily during activity—while taking an evening stroll or swinging on the swing. Often the narrative of a book provides a perfect chance to ask, "Have you ever felt that way?" Or it may inspire a child to tell you: "I found a frog today that looks just like that one."

Having the energy to be this spontaneous is perhaps one of the most difficult but important requirements of parenting. Adults can store up their experiences and wait until Friday night to share them with each other (in a "quality time" exchange), but children really can't.

Sometimes children can be downright elusive or secretive. Usually this is because they don't want to be caught at wrongdoing or failure, or they're afraid answering will necessitate telling a lie. "Maybe if I don't answer, I won't have to tell him I lost his keys [or flunked my test]" is the thinking.

Help children to admit their mistakes honestly by not putting excessive pressure on them to succeed. Don't blow up at them when they've done something foolish. A child who is traumatized by your (understandable but unhelpful) rage will not be able to assist in finding the keys, nor will he admit to future mistakes. (See also *Secretiveness* and *Lying*.)

If a child has a speech or language problem, he may be embarrassed to talk, especially if peers have teased him. Such a child should see a speech and language pathologist. (See *Language and Speech*, *Articulation Problems*, and *Hearing*.)

Every once in a while, a child simply refuses to speak. Elective mutism is an uncommon and extreme behavior that may have to do with control, oppositional behavior, extreme anxiety, or abuse. This is a child who understands language and is able to talk, but in a particular situation, usually school, refuses to utter a word. The disorder is slightly more common in females, according to the American Psychiatric Association's diagnostic manual, and usually lasts only a few months. Often the child just miraculously begins to speak on a day of *her* choosing.

Don't wait for a child to come around on her own, however. Seek professional help in any situation in which your child refuses to speak at school, and get to the root of the problem.

Regression

Regression means temporarily losing a skill a child has already mastered. Backsliding in toilet training is probably the most common form of regression, which can happen for a variety of reasons: the arrival of a new baby, beginning nursery school, moving into a new neighborhood, divorce, or the death of a relative. A child who suddenly begins wetting his pants after months of being dry, becomes unusually clingy, or stops using words he knows may be reacting to change with anxiety. (See *Reaction to Loss*, *Reaction to Parental Conflict*, and *Anxiety*.)

Usually given some time to adjust and some supportive understanding from parents, his more mature behavior will return. Try to discover what might have prompted his regression and talk about it with him. Avoid shaming a child with: "You're acting like baby." Praise his accomplishment when he regains his skill.

Pronounced regression is likely to have more serious causes. Sometimes it is a symptom of Post-Traumatic Stress Disorder, brought on by a child experiencing a traumatic event. Regression can also occur when a child has been abused, or if there is an underlying and untreated medical illness. (See *Post-Traumatic Stress Disorder* and *Sexual Abuse*.)

Recommended reading for children: *When You Were a Baby*, by Ann Jonas (Greenwillow).

Risk-Taking

At some point parents have to step back, hold their breath, and let a child try something new. Otherwise, you'll breed hesitancy. When a toddler is surefooted and wants to go down the tall slide or when a nine-year-old knows how to dive safely off the low board and wants to try the high board, you must let him.

Such risk-taking allows a child to test, improve, and gain confidence in his abilities and in himself. It is particularly important to the eight- to twelve-year-old in a developmental stage Erik Erikson called "industry versus inferiority." During this time, children define themselves and build self-esteem according to the activities they can master and enjoy. (See the Developmental Tasks Appendix.)

The key is to allow *calculated* risk—meaning the likelihood that they will succeed is much greater than the chance they'll get hurt. Make sure they're ready emotionally and prepared for the challenge. Much of your decision will be based on the child's nature, skill level, and good old common sense.

The child to watch is the high-energy thrill seeker. A persistent tendency to impulsive acts needs to be evaluated. If your child is constantly running off, climbing dangerously, or lunging for things despite your objections and warnings, he may have Attention-Deficit Hyperactivity Disorder (ADHD). (See *Attention-Deficit Hyperactivity Disorder.*)

Rocking

It's very common for babies to rock rhythmically back and forth once they've mastered sitting up. Toddlers often do it as they make the transition from crawling to standing. They use the momentum of rocking to pull themselves up onto their wobbly legs. In both the sitting baby and the standing toddler, rocking has something to do with the rhythmic motion needed to achieve the physical act.

Rocking might be the symptom of a problem, however, when children do it habitually, as if to block out their surroundings. Children should be evaluated by a pediatrician, especially if rocking is coupled with frequent head-banging. The behavior may suggest a neurological or developmental problem, and sometimes is a sign of autism.

Rudeness and Developing Manners

Being polite may not always be easy, but it is an important sign of respect for the rights and feelings of others. Manners are society's code of conduct that make living with one another easier and more pleasant. Manners reduce the number of misunderstandings between people and make them feel that they and their good acts are appreciated and, therefore, worth doing. Rudeness alienates people. Ultimately, children with good manners will be better liked by adults and by peers. And knowing a few tools of etiquette will make going into unfamiliar situations far easier for children because they'll know how to act properly.

Of course, children may not be able to understand all the above reasons for having good manners. Older children in particular, who might like to have burping contests with their buddies, are going to try to dismiss polite behavior as being boring and insincere. Why use a fork when it's more fun to toss a pea into your mouth? Why write a thank-you note to Grandma for ugly socks? But deep down children are reasonable. If you can explain that good manners are a way to ensure easier and friendlier relationships—a system of do-unto-others-as-you-would-have-them-do-unto-you—children are more likely to buy into the proposition.

Begin teaching manners as early as possible. A preschooler leaving a friend's house is perfectly capable of turning to her host and saying, "Thank you." Gently remind children in private, not in front of their friends, about lapses in manners. And be sure to compliment them when they do say "please," "thank you," "excuse me," or "I'm sorry." Add, "I'm proud of you." Setting up a reward system for mannerly behavior during holiday gatherings may be a positive strategy. With positive feedback, polite behavior will eventually become habit rather than a chore. (See "Reward Systems" in the Parenting Skills Introduction.)

Decide what really matters to you. Basic manners probably include the ability to look at people as they speak, to say "please" and "thank you," and to say "excuse me" when one must break into a conversation. "Hello" and "goodbye" are easy-to-do niceties that teenagers often forget. (Sometimes it helps to explain the origins of behavior. Handshakes, for instance, developed as a way for strangers to show one another they were unarmed.)

234

Good table manners (chewing with mouth closed, for instance) keep mealtime pleasant for all. Adults also appreciate and like a child who writes thank-you notes, puts things back where he found them, displays gratitude for gifts, and holds doors open for the elderly.

Finally, remember that you must model whatever polite behavior you want to instill in your child. That means showing children the same respect and courtesy you want them to display to others.

Recommended reading for parents: *Miss Manners' Guide to Rearing Perfect Children*, by Judith Martin (Penguin Books).

For children: *What Do You Say, Dear?*, by Sesyle Joslin, illustrated by Maurice Sendak (Harper Trophy); *Manners Can Be Fun*, by Munro Leaf (Harper & Row); *Manners*, by Aliki (Greenwillow); *Brats*, by X. J. Kennedy, illustrated by James Watts (McElderry); *Mrs. Piggle-Wiggle*, by Betty MacDonald, illustrated by Hilary Knight (HarperCollins); *Eloise*, by Kay Thompson, illustrated by Hilary Knight (Simon & Schuster); and *Telephone Time: A First Book of Telephone Do's and Don'ts*, by Ellen Weiss, illustrated by Hilary Knight (Random House).

Rumination

(See *Vomiting*)

Running Away from Home

At some point, in anger, your child may threaten to run away from home. It'll probably follow fast on the heels of your denying a request, setting a limit, or having to impose a consequence for his breaking a rule. The threat of running away is the biggest weapon he can think of in his retaliation arsenal. It is not unlike the temper tantrums that he may have thrown as a toddler.

Don't help him pack (as our parents might have done) in an attempt to defuse a child's resolve. Nor should you give too much attention to the threat itself, as that might encourage him to use it again. Your best response is to sit down and discuss what caused his anger or disappointment. Try to view the event as an opportunity to improve your communication. Let him know it's okay to feel angry and to verbalize it, but that he must find more appropriate, productive ways to express himself than simply making threats or shouting, "I hate you." (See *Anger.*)

If he continues making threats when he's angry, perhaps make a behavioral contract with him. If he can talk about his feelings the next time he's upset, without yelling or threatening to run away, give him a prearranged reward, such as playing basketball with Dad for thirty minutes.

Children who really do run away are generally fleeing a bad situation at home. Overly strict authority, criticism, constant fighting, or a parent's alcoholism or depression can easily cause a child to run away. Again, address whatever caused a child's upset and flight. If he runs away several times, you need to seek family counseling to improve communication around the household.

Parents might want to consider the safety precaution of having their children fingerprinted. Police departments provide this service and will give prints to the parents, so that there's no police record made. But parents have the prints in case they need to ask police to help find their children.

Chronic adolescent runaways are generally known as "throw-away kids." They are children who feel that they really aren't wanted at home or are fleeing terrible circumstances.

Recommended reading for young children (when the idea of running away first occurs): *Where Are You Going, Little Mouse?*, by Robert Kraus, illustrated by Jose Aruego and Ariane Dewey (Greenwillow); and *The Runaway Bunny*, by Margaret Wise Brown, illustrated by Clement Hurd (Harper Trophy).

Sadness

Sadness is a common and normal emotion. After all, the ability to reflect upon the meaning and import of events or relationships is what elevates humans above animals. Think of poetry and prose across the ages—some of the most spectacular and moving are those expressing sad thoughts.

Adults become nervous when a child is sad. We don't want them weighted down by unhappiness. Seeing a child's face so stricken can be enough to drive a parent to tears, too.

But children are entitled to their emotions. Of course they will grieve when a pet dies or runs away, when a favorite playmate moves to another city, or when they haven't achieved something for which they have tried very hard. (See *Reaction to Loss.*) Try to recognize the good in such emotions—it means a child is connecting with others and placing importance on events. Complacency is not really a desirable alternative.

That doesn't mean you should let a child struggle with his sadness all alone. Talk to him about what he's feeling, acknowledge his loss, and ask him what would help him feel better. Take this opportunity to talk about different emotions with him, to explain and normalize them, to discuss how long and why a child might feel unhappy, angry, or uncertain.

For a young child, experiencing true grief for the first time can be frightening. The emotion seems far more dramatic because it's novel. Talking about it helps him learn how to work through powerful emotions. It also helps you accept them and their natural progression within your child so that you don't put undue pressure on him to feel better before he's ready.

However, if sadness keeps a child from his usual activities or seems to last longer than a few weeks, watch for other signs of depression: sleeplessness, loss of appetite, headaches. (See *Depression.*) Clinical depression, with the physical symptoms seen in adults, is less common in people under the age of twelve, but it does occur.

Also, be aware that constant arguing and parental conflict may make a child sad or fearful. Divorce represents loss to them as well as to adults, and children may need some counseling to help them adjust to the change in life-style it brings. (See *Reaction to Parental Conflict*.)

School: Anxieties, Performance Problems, and Phobia

School is where a child comes into his own. It's a place exclusive of home, beyond the design and control of parents. It is the arena in which a child will have some of his greatest challenges, dilemmas, triumphs, failures, self-affirmations, and embarrassments.

It is at school that a child will learn about how the world works—not only its history, philosophies, sciences, and physical properties, but also about how negotiations are made, how people outside his family interact with one another, differentiate among one another, and accept one another. He will learn about himself, his strengths, his weaknesses, his interests, and who he is socially. He will have to perform in a way he never has had to at home. He has to live up to his potential academically, make friends, and detach himself from his parents.

These are tall orders. School can be great fun, of course, but it also has nerve-racking, overwhelming moments. So it's perfectly normal for children to show some anxiety about school. That's especially true when a child first attends, or at the beginning of each new school year, or perhaps when he's just entered a different school. Other pivotal pressure times are around third grade (when most schools begin grading and comparing children academically) and seventh grade (when schoolwork demands longer homework readings and a higher level of organizational thinking and comprehension).

In fact, a little healthy apprehension about tests, book reports, and school plays probably helps motivate a child to prepare himself better. Parents can help ease children's tension about school by having a supportive, encouraging attitude while accepting a child's natural limits, as well as helping him learn *how* to study. (See *Motivation*, *Procrastination*, *Perfectionism*, and *Self-Esteem*.)

Keep in mind, however, that school should often be as much about socialization as it is about intellectual growth. Because of that fact, children will also be troubled at times by arguments with their friends, by playground competition, or by poor relationships with their teachers. These are things that parents can and should try to help children overcome by giving a little empathetic advice.

When a child has a serious problem, it is often at school that it first presents itself clearly. If he cannot inhibit his aggressiveness or contain his impulsivity; if he cannot learn at a developmentally appropriate pace; if he has difficulty separating from parents; if he is emotionally troubled by something at home; or if he is so painfully shy that he cannot relate to others—these problems will suddenly become obvious in school, because a child is now in the context of his peers. Surrounded by them, he looks different. His behavior or progress may seem a little off.

Often a learning disability, a language and speech problem, or Attention-Deficit Hyperactivity Disorder (ADHD) is the root cause of serious school trouble. He may also have a hearing or sight impairment that simply needs correcting with hearing aids or glasses. (See *Attention-Deficit Hyperactivity Disorder*, *Hearing*, *Language and Speech*, and *Learning Disabilities*.) Or he may be distracted and unable to concentrate because of a recent loss, illness, or trouble at home. (See *Reaction to Loss, Reaction to Parental Conflict*, and *Depression*.)

If a child's problems are serious enough to affect his functioning at the level he desires, he may become overly anxious, perhaps even avoidant or phobic, about school. A child with *school phobia* has an intense dread of school. He may develop recurrent psychosomatic ailments—headaches, stomachaches, nausea, or dizziness—that prevent attendance. Typically these complaints follow a pattern, occurring on Monday mornings or following vacations. That doesn't mean that a child is not feeling real physical distress—many of us have been nervous enough for our stomachs to hurt at some point in our lives. (See *Headaches*, *Stomachaches*, *Fears and Phobias*, and *Psychosomatic Disorder*.)

* * *

239

If his phobia is not situational, (i.e., caused by a specific thing, such as an overly authoritative teacher or a class bully), or the result of ADHD or learning disabilities, then it generally stems from separation anxiety. A child may really be more terrified about leaving home than he is about going to school—he may fear something horrific will happen to his parents during his absence. In this case, he probably has not achieved a developmentally appropriate independence from his parents, most typically his mother.

Separation anxiety is normal in preschoolers but should have largely resolved itself by kindergarten. The mothers of school-phobic children are often overprotective and ambivalent about a child's autonomy. They may even suffer from depression or an anxiety disorder themselves. (See *Anxiety* and *Anxiety Disorders*.)

Ironically, if ADHD and learning disabilities are not involved, many school-phobic children can actually do well academically and are of average to above-average intelligence. This is very different from the truant child, who typically is a poor student, has a conduct problem, dislikes school, and skips it, usually without his parents' knowing.

According to the American Psychiatric Association's diagnostic manual, school phobia occurs equally in boys and girls, and most often between the ages of five and seven (at the start of elementary school) and the ages of eleven and fourteen (the beginnings of junior and senior high school). It is critical that school-phobic children be sent back to school. The longer they go without attending, the more entrenched their anxieties become, and the harder it will be to return. Heaped onto their original fears will be secondary worries about missed work and the reaction of classmates and teachers.

What to Do

If your child has predictable, general worries about school, be reassuring and responsive to his specific troubles with studying or fitting in on the playground. Be firm about attendance and help him work at making school a good experience. Ultimately, school is a child's job.

When a child first attends kindergarten or first grade, it's normal for him to feel anxious about being away from parents for what seems like a long day. Let him take a picture of you to keep in his knapsack or desk to look at when he's homesick. (His old blanket or teddy bear, on the other hand, are not good options, as his classmates are sure to tease him.)

240

Sometimes making sure he gets on the bus with a favorite playmate or carpooling with that friend makes the daily transition from home to school easier for a child. Make the getting-ready-for-school ritual as stress-free as possible. Perhaps lay out all his notebooks and clothes the night before. (See *Dressing*.)

Teach a child self-soothing techniques for anxiety-producing events such as tests. Tell him to take deep, slow breaths, or think positively: "I can do this, I can do this." (See *Fears and Phobias* and *Anxiety*.)

If he seems worried, try to ask him specific questions to prompt productive discussions: "I know that sometimes kids are a little afraid of school because they're not sure where things are, or because they have problems with work, or the teacher, or a classmate. Is something like that bothering you?" Admit that you were fearful of something at school as a child and that many people have similar concerns.

Then, when he describes the problem, acknowledge his feelings and discuss strategies for changing the situation to his benefit. Help him practice free throws, for instance, if classmates have been teasing him on the basketball court. Or invite one classmate over to play with him after school to facilitate a budding friendship. (See *Anxiety*, *Shyness*, and *Making Friends*.) If a child feels he's constantly being rejected by his peers, try to assess if he is actively doing something to alienate them and talk to him about better conversation techniques. (See *Clowning*, *Talkativeness*, and *Boasting*.) If he's being bullied, contact the school or his tormentor's parents. (See *Bullying* and *Teasing*.)

If it seems that a child can't describe entirely what's wrong, talk to his teacher. Teachers have seen many children over the years in the same setting and can usually pinpoint a problem. If severe school refusal or anxiety persists beyond the second week of school, seek professional guidance.

If schoolwork and test performance are what concern him, first make sure that there is not some physiological problem hampering him. Children with a slight hearing loss may have difficulty absorbing everything the teacher has to say. (See *Hearing*.) If he needs glasses, he may not be able to see what she writes on the chalkboard. Also, if you suspect your child has a learning disability or Attention-Deficit Hyperactivity Disorder (ADHD), be sure to have him evaluated by a professional. Those are problems you and he cannot correct or overcome alone.

Many children need help to study more efficiently and productively. Schedule a set, daily time for homework in a quiet place where he won't be interrupted. Help him prioritize what he studies first that day, building in time for long-term projects. Children are not really capable of such organized thinking and need you to help them learn how to do it. (See *Procrastination* and *Disorganized.*) Sometimes a tutor may be necessary, especially when school problems begin to strain the parent-child relationship.

A child's school experience is largely colored by whether his parents have helped prepare him emotionally for the challenge, whether his self-esteem is strong, and whether they praise his accomplishments while accepting his limitations. You can exacerbate a child's anxiety and damage his motivation by projecting your own ambitions onto him; being disappointed by any grade lower than an A; pushing a child to succeed in activities *you* pick (with no regard for the child's desires); and doing his homework for him. (See *Self-Esteem.*)

Set realistic goals and reward improvement. Try to instill the idea that *learning*, not necessarily being top of the class, is what school is really about. (See *Competitiveness.*) Be sympathetic and nonaccusatory when he does poorly.

Recommended reading for children: *Timothy Goes to School*, by Rosemary Wells (Dial Books for Young Readers); *Will I Have a Friend?*, by Miriam Cohen, illustrated by Lillian Hoban (Macmillan); *Today Was a Terrible Day*, by Patricia Reilly Giff, illustrated by Susanna Natti (Viking); and *Nothing's Fair in Fifth Grade* and *Sixth Grade Can Really Kill You*, by Barthe DeClements (Viking).

School Phobia

(See *School*)

School, Skipping

(See *Truancy*)

Screaming

(See *Crying*, *Temper Tantrums*, *Attention-Seeking*, and *Anger*)

Secretiveness

Like so many behaviors that may seem odd to parents, secretiveness is normal and age-appropriate during a particular developmental stage. Parents may not like it, but children aged eleven and twelve begin to become far more reticent about their lives away from home. They will not be as open about their activities, friends, school days, or hopes and dreams. That doesn't necessarily mean they are hiding dark, illicit secrets. At this age, a certain level of guardedness about their thoughts and feelings is just part of the process of separating from parents and building their own identity.

Don't be discouraged and give up trying to be included, however. It will just require a little more work, patience, and careful listening, as well as showing respect for children's privacy. (See also *Refusing to Speak*.)

Before age eleven, secretiveness is a little less common, although most children will be closemouthed about a deed they know was inappropriate or against the rules. Show some discretion about the severity of minor incidents. A child who denies spilling the milk is very different from one who swears he hasn't been smoking in the

243

basement when he's been doing so daily for the past month. (See *Lying.*)

Secretiveness may also be an element of temperament. Some children are naturally more reticent than others, particularly if their parents are also rather private. All in all, secretiveness is not a problem in and of itself. But on rare occasions, it may be a red flag to other problems in certain situations, and you may need to watch for other behavior patterns if a child is very secretive, especially before the age of ten or eleven. For example, a child who is furtive about her eating habits, stashing food in her room or disappearing into the bathroom after meals, may have bulimia or anorexia. (See *Eating Disorders.*) Sometimes children secretly hoard items they've stolen. (See *Stealing.*) Occasionally, a child seems secretive when he's really had a disassociated episode and is confused about a lapse in his memory. But this is rare. (See *Staring Episodes.*) Finally, an abused child may become clandestine about his whereabouts or relationships because he has come to believe his victimizer's claim that he is responsible for the abusive events happening. (See *Sexual Abuse.*)

Self-Consciousness

Around the age of ten or eleven, there is likely to be a dramatic increase in a child's self-consciousness. She will embarrass more easily. One of her greatest fears will be public humiliation before her peers. Their opinion suddenly becomes paramount. Seemingly insignificant things like shoes, hairstyle, and whether socks are pulled up or scrunched down become critical to the image she wishes to present to her friends. Welcome to the dawn of adolescence.

Try to view this change as an opportunity to help a child build her self-esteem and self-concept. It's important that you do it now, because by the time she's fourteen years of age, she'll be less likely to listen to or solicit your opinion about the validity of her peer group's values. If she isn't already capable of analyzing and dismissing peer pressure by then, it will be much harder for her to develop that kind of confidence.

Hear her out about an embarrassing moment, but try to do a little "reality testing" as well. Is a small embarrassment (not knowing the answer in class, a boy snubbing her in the hall) *really* the end of the world? Be gentle about it. Try to recall some hurt or embarrassment in your own youth that you can point to and say, "I remember how awful that was. But, you know, the next year I didn't even care what Billy said about me. I had met some friends who were much nicer and liked me for what I was, not what I tried to be." One of the gifts parents can give children is a sense of future, of context, that tomorrow they can try again or try something completely different.

Bolster a child's self-esteem by helping him practice for events he's self-conscious about: singing in a concert, giving a speech, even dancing at a dance. That way you're setting up situations so that your child is more likely to succeed than fail, reducing the risk of public embarrassment.

Remember that if your child has always been shy or reticent, this is likely to be a very hard time for her. When she asks for help, talk about social skills (about asking for and listening to other people's opinions) and help her identify situations that make her most anxious. Then discuss alternative ways of handling those circumstances. Help her find activities she really enjoys and has a talent for, where it will be easier for her to find friends and people like her. (See *Shyness.*)

Finally, if a child is self-conscious about her body, talk up her other good character attributes. (See *Eating Disorders* and *Precocious Puberty.*) Or if she's upset that she's not developing fast enough, assure her that those growth spurts will come soon enough. Don't pressure her to be perfect at everything or to be popular; and don't tease her in front of her friends.

(See also *Self-Esteem, Perfectionism, Making Friends*, and *Popularity.*)

Self-Esteem

If a person has a healthy self-esteem, he believes in his abilities, his inherent worth, and that he is deserving of love. Healthy self-esteem should bring self-confidence and a low level of anxiety. That doesn't mean a person is conceited. It means he trusts himself. He knows that if he applies himself he will succeed to a satisfactory degree and will be able to survive a crisis. He's willing to try.

Self-esteem is tied up with self-concept: the way in which a person defines himself in terms of his talents, intelligence, and personality traits. He likes who he is and accepts what he is not. He strives to achieve, not to impress others or solely to garner their approval, but to satisfy himself. If a person's self-concept is strong, he won't be shaken by peer pressure or dependent upon the opinion of others.

Good self-esteem is the emotional foundation of a person's general well-being. It is built during childhood predominantly by two things: by parental affection and approval, and by a child discovering his innate talents and interests. The two components—the loving influence of parents and a child's self-realization—are often intertwined. If parents don't support a child's explorations, he may never discover what endeavors he most likes and in which he can blossom. Self-esteem is built by a child mastering skills on his own, discovering for himself what he likes to do, what he is good at, and being allowed to pursue those interests. (See "initiative versus guilt" and "industry versus inferiority" in the Developmental Tasks Appendix.)

That said, it is vital to remember that self-esteem comes not from being perfect, but from a child accomplishing something that he knows he achieved himself. There is a fine line between parents helping a child and parents doing a task for him. Parents who complete a child's science project, for instance, may win him the A he so badly wants, but it probably sparks some self-doubt as well. If you don't believe he can do a good enough job on his own, why should he? (See *Perfectionism.*)

Children must be allowed to "individuate," to find hobbies that complement their innate talents. They may not be what interests a parent, or what a parent abstractly envisioned for his child. An avid golfer, for instance, needs to accept a child's preference for painting or tennis. Achievement, motivation, and a subsequent healthy self-esteem come largely from enjoyment.

Helping a child build strong self-esteem is probably the greatest, longest-lasting, and most far-reaching gift parents can give a child.

Warning signs that a child's self-esteem may be low include boastfulness, aggression, social withdrawal, jealousy, competitiveness, perfectionism, and blaming others for failure.

What to Do

The first thing you must do for children's self-esteem is to build an environment where it's clear that they are loved and valued. That means hugging them, accepting their limitations while praising their strengths, and adopting a style of parenting in which you listen to and respect differing ways of seeing and doing things. It also means spending "special time" with your child each day, playing or talking on a one-to-one basis, and frequently asking his opinion (and really listening to it) during conversation. (See the Parenting Skills Introduction.)

When correcting a child's inappropriate behaviors, be sure to label the behavior, *not* the child, as being bad. Never belittle. Try to put constructive criticism in a positive context. If a child snatches a toy from a younger sibling, try saying, "You're usually so good at sharing; I know you know better than that." If you expect the best of a child and say so, he is more likely to improve.

After a time-out or other behavior modification is over, be sure to follow it with some happy, affectionate time together to help show you love a child no matter what he does. Find something to praise, especially if he corrects the behavior that caused trouble.

When giving compliments, target specific deeds or talents so that a child knows you are discriminating and sincere in your praise. When he does uncover a gap in his talents, put it in the context of his entire personality and life. Compliment him on the things he really does well. Remind him that accomplishment is found down many different avenues. Being an attentive big brother is just as valid and important as being the star of a football team. Tell him about something you have difficulty doing and add, "No one is good at everything." (See *Perfectionism.*)

Set consistent limits. Children may seem to want parents to be endlessly permissive, but they are actually frightened by too much freedom. They also may feel that you don't care enough about them to set rules, and their self-esteem plummets. If you don't care about them, why should they care about themselves? As children grow older, explain your rationale for rules and show some appropriate flexibility. If your eight-year-old is responsible and careful, for instance, it may be permissible for him to cross a low-trafficked neighborhood street alone to his friend's house. Listen to his opinion, even if the answer remains no. (See also *Self-Sufficiency.*)

Don't compare siblings or label them as being "the shy one," "the smart one," "the musical one." In fact, avoid comparisons altogether as they seem to say that performance is only of value when it exceeds someone else's. (See also *Competitiveness* and *Sibling Rivalry*.)

Allow children to try their hand at tasks as soon as they show an interest in doing so. Set it up so that it is highly likely a child can accomplish those tasks. For instance, a toddler may want to dress herself but may not be capable yet. If you let her try completely unaided, she may fail, become frustrated, and perhaps give up trying. Instead, put her shirt over her head, then let her push her arms through, so that clearly she's helping to finish the task. Praise her for being "such a big helper."

Don't rush in to help her build a block tower. She will feel the greatest sense of accomplishment if she is allowed to struggle, fail, then finally succeed. She'll know that her persistence resulted in her own success. Let a child try unorthodox ways of doing things and find out for herself if they work. Encourage her to have pride in her initiative, even if her efforts weren't completely satisfactory.

Give children age-appropriate household chores. That makes them feel competent, responsible, important to a team (your family), and that you trust them with a task. When a child completes a chore, give specific feedback such as "You did a very nice job putting away your toys." If he didn't quite finish mowing the grass the way you like, don't criticize or redo what he did. Instead, try saying, "You did a really good job over there. Thank you. Let's just finish up these few spots together." He still feels a sense of accomplishment, while learning that a task well done can still stand a few improvements. (See *Chores and Cleaning Room*.)

Allow a child to experiment with many different hobbies or activities until he strikes upon the one that he enjoys most. Don't allow him to quit mid-season, however, if he hates soccer, because that might actually damage his self-esteem. No one feels good about quitting. Encourage him to finish out the season and then stop if he still doesn't like it. Who knows? The next game he might make a goal. It's important for children to understand that trying is what matters and is admirable. Winning is great, but shouldn't be the sole option or motivation. Tell him how proud you are of his efforts and his perseverance. (See *Perfectionism*.)

If a child really isn't particularly athletic but remains very interested in sports, suggest he try out for an individual sport such as swimming or track and field, in which his performance is important but not as critical or immediately apparent to teammates. This is also a particularly good option for children who are easily rattled by peer pressure or are shy.

Finally, model self-respect. If you are harshly critical of yourself or easily upset by disappointments, your child will probably be the same way.

Self-Injurious Behavior

Because they are inexperienced and often don't realize that an activity could be harmful, very young children may sometimes do things that adults view as clearly dangerous and self-destructive. One of the most common is sticking objects into body openings: ears, nose, or anus. (Take a child to the pediatrician to remove objects when they're wedged in.) And without adult supervision, toddlers and preschoolers are at risk of darting into the street because typically they aren't yet capable of *understanding* in the abstract just how dangerous a moving car is. (See *Risk-Taking*.)

Self-injurious behavior, on the other hand, carries the *intent* of harm. This is different from a toddler not knowing better or an older, impulsive child being unable to contain his curiosity or daredevil attitude. A child who continually jumps from dangerously high places; purposefully burns, stabs, or cuts himself; or consumes substances he knows are toxic may be deliberately trying to hurt himself.

Autistic children are at high risk for self-injurious activity, as are the mentally handicapped. Nondisabled children who engage in such behavior are often emotionally troubled. They may even be suicidal, without recognizing it.

Suicides among preadolescent and younger children are less common than in teenagers. But each year about 12,000 children aged five to fourteen are hospitalized for deliberate self-injurious acts, according to the National Institute of Mental Health. Experts speculate that a child who purposefully places himself in danger or hurts himself is usually

249

clinically depressed. (See *Depression.*) Contact a professional if your child continues to hurt himself despite warnings and despite his experiencing bodily discomfort.

Self-Stimulation

(See *Masturbation*, *Habits*, and *Depression*)

Self-Sufficiency

A self-sufficient person is able to take care of his own needs without external assistance and has confidence in his own resources, capabilities, and judgment. It probably also means that he won't be afraid of having to make a decision or of saying no to peer pressure; he has the self-confidence and consequent courage to do both.

Helping a child become self-sufficient is one of the primary goals of parenting. But it must be accomplished slowly and carefully. Parents need to watch a child's evolution to know when he's ready for new challenges or responsibilities. That judgment must be made according to a child's temperament, his cognitive level, his emotional maturity and sense of security, his developmental stage, plus his ability to discriminate between foolhardiness and reasonable risk. It means parents must know their child well.

Each level of independence lays the foundation for the next. Try to hand a child tasks that push him to grow but which he is also likely to achieve. (See *Self-Esteem.*) Don't hand him chores that overwhelm and defeat him, thereby lowering his confidence and motivation to try to do things on his own. (See *Chores and Cleaning Room*, *Motivation*, and *Procrastination.*) Avoid doing for a child what he has become capable of doing for himself, and allow him to make choices. (See *Dressing* and *Food Refusal.*)

Self-sufficiency also requires self-respect. Foster self-respect by listening to a child's opinions and helping him learn a deference for the rights and views of others. If you demonstrate that you trust your child and believe he's a good, worthy person, he'll usually rise to your expectations.

Finally, assess a child's level of impulsivity when deciding whether or not he's ready to play in the backyard by himself or cross the street to a friend's house. (See *Risk-Taking.*)

There is a phenomenon in our society that raises the issue of self-sufficiency in children far earlier than used to be the case: dual-career couples. Today more than half of all mothers work outside the home, predominantly out of economic necessity. That means that thousands of children come home from school to empty houses. Commonly they are known as "latchkey kids."

Being a latchkey child certainly isn't harmful by definition, as long as parents handle the situation well. Ideally, parents and their employers should work out a more flexible schedule so that one parent can be home at least a few afternoons a week. Perhaps parents could alternate with each other.

No one really knows yet the long-term impact of both parents working, although there is some suggestion that children of dual-career couples tend to be more resourceful, self-reliant, and goal-oriented and better students. Much of that may have to do with the educational level and affluence of their parents. It also gives children role models of success, and helps develop a child's sense of individual responsibility and teamwork (particularly true for adolescents).

A few tips: Pay attention to children when you are at home and don't allow them to think that careers are all that matter. Don't put unreasonable stress on children. Try to give age-appropriate responsibilities that don't overburden. Younger children, for instance, need baby-sitters. Older children may come to feel resentful and overwhelmed if they are constantly expected to prepare their own meals from scratch, take care of housework, and spend long hours watching younger siblings. (The latter may heighten sibling rivalry and make afternoon hours when you're not there to mediate particularly contentious.)

Call after school. Ask them how their day was, not just, "Are you doing your homework?" Let them know that they can call you with problems. If it's impossible for you to talk to them right then and there, promise to talk after dinner. Then, stick to your word and do so.

Try to set up pleasurable afternoon activities or arrange for them to visit a neighbor until you return. If you don't, they may spend their time in front of the TV. On the other hand, try not to overschedule them either. Children need some time just to "hang out" and regenerate their energy after a school day.

Continue to set loving, reasonable limits even if you feel guilty about working. Don't be lax about rules or children might believe you don't care about them. (See *Self-Esteem* and the Parenting Skills Introduction.)

Selfishness

At certain ages, selfishness will be more prevalent in children. Infants, toddlers, and preschoolers are naturally egocentric, meaning they perceive and understand the world only through their individual point of view. The ability to empathize comes only with time, cognitive development, and socialization through peers and parents.

By the time a child is five or six years of age, he should know how to share and play nicely in a group. By third grade, he should understand and respect the rights and feelings of others. If not, he has not responded to peer pressure or parental disapproval and behavior modification. (See *Insensitivity* and *Aggression*.)

A selfish school-aged child may have been overindulged or overprotected at home or, conversely, he may have come from a large family in which there is intense competition for resources and parental attention. (It should be noted that even the most polite, generous children are apt to become more greedy and grabby with their siblings. It seems to be part and parcel of sibling rivalry.)

Selfishness can also stem from emotional insecurity or anxiety. If the behavior seems to grow from nervousness about his safety or capabilities, you should explore these issues. (See *Anxiety*, *Reaction to Loss*, *Reaction to Parental Conflict*, and *Self-Esteem*.)

Around the age of twelve, children will again become more preoccupied with themselves as they begin deciding who they really are.

What to Do

Model sharing and empathy for others in your own actions and attitudes. Discuss manners and respecting the rights and needs of others. (See *Rudeness and Developing Manners*.)

Praise children when they do share and don't respond when they try to garner your attention by purposefully acting selfish. Condition them to show some patience and don't immediately give them whatever they demand. (See *Demanding*, *Impatience*, *Bossiness*, *Attention-Seeking*, *Making Friends*, and *Competitiveness*.)

With siblings, try to treat them equally to dampen one child's need to prove he's the best simply because he has more possessions or receives more attention. (See *Sibling Rivalry*.)

Finally, the strongest lesson may have to come from a child's peers. Selfish children lose friends.

Sensitivity

(See *Temperament*, *Adaptability*, and *Self-Consciousness*)

Separation Anxiety

(See *Anxiety*)

253

Sexual Abuse

It is a sad but true fact that sexual abuse happens most often with relatives and family members, not with the proverbial stranger. That's why it's critical for parents to teach a child to act on instinctual feelings of discomfort rather than to rely on clichés such as "Don't take candy from strangers."

Start young. Allow a toddler to choose whom he wants to embrace. Don't make him hug or climb into the lap of an adult just to be polite. If you insist that he kiss Grandma or family friends when he really doesn't want to, you may unwittingly render him more susceptible to molestation. Pedophiles use their authority as adults to coerce children. To be able to protect himself, a child needs to have a firm understanding that his body belongs to him, and the confidence to say no.

That means respecting those feelings yourself, even if it means allowing your toddler not to kiss you goodnight because he's mad at you for not reading his favorite book one more time. Say, "I'd like to give you a kiss, but you don't have to if you don't want to."

Tell him that the parts of his body covered by his underwear are "private," and that no one other than you, his doctor, or his most trusted baby-sitter should ever touch him there, and then only for the purposes of a medical exam, bathing, or dressing. Approach it as a safety issue rather than a sexual one and it should be easier for you to feel comfortable discussing it.

The other important idea to teach children is that there are no "secrets" in your house. Use the word "surprise" rather than "secret" when talking about holiday or birthday parties and gifts. "This is our little secret" is a common pact made by sexual abusers. Instruct your child to tell you if anyone ever asks him to break rules (such as never going anywhere without telling you first) or to make a secret bond. Always believe a child first if he tells you that he's been abused. Remove him from potential danger and *then* investigate what happened.

A child who has been abused may exhibit extreme or unusual behaviors. An abused toddler may engage in hostile, aggressive play or try to physically harm himself.

Many preschoolers masturbate (see *Masturbation*), but an abused preschooler would probably also use sexual language that he couldn't

254

have learned under normal circumstances. He may try to stimulate other people as well as himself. This will be different from "playing doctor" and the kind of normal curiosity children exhibit about body parts. It will be done expressly to promote sexual arousal. He might also draw pictures depicting abuse or sexual organs.

Older children may display signs of depression or begin to abuse substances because their self-esteem has become so low. They may start victimizing other, younger children.

An abused child may also seem ashamed, believing his victimizer's claim that he is responsible for the abuse. Pedophiles try to secure a victim's silence by telling the child that he provoked or deserved abuse because of bad behavior. They may also try to coerce a child by trying to instill guilt, asking, "Don't you like me anymore?"

Finally, an abused child might be clandestine about his whereabouts, relationships, or doings because he's terrified that his abuser will harm him if he tells. Because they generally are well known to a child and to his family, pedophiles know exactly when and where to catch their victim and hurt him.

Many children also speculate that no one would believe them if they did tell. That's why it's so important for you to say you do believe him when he initially comes to you. If a parent's first reaction is: "What were you doing there in the first place?" a child may become convinced that the abuse was, indeed, his fault.

If you suspect your child has been abused, take him for evaluation either by a pediatrician or by a mental-health professional. Do not put him back into situations with people he's accusing until you know for sure that no harm will come to him.

Recommended reading to help prevent abuse: *The Safe Child Book: A Commonsense Approach to Protecting Your Children from Abduction and Sexual Abuse*, by Sherryll Kerns Kraizer (Delacorte Press); *Protect Your Child from Sexual Abuse: A Parent's Guide*, by Janie Hart-Rossi and *It's My Body: A Book to Teach Young Children How to Resist Uncomfortable Touch*, by Lory Freeman, illustrated by Carol Deach (both books published by Parenting Press, PO Box 75267, Seattle, WA 98125).

Sexualized Behavior

(See *Masturbation*, *Sexual Abuse*, and *Secretiveness*)

Sharing

(See *Aggression*, *Insensitivity*, *Selfishness*, *Making Friends*, *Sibling Rivalry*, and *Teasing*)

Shyness

Shyness is often an inborn personality trait that can be fueled or diminished but rarely expelled entirely by parents and environment. (See *Temperament*.)

Shyness tends to run in families. Bashful children are likely to have at least one introverted parent. That generational link may produce conflict between parent and child. Parents who were shy as children and who may have felt excluded or lonely as a result sometimes are determined that their child will become gregarious and popular. They may push him to become something he's not, and the result is usually a very unhappy child. The reality is that shyness is one of the most persistent of temperamental traits and many shy children will grow up to be relatively shy adults.

The real issue is whether or not a *child* is comfortable being that way and whether or not she is making friends despite her shyness. Shy children tend to befriend one another and may be perfectly content with just one or two playmates. Number isn't important; significance of the relationships is. The child who should worry parents is the one

256

without *any* friends, who won't leave the house because she's so afraid of people, or who seems sad because of her reticence.

That doesn't mean parents can't or shouldn't help a child learn social skills or how to increase her comfort level. Adults need to recognize that shy children are constantly forced into public endeavors that can be daunting to them: show-and-tell, book reports, dodgeball. Shy adults can pick their niches, finding jobs where they don't have to interact much with others. Children, on the other hand, are constantly forced to perform and typically in public view. If they won't speak up in school, teachers may mistakenly conclude they haven't prepared for class or aren't very intelligent. Peers may think them aloof.

Sometimes preteens go through a shy period as they become more self-conscious and are afraid of making mistakes in front of their peers. This is different from lifelong shyness and usually will pass with some empathetic conversations with parents or simply the passage of time. (See *Self-Consciousness.*)

What to Do

Gently encourage the shy child. If she feels she's disappointed you, this will only add to her unhappiness. Try not to overprotect, either. For toddlers and preschoolers, actively search for a parent and child of like temperament to befriend. (Or maybe try to encourage a complementary relationship with a more gregarious child who can help your child come out of her shell.) Do as much as you can to help foster that relationship by always being open to playtime at your home. Sometimes a slightly younger child is easier for a shy child to engage. (See *Making Friends.*)

Don't hurl a shy child into a crowd and leave her in a sink-or-swim situation. Carefully explain a new experience beforehand; listen to her concerns about it and then reassure her by giving as much information about the situation as possible. Drive her by her new school; play in the playground after hours with her to familiarize her as much as possible with the environment. (See *Adaptability.*)

Rehearse scary situations such as show-and-tell. Try to find activities that your child enjoys and will, therefore, be more at ease doing with others. Help him develop skills in those endeavors—basketball, for instance—so that he has more self-confidence when asking to join in a game. A child who has practiced free throws by himself so that he hits them under pressure will be seen as an asset by his peers. They'll be more likely to ask him to participate and he'll be more likely to do well enough to assimilate himself. Another option is to suggest a child try out for an individual sport, such as track and field or swimming, which allows him to be part of a team without being forced into a lot of pressured interaction. Or, if a child is musically inclined, playing an instrument in a band promotes group interaction without having to talk too much.

Finally, focus on a child's attributes and never refer to his shyness in a derogatory manner or as an insurmountable impediment. (See *Self-Esteem*.)

Recommended reading: *The Shy Child: A Parent's Guide to Overcoming and Preventing Shyness from Infancy to Adulthood*, by Philip G. Zimbardo and Shirley L. Radl (Doubleday/Dolphin). For children: *Shy Charles*, by Rosemary Wells (Dial); *A Tiger Called Thomas*, by Charlotte Zolotow (Lothrop Lee & Shepard); *Stage Fright*, by Ann M. Martin (Scholastic); *I Want to Play: A Children's Problem Solving Book*, by Elizabeth Crary, illustrated by Marina Megale (Parenting Press, PO Box 75267, Seattle, WA 98125); and *Chatterbox Jamie*, by Nancy Evans Cooney, illustrated by Marylin Hafner (G. P. Putnam's Sons).

Sibling Rivalry

The word "rivalry" comes from the Latin word *rivalis*, which means having the right to the same stream. It is a particularly apt derivation in terms of sibling rivalry since brothers and sisters come from the same source of sustenance and must tap that source to live and grow. The sibling relationship is built upon the ability to share the many things that contribute to a child's well-being—independent time with parents, space, economic resources, and attention from relatives.

Young children don't understand that parents can have enough love to go around. They seem to think there is only a meager stream available and that the attention a new baby receives must be taken from their supply. No wonder children can become so territorial and competitive.

However, our self-definition comes as much from reference to our brothers and sisters as from our parents. That's where the ultimate importance of the sibling bond comes in. The relationship people have with their brothers and sisters is probably the longest they'll have throughout their lives. In childhood, it offers us the chance to find out about resolving conflict, tolerating people's idiosyncrasies, sharing, and accepting the fact that you can feel both good and bad emotions about someone you love.

As such, the relationship between siblings is the practice field for future bonds. And in families with dysfunctional parents, siblings often help one another survive, nurturing one another's emotional needs. In fact, the youngest child is typically the one most harmed by a parent's depression or alcoholism because he remains behind to deal with the disease alone, after older siblings have left home.

Many people's fondest memories are of childhood moments with brothers and sisters. In *One Writer's Beginnings*, novelist Eudora Welty wrote about herself: "I can't think I had much of a sense of humor as long as I remained the only child. When my brother Edward came along, we both became comics, making each other laugh. We set each other off, as we did for life, from the minute he learned to talk."

Parents who have withstood constant name-calling from the backseat of their car may think this is naive idealization, but Welty's sentiment is probably what they dream of for their own family. It's very painful for parents to listen to the antagonism between their children. After all, these are the people they love most in the world, and if anybody else called a child of theirs "a liar" they'd come to his defense.

While no parent can make siblings like one another (some are just so different in their temperament and hobbies that they have no basis for a strong bond), you can help them respect one another. And ultimately, respect may be a more resilient bond than affection. Avoid exacerbating already existing tensions. Don't compare children or favor one over another.

Parents need to come to think of their children as an intact subset of their family—just as they are a subset as a couple. Teach children to negotiate, and as long as they are not physically or emotionally harming

259

one another, it's best to let them work things out for themselves. That will bind siblings together while helping each individual child grow and learn about the day-to-day mechanics of relationships.

What to Do

Start by handling the arrival of the second child (and additional siblings) in such a way so as not to disenfranchise the firstborn. When you tell him the news of the impending birth, say, "*You're* going to be a big brother." Take his photo to the hospital with you, and call him to see how *he* is doing. After he's told you all his news, you can fill him in on his new sibling.

When you return, make sure to schedule some private time with him. Expect him to slip some in his abilities, such as toilet training, or to become more clingy and demanding. When he sees you cuddling or nursing an infant, he's going to want to climb into your lap, too. Let him express his jealousies and help him put words to his emotions. However, don't leave an aggressive two-year-old alone with a baby. He's not yet capable of knowing that a punch of anger could seriously harm an infant. (See *Regression* and *Anger.*)

When visitors come, be sure to talk about your firstborn. He needs the attention and praise, while a newborn baby is blissfully unaware of it. Ask that they bring him a token gift or card if they're bringing presents for the baby. Praise your firstborn for "nice" behavior.

As siblings age, don't expect or push them to be best friends. An introverted, bookish child may be totally uninterested in spending a lot of time with a boisterous athlete. That's okay. Remember that each child is temperamentally different and that shared blood does not guarantee a complementary pairing of personalities.

Schedule and spend special, private time with each child. (See "Special Time" in the Parenting Skills Introduction.) The trick is to try to treat each as an individual. If a child has a problem—is a lesser student, for instance—respond to it in the context of him alone, not in comparison to his siblings' abilities. It will only drive a wedge of resentment and competition between them.

When they do fight, take a deep breath and remember several things: Children often seem most selfish and aggressive with their siblings. The stakes in their competition, after all, are big. The prize is your attention.

260

So don't feed it by constantly playing the referee. Children fight most in the presence of their parents (particularly mothers). Walk away and the fight just might stop, just as tantrums did during the "terrible twos." Intervene only when they are physically harming, demeaning, or humiliating each other. Give your attention to the victim, not the aggressor. (See also *Selfishness* and *Aggression*.) If you don't know which is which (often the case in a busy household), be clear that the consequences (no TV, for instance) are for *all* children involved.

Give them guidelines for negotiating their differences. Talk about how to come up with compromises, about alternatives for their bickering. But then step back and let them do the rest. If you constantly swoop in as the authority to resolve disagreements, children may grow up expecting others to solve their problems for them. Model compromising in your own disagreements with your spouse. (See "Arguing" under *Reaction to Parental Conflict*.)

Teach children not to respond to teasing or name-calling and that such behavior is inappropriate. (See *Teasing* and *Aggression*.) If siblings bring their complaints to you, listen to both sides, acknowledging how each feels. Don't play favorites. If one tattles on the other about something you didn't see, it's probably best to stick with the teacher's technique of disciplining either all or none. (See *Tattling*.) Regular family meetings are effective ways to resolve problems before they escalate.

And one final note on persistent squabbles in the car: Defuse them by pulling off to the side of the road and saying calmly, "I can't concentrate on driving safely with all that noise." Turn off the car and wait for them to stop.

Recommended reading for parents: *Siblings Without Rivalry: How to Help Your Children Live Together So You Can Live Too*, by Adele Faber and Elaine Mazlish (Avon); *The Sibling Bond*, by Stephen P. Bank, Ph.D., and Michael D. Kahn (Basic Books); and *He Hit Me First*, by Louise Bates Ames, Ph.D. (W. W. Norton).

For children: *101 Things to Do with a Baby*, by Jan Ormerod (Lothrop, Lee & Shepard); *A Baby Sister for Frances*, by Russell Hoban (HarperCollins); *Outside Over There*, by Maurice Sendak (Harper-Collins); *Secrets of a Small Brother*, by Richard J. Margolis, illustrated by Donald Carrick (Macmillan); *When the New Baby Comes, I'm Moving Out* and *Nobody Asked Me If I Wanted a Baby Sister*, by Martha Alexander (Dial); and *Little Women*, by Louisa May Alcott (Little, Brown).

Sitting Up

Most babies begin sitting independently at around six months of age. This is an important "gross motor" milestone. (Gross motor involves large muscles such as the neck or torso.) It is also a wonderful independence milestone. No longer does Mommy or Daddy always have to figure out what it is a baby wants and then hand it to him. Now, if a baby drops a toy he can reach down and pick it up for himself.

Remember that six months is an *average*. Any concerns about a baby's motor development should be shared directly with your pediatrician. (See also the Developmental Tasks Appendix.)

Sleep

Ah, to sleep. For many parents, a good night's sleep is merely a fond memory. Although there is always that one smug parent whose child came home from the hospital and slept through the night, most children are simply not physiologically predisposed to sleep for long stretches. In fact, a great many young children can sleep only about six hours at a time. Expecting ten hours of uninterrupted slumber, then, may simply be unrealistic for a large percentage of children.

Then there are other individual variables. Many children toss and turn during their sleep (and subsequently awaken) because they are temperamentally active children. Plenty of babies have colic, which wakes them. Others may suffer painful ear infections or allergies, which make falling asleep difficult. Many more have disrupted sleep when separation anxiety or toilet training begins, or when a new sibling is born.

These predictable sleep disruptions are probably then compounded by parents' reactions to them. Holding a child until he falls asleep or sleeping with him can set up secondary complications—now he will fall asleep only in the company of a parent. These are habits that are difficult to break.

All in all, about one third of all children between the ages of one and four have significant sleep problems. If your family seems to engage in nightly bed-tag, you are in large and good company.

What's important is whether getting up in the night causes you trouble or whether you have the emotional fortitude to listen to a baby cry himself to sleep. Many parents find the latter inhumane. There is also substantial evidence that answering a baby's cries actually makes him more confident and capable of soothing himself in the long run.

On the other hand, sleep deprivation can render a parent impatient and less nurturing by virtue of sheer exhaustion. Depression can also set in, especially when a weary mother (typically it is the mother who takes nighttime duty) believes the criticism that she must be doing something wrong. Marital problems can also result from lack of bedtime privacy and arguments fueled by fatigue and irritability.

Parents need to decide what they need, what their child is actually capable of achieving, and what they are willing to do to reach that goal *before* embarking on a planned course of action.

Keep in mind there are certain bedtime techniques that make going to sleep easier and help prevent sleep disturbances from snowballing. For instance, set up a consistent, tranquil bedtime ritual; make bedrooms, or the crib area, a haven for rest, not a place of playtime or punishment. That way, a child can fall asleep contented, and if he does wake in the night is more likely to be capable of settling himself down.

All children will sleep better as they age because they are more active during the day. They are also neurologically more mature. But parents can help speed that natural evolution. With a little empathetic but firm reassurance that everything is just fine, with patience and resolve and *realistic* goals, a good night's sleep is not an impossible dream.

Infants

A baby's natural sleep rhythm is disrupted from the moment of his birth. To ensure that he's healthy and hydrated, hospital nurseries wake a newborn every two or three hours to feed him. It may be that such practices set up babies for irregular sleep patterns. Most babies, in fact, don't develop a dependable sleep cycle until they're between three and six months of age. The majority don't sleep "through the night" until about six months of age.

The average newborn sleeps sixteen hours a day. (Remember that all babies are different and there are always individual exceptions for every average, usually through no fault of the parents.) But those hours are accumulated in a series of short, nap-like slumbers. By the time he's eighteen months old, a baby sleeps less, about thirteen hours a day.

During the first eight or nine months of his life, a baby will wake because he's hungry, wet, or otherwise uncomfortable. He may also have colic, which adds another layer of anxiety onto both him and his parents. (See *Colic.*) If he's fed and dry and still crying, what he wants is stimulation. He is not afraid of the dark or of being separated from his parents. That kind of fear and cognition develop later.

What to Do

Parents should promptly respond to a newborn's cries, thereby building his trust in the world, that he has nurturing parents and that he can influence his environment positively. (See *Crying.*) By the time he's four months of age, once you're sure that he is dry, fed, warm, and physically safe, help him nestle back to sleep on his own. Don't rock him to sleep if you can help it.

Put babies in their cribs after feeding them, while they're drowsy but not fully out. That way they associate falling asleep with the feel of their mattress, not your arms. Don't tiptoe or whisper once he's down, as that may lower the threshold of his sound tolerance so that he wakes at the sound of a door opening. (Of course, some children are born with a high sensitivity to noise and will need a fairly quiet environment. See *Temperament.*) Some parents find that playing a tape of soft lullaby music helps their child nod off.

If a child fusses during the night, go in and check to make sure everything is all right. Many babies will need at least one nighttime feeding. If he had a bottle an hour ago, however, speak to your baby soothingly, and then go out again. If his diaper is dirty, try to change it by the night-light and with as little interaction as possible. Don't turn on lights, as that will completely wake him up. He'll cry then because he wants to play. Babies need to learn that nighttime is a period of rest, not playtime.

Of course, all this advice will have little benefit if a child is truly colicky or in physical distress from an ear infection or is teething. (See *Colic* and *Crying.*) It is during these times that many parents, exhausted and at wits' end, either fall asleep in a chair while holding their baby or take him back to sleep in their own bed. This is a personal decision. There is nothing intrinsically wrong with children sleeping with their parents as long as there is nothing pathological going on (no inappropriate emotional dependence between a parent and child so that the child is being used as a wedge in an unhappy marriage, and no inappropriate physical contact). In fact, some people believe the family bed makes children more confident and secure. (In some cultures this is common practice—parents think nothing of allowing a frightened child to crawl into bed with them until morning.)

Keep in mind, however, that things might get a little crowded, and that once you start it, a child is going to want to continue sleeping with you. It is when a baby becomes a toddler or preschooler and takes up a great deal of space that parents are apt to want to break the habit. And by then it is truly a habit that will require some calculated persistence to change.

Toddlers

There are several major sleep problems facing toddlers: the onset of separation anxiety, toilet training, and the baby's ability to get out of a crib, followed by the move into a big bed.

Separation anxiety hits its peak in toddlerhood. (See *Anxiety*.) It is at this time that many parents report that children who used to sleep through the night are now waking three or four times and are unable to go back to sleep. Their cries have a new timbre to them—they sound terrified. And, indeed, children this age may be. They are now cognitively capable of waking up and realizing that it's dark and that they're alone. They're afraid. They haven't yet developed the understanding that Mommy and Daddy must be down the hall, so everything really is okay.

If a child is able to climb over the crib's rail and go look for his parents, the problem is compounded. Switching to a bed to keep him physically safe may exacerbate his anxiety, because the bed is unfamiliar and seems so big. Toilet training may also worry him if he wakes because of the urge to urinate.

Don't forget that in a preverbal child, who can't always tell you what's hurting, wakefulness can also be a sign of physical illness. Check for fever and other symptoms.

What to Do

First, predictable routines become increasingly important to a child's sense of well-being and control over a world largely dictated by others. Make sure each evening follows a pattern: for example, a bath, followed by putting on pajamas, followed by toothbrushing and a book or a few songs. Don't engage in rambunctious play. The idea is to help lull a child into sleepiness.

This is probably the time to gradually remove yourself as a child falls asleep, as Richard Ferber, M.D., describes in *Solve Your Child's Sleep Problems*. (Going cold turkey—putting a child in his room and not returning—may work after a night or two, but parents have to be willing to wait out the hour or so of screaming that it may take. Many can't.) The process Ferber outlines and we at Children's recommend works like this: The first night, let your child cry a short time: two to five minutes. Go in, reassure him that you're there and that everything is fine. Don't pick him up. Then leave.

Repeat the scenario after the same interval of time has passed for as long as it takes for him to fall asleep. The next night increase the waiting period by a few minutes. The next night do the same, gradually elongating the time before you respond. Some parents find that just going to the door and gently saying, "Shhh, I'm right down the hall, everything is fine" is enough. The point is to reassure the child in the throes of separation anxiety that you still exist and will come if he needs you.

The process usually takes about a week. Don't instigate this technique at a time you can't see it through: when a child is sick, you're on deadline, or Grandma is visiting. Giving up after a half hour of a child's crying will serve only to double the length of time he will cry the next night.

Of course, there is always the exception to the rule—the child who is emotionally volatile and anxious by temperament, and who can whip himself up enough to vomit, for instance. (See *Temperament*, *Adaptability*, and *Vomiting*.) Follow your gut instincts about what is right for your child and for you.

If worries about toileting "accidents" seem to be causing a child's sleep disruption, rethink the amount of attention being spent on toilet training during the day. (See *Toilet Training* and *Bed-Wetting*.)

* * *

Once a child can get out of a crib, you'll need to put him in a bed for his own safety. (Some children can lift themselves over the side of their crib and slide down safely, but there is a real danger of a fracture if a child falls. Be firm that climbing out is a no-no. But if a child persists, make the change.) Introduce the bed gradually, during naptime, perhaps, without taking the crib away at first. If he refuses to stay in his bed, take him back to his room and tell him that as long as he stays in his bed, the door can remain open. Most children will eventually comply, because they prefer the door to be open. Remain firm.

Fill the bed with his favorite stuffed animals so that he feels safe and in good, familiar company. In fact, promote the idea of "transitional" objects, things of your child's own choosing that help him make the transition from you to being without you. It can be an animal, a blanket, or even a small piece of clothing. Let him hold it as he sleeps.

Finally, if a child seems to be waking up very early, he may be napping too much during the day. Usually one afternoon nap (rather than two a day) is best for two-year-olds and promotes longer sleep at night. These naps might also need to be kept fairly short.

He might also be hungry. Try a light, nutritious snack before bedtime, such as Cheerios or crackers and cheese. (A heavy or sweet snack may keep him awake.)

Preschoolers

Preschoolers will begin to have nightmares and fears. (See *Fears and Phobias* and *Nightmares and Night Terrors*.) At this age, they engage in magical thinking. The line between reality and fantasy or a dream is very thin. To them a dream is just as real as what goes on when they're awake. Parents may need to prepare themselves for a new round of nightly awakenings. (See also the Developmental Tasks Appendix.)

What to Do

Continue following your established bedtime routines. There are all sorts of lovely books about bedtime that have soothing, rhythmic language not unlike lullabies. (See below for recommendations.)

Leave a night-light on so that when a child wakes, he can see for himself that there is nothing lurking in the dark. Let him keep that transitional object (see above), as it remains a healthy way for him to self-soothe.

Avoid dismissing a child's fears. For one thing, he will not believe you when you say there is no such thing as monsters. Better to give him power over them. Perhaps endow a beloved stuffed animal with magic powers or go through a monster-purging ritual before bed. Perhaps open the closet and say, "Go away, monsters." Or tell him that you'll always take care of matters: "If there really were monsters, I would make them go away. That's my job as your Mommy [Daddy]." (See *Fears and Phobias* and *Nightmares and Night Terrors*.)

Try to recognize a correlation between daytime events and nightmares. Are they more frequent after watching a scary television show or reading a specific fairy tale? If so, perhaps curtail those for a while. If his anxiety seems the result of a move or of the birth of a sibling, it will probably pass on its own, given some reassurance. (See *Reaction to Loss*, *Sibling Rivalry*, and *Anxiety*.)

Recommended bedtime reading: *Goodnight Moon*, by Margaret Wise Brown, illustrated by Clement Hurd, and *A Child's Good Night Book*, also by Margaret Wise Brown, illustrated by Jean Charlot (both Harper Trophy books); *When I'm Sleepy*, by Jane R. Howard, illustrated by Lynne Cherry (E. P. Dutton); and *Into the Night*, by Deborah Heiligman, illustrated by Melissa Sweet (Harper & Row).

School-Aged Children

Sleep problems at this age generally have to do with stress at school or some other situational disturbance, such as a move or parents splitting up. Or it may be a simple matter of schedule. Forcing a child to go to sleep too early can make him wakeful. The solution may be as simple as letting him go to bed an hour later.

If a school-aged child has been sleeping in your bed, he should have decided for himself by now that he's far more comfortable in his own room. If he hasn't, parents need to help him make that switch, especially since the majority of parents are likely to have become appropriately uncomfortable with the arrangement.

What to Do

Continue to make sure that the hour before bed is a time to unwind. Don't let a child study right before going to sleep, as he might carry those worries into his dreams. Also, don't let him engage in wild play with siblings or with you. Older children may want some private time to read or listen to the radio before they go to sleep. Time for bed may be separated at this age from time to sleep.

If he has been sleeping in your bed, suggest that he's too big for that now. There's not enough room. Try putting a mattress on the floor of your bedroom for him. Then gradually move the makeshift bed into the hall and finally into his room.

Recommended reading for parents: *Solve Your Child's Sleep Problems*, by Richard Ferber, M.D. (a Fireside book / Simon & Schuster); *Healthy Sleep Habits, Happy Child*, by Marc Weissbluth, M.D. (Fawcett Columbine); and *Nighttime Parenting: How to Get Your Baby and Child to Sleep*, by William Sears, M.D. (New American Library).

Sleeps Too Much

Sometimes children are such heavy and long sleepers that they have trouble getting up in the morning. Part of this may be due to temperament. Bed-wetters are also often described as heavy sleepers.

Trouble begins when a child starts school and can't get himself up and moving fast enough to get ready in time. Parents should consider putting him to bed earlier, if he sleeps late. Also consider whether or not he gets enough physical activity during the day, if he's obese, or if he watches too much television—all these things can cause a child to sleep too much. The best solution is often to get into a more comfortable morning routine in which enough time is set aside to prepare for school. (See also *Dressing*.)

Sleeptalking

Talking in one's sleep is very common but has a wide range of variability. Some children and adults talk regularly and loudly. Others mumble infrequently. Some never talk at all. Stress is thought to increase the frequency and duration of sleeptalking.

Sleeptalking is usually not a problem, except for those who are awakened by someone's nighttime chatter. If a child talks often, it is probably best for him to have his own room, so that he doesn't disturb his siblings. Sleeptalking is sometimes associated with sleepwalking; such cases should be brought to your pediatrician's attention. (See also *Sleepwalking.*)

Sleepwalking

Sleepwalking is an unnerving but not uncommon behavior in children between the ages of two and twelve. Usually sleepwalking is transient, and it may be stress-related. A child generally sleepwalks early in the night, about an hour or two after he has gone to sleep.

What's happening is that part of a child's brain—the part that regulates motoric activity—is still working. He can walk about the room; his eyes are open and he sees, but he is still asleep. Sleepwalking is related to night terrors and should be brought to the attention of a child's pediatrician. (See *Nightmares and Night Terrors.*)

Parents need to make sure that the house is safe for a sleepwalker. He can physically do in his sleep everything he can when awake. Make sure doors are locked. If he has trouble safely negotiating stairs, put up a gate. Have childproof locks on medicine cabinets and cover stovetops.

Unless he is awakened, a sleepwalking child will not remember his nighttime travels. Lead him back to bed when you find him up. Contrary to the old wives' tale, it is not dangerous to wake him up, but you may have trouble getting him back to sleep.

Sloppiness

Children, particularly preteens, rarely have the sense or need of order and neatness most adults do. What looks like chaos to you may be completely acceptable to a child. But, if you want your child to be neater, help him devise a manageable system. Most children's rooms are messy because they don't have the first idea how to put things away. Provide containers, shelves, and organizers to help him, and give positive reinforcement when he improves. (See *Chores and Cleaning Room*, *Disorganized*, *Dressing*, *Procrastination*, and "Reward Systems" in the Parenting Skills Introduction.)

If a child's sloppiness is sudden and out of character, or associated with sadness, a change in appetite or sleep, an abrupt shift in friends, or a general disregard for personal appearance, watch for depression. (See *Sadness* and *Depression*.)

Slow to Warm

(See *Temperament*, *Adaptability*, and *Shyness*)

Smiling

In the first few weeks of life, a baby's face may relax into a smile as he nurses. He's content and experiencing pleasure. He is not yet *really* responding to the human who is feeding him. That happens around two months of age, when an infant recognizes the human face as the purveyor of sustenance, milk, and cuddling. That smile is truly a happy response to that person's presence. The baby anticipates that he's

271

about to experience satisfaction. His smile is an important step in making a connection with other people.

When he's around eight months old, a baby may smile at his parents by way of greeting because he distinguishes their faces from other people's. He knows for sure that he's looking at Mommy or Daddy and that pleases him. The more parents engage with him, smile, talk, and sing, the more stimulating a child's environment is, the more likely an infant is going to smile back at the world. (See also *Play*, *Eye Contact*, and the Developmental Tasks Appendix.)

Smiling continues to be a natural result of amusement, affection, happiness. A child who doesn't smile very often may be a temperamentally solemn person, but a previously happy child whose face no longer lights up may be depressed. (See *Reaction to Loss*, *Reaction to Parental Conflict*, *Sadness*, and *Depression*.) A baby who never smiles or avoids eye contact may have a serious developmental delay and should be evaluated by a pediatrician.

Social Isolation

"Socially isolated" is a term used to describe withdrawn or lonely children. One of the jobs of childhood is to interact with and befriend peers. Some children are simply born shy or "slow to warm" to new situations and will never have a large circle of friends, but they would not be described as socially isolated. One or two close playmates is all a child needs. It's really the ability to connect with others that is vital to growth and to a sense of well-being. (See *Shyness* and *Making Friends*.)

Children who suddenly break off from existing friends or show no interest in them whatsoever should concern parents. Support networks are important to all humans, no matter their age, and a lack of them can render a person vulnerable to depression. Once a child has entered school, friends should take on more and more importance as he steps out of the safe confines of home into a world increasingly of his own making. Peer approval and friendship are particularly significant to preteens, who typically run in packs to the mall, to sports events, to parties.

A child who is truly isolated socially is not just missing out on some fun, he may also develop low self-esteem. Try to arrange playtime with neighborhood children, involve him in church groups or sports he enjoys. But never force a child into a situation that frightens him and then desert him. Mothers of shy toddlers know to stay within view during playgroup or risk turning the outing into an ordeal rather than productive pleasure.

An older child who suddenly spends all his time in his bedroom and has no contact with peers may have suffered an embarrassment or rejection. If so, watch for other signs of depression or anxiety. (See *Depression*, *Anxiety*, and *School*.)

Soiling

Sometimes children who suffer constipation (having stools that are difficult to pass) try to retain their bowel movements. Because they hold back, the fecal mass gets even larger, and a child will leak a watery diarrhea around the blockage, thereby "soiling" his pants. This can happen to one-year-olds as well as to toddlers.

Children generally get into this cycle if they are having a hard time with toilet training and are worried about bowel accidents. They may also be afraid that their bowel movement will hurt. If they have been holding back, the unfortunate reality is that it probably will. Sometimes parents make the mistake of thinking a child is purposely fighting toilet training. In fact, soiling seems to be more an act of fear (of pain or embarrassment) than of defiance.

To avoid soiling problems, take a more low-key approach to toilet training. (See *Toilet Training*.) Also, consult your pediatrician about ways to help ease constipation. If a child has several soiling accidents in a row and has abdominal pain, see a doctor immediately.

Speech Problems

(See *Language and Speech*)

Staring Episodes

Generally, when a child stares off into space he is only daydreaming. Fantasizing is a common and desirable release for a child, and probably is evidence of a creative mind. (See *Daydreaming.*)

A child who gazes vacantly, seems oblivious to your presence (you cannot snap him out of it by calling his name or waving your hand in front of his face), and then is unaware of what occurred when he does "come back" may have had a petit mal (or absence) seizure.

During these seizures both hemispheres of the brain are affected and a child temporarily loses consciousness. Bring them to the attention of your doctor, since they can be controlled with medication. The seizures can be alarming to a child when he recognizes that he has no awareness of the past few seconds or that he has gaps in his memory of a day's events. Additionally, seizures can be dangerous if the episodes occur in precarious situations.

Because they last only a few brief moments, petit mal seizures can be easy to miss at first. You may notice a pattern of staring episodes, or a child may actually ask, "What was I just doing?"

In very rare cases, a child may actually be hallucinating. While a young child will usually tell parents what he sees if asked, a child of six or seven may realize the vision is odd and try to fib about it. Children with this kind of problem should be evaluated by a child psychiatrist.

Stealing

Stealing is an act that violates societal rules. Keep in mind that most children try to steal, usually because they don't understand that it's wrong. Find out the child's motivation—did he do it impulsively or under peer pressure, or did he do it for thrills? Did he *know* he was doing wrong?

The seriousness of stealing needs to be gauged along developmental stages, much as cheating or lying are. Before the age of six, children don't know the implications of taking something from a store without paying for it. They don't yet understand the system for purchasing goods. That comprehension doesn't come until around six or seven years of age, when a cognitive change called "concrete operations" takes place. After that children are capable of understanding logical connections, cause and effect, rules and procedures. They are able to check their impulses, to stop and consider, "If I do this, what are the consequences?" (See the Developmental Tasks Appendix.)

Children five years of age or younger steal because they see something in a store that they want. They reach out and take it. They are egocentric beings; the world is there to entertain, nurture, console them.

Older children know better. Shoplifting during elementary-school years is more unusual and probably has a lot to do with impulsivity. (See *Impulsivity* and *Risk-Taking*.) Children may steal simply because they want something (that their parents won't give them) badly enough. Stealing and other conduct disorders may indicate "masked depression"; that a child doesn't feel loved and is trying to grab a parent's attention; or he's responding to a specific loss or trouble at home. (See *Reaction to Parental Conflict, Reaction to Loss,* and *Depression.*)

Preteens, who are so worried about impressing peers and showing loyalty to their cliques, may begin to shoplift under a "dare." These children may have some self-esteem problems if they can't refuse inappropriate suggestions made by their friends. If stealing becomes frequent and seems to be generated by thrill-seeking, it is probably part of a more serious pattern of antisocial behavior. (See *Oppositional-Defiant Disorder* and *Conduct Disorder.*) If a child is stealing large quantities of food, she may have an eating disorder like bulimia. (See *Eating Disorders*.)

What to Do

If this is the first time your child has stolen something, remain calm. Try to view it as an opportunity to talk with him about values and to build on his trust in your ability to listen and help him. If it's the tenth episode of stealing despite your attempts to stop the behavior, seek the help of a mental-health professional.

With a young child who honestly didn't know taking the candy bar was wrong, gently and simply explain that people must pay for things at a store. Many parents have taken children back to the store to apologize and pay for the stolen item. Handled well, this is probably a good response. You're there to support a child through his apology, but you're making him take responsibility for his actions.

It's impossible to give a young child a conscience overnight, so help him build one by first imposing your own code of ethics on him. Tell him stealing is unacceptable behavior. Give a logical consequence such as going back to the store to apologize. Then monitor him more carefully the next time you're in a store. Remember, a child under five years of age is not going to contain his desires because he comprehends the abstract notion of right and wrong. He does so because he doesn't want to lose your approval. (See also *Insensitivity*.)

Ask why he stole. If it was because he desperately wanted that item, help him think of alternative ways to obtain it. (If you refuse even to consider a child's request for a toy and won't help him find a way of purchasing it, don't be surprised if he simply takes it.) If the item was too expensive for him to purchase with his usual allowance, find extra work around the house that he can do to help pay for it.

You are your child's guide. It's your job to help him learn to think through options so that he can grow into a self-regulating adult. Remember, too, that you are a child's model for values. If he sees you bringing home paper clips and stationery from the office for personal use or for his art projects, or if he watches you let a cashier give you too much change, it may be hard for him to understand the difference between that and taking some chewing gum. Hold yourself to the same standards you do him.

If stealing persists despite your best attempts to curtail it, seek consultation from a qualified mental-health professional.

Stepfamilies

(See *Reaction to Parental Conflict*)

Stomachaches

Stomachaches can be part of medical conditions as simple as the flu or as serious as appendicitis. Any severe stomach pain should be evaluated promptly by a pediatrician.

Sometimes anxiety can produce "nervous tummy." Many adults experience an upset stomach when they're pressured by work deadlines or worried about their families. Children are no different. Tests, science projects, playing in a semi-final game, and show-and-tell are all potential anxiety producers, especially for the shy or reticent child.

Like some chronic headaches, tummy trouble may seem to have no apparent physical cause. If a child complains about stomachaches only on school days and seemingly as a way of avoiding going to class, he may have school phobia. (See *School* and *Anxiety*.) Still, parents must remember that the pain is very real to a child. It's increasingly evident that emotional stress can produce very real physical symptoms.

If anxiety seems to be causing your child's stomach trouble, find out what is worrying him and try to help him deal with his concerns. In the case of school phobia, the best medicine is to send the child to school, making arrangements for him to lie down in the clinic if he has a stomachache. Keeping him at home day after day will only heighten his phobia. (See School Phobia under *School* for further advice.)

277

If a child frequently complains of stomach cramps and vomits often, but doctors have found no underlying medical condition, you might need to watch a child's overall eating pattern. If an older child, particularly a girl, seems preoccupied with her weight, has strange rituals around eating, and frequently disappears into a bathroom after a meal, she may be experimenting with bulimia. (See *Eating Disorders*.)

Constant stomach trouble accompanied by a sudden shift in a child's sleeping, eating, and social habits may suggest he is depressed. (See *Reaction to Loss, Reaction to Parental Conflict*, and *Depression*.) If constant stomachaches are coupled with other, more severe symptoms such as limb paralysis, a child may be suffering a psychosomatic disorder. In such cases, once medical causes have been ruled out, it's time to seek consultation with a qualified mental-health professional.

Stranger Anxiety

(See *Anxiety*)

Stress

(See *Reaction to Loss, Reaction to Parental Conflict, School, Competitiveness, Perfectionism, Popularity*, and *Achievement Issues*)

Stubbornness

(See *Oppositional Behavior*)

Stuttering

Many children repeat words or parts of words as they learn to speak. "Mommy, Mommy, I want milk, milk, milk" is a typical singsong pattern of a three-year-old and is considered a normal developmental phase. There should be no physical distress or behavioral struggle involved in the repetition.

Stuttering is different. A child who stutters is experiencing vocal tension and will show physical signs of a struggle in his lips and jaws. He tends to repeat syllables and parts of words—"s-s-s-s-say" rather than "milk, milk, milk." He trips most frequently over long words and those that begin phrases or have the greatest importance within a sentence.

About 5 percent of all children stutter, according to the American Psychiatric Association's diagnostic manual. The peak age of onset is between two and three and a half (as a child is learning to speak), and then again between four and a half and six (as he begins school). Boys stutter more than girls, at a ratio of three-to-one. Many researchers think stuttering has a genetic predisposition, that there is something physically wrong within the brain's regulation of the motor control of speech. Precisely what that problem is remains unclear.

The offspring of a stutterer, however, is not preordained to stutter himself. A genetic predisposition can remain completely dormant if it's not triggered by some environmental stress. Researchers speculate that stuttering is the result of complex interactions between a child's genetic and physiological makeup and his environment. Parental conflict, a move, beginning school, the birth of a sibling, even learning to talk—anything that stimulates a lot of feelings in a child—may trigger an inherited vulnerability.

Three out of four children who begin stuttering between two and seven years of age will be stutter-free by the time they are twelve. That good news has sometimes led pediatricians and parents to overlook the condition, thinking a child will grow out of it. Meanwhile, however, during a prolonged period of stuttering a child may experience subsequent developmental or social problems.

Children who stutter may be embarrassed, inhibited, or depressed by their speech. And for the one out of four who do become "persistent stutterers" (one percent of all adults), life can be far more difficult than

279

need be. Children who receive language and speech therapy and break the pattern before the age of five typically remain stutter-free no matter what emotional trauma confronts them later in life.

What to Do

Don't wait to get help. See a pediatrician within a few weeks of the onset of stuttering. Your pediatrician should refer you to a speech-language pathologist, who will use therapy techniques appropriate to a child's age. For the preschooler, a speech and language pathologist may work on slowing the rate of discourse, by reading stories and speaking in "our slow way of talking." If a child learns to respond to the modified rate, the frequency of stuttering usually decreases.

The professional will probably work with parents, as well, teaching them how to reduce the stress of talking at home. For instance, avoid finishing a child's thought for him. Ask a child about his day when you can really stop and listen carefully and patiently, not in the car or when the family is rushed. Reducing tension in the home environment in general will also serve to make a child less anxious and less likely to stutter.

Stuttering becomes far more difficult to tackle when the pattern is ingrained. Some children may need more formalized training programs. Controlling breathing, speaking slower, and minimizing inflection are techniques a child may practice and use all the time.

Mental-health professionals suggest that if a child doesn't respond to speech and language therapy within six months, parents should consider that there may also be a psychological underpinning to the stuttering. Stammering problems often simply mask other issues. A child may have strong feelings he is afraid to express; perhaps he is nervous about school; or he might have experienced abuse.

In these cases, child psychiatrists or psychologists may need to assist speech and language pathologists in unearthing psychodynamic or situational contributors to stuttering. Serious disorders sometimes associated with stuttering include Attention-Deficit Hyperactivity Disorder and anxiety disorders. (See also *Language and Speech*, *Articulation Problems*, and *Hearing*.)

For more information, contact the American Speech-Language-Hearing Association, 10801 Rockville Pike, Rockville, MD 20852 (1-800-

638-8255); or the American Academy of Child and Adolescent Psychiatry, 3615 Wisconsin Avenue, NW, Washington, D.C. 20016 (202-966-7300).

Suicide

Suicide is the third leading cause of death among adolescents. Each year about 5,000 teenagers take their own lives, a rate of frequency that has tripled in the last three decades, according to the National Institute of Mental Health (NIMH). The riskiest time seems to be in college, as young adults grapple with increasing social and academic challenges and as a consequence perhaps meet with their first real failures. But in particularly competitive urban environments, high schools also seem to be a breeding ground for suicidal feelings. Most suicides are by males, since they tend to use the deadliest means, but females attempt to take their own lives four times more than males.

Suicides among younger children are rare, according to the NIMH, but suicidal behavior is not. Each year about 12,000 children aged five to fourteen are hospitalized in the United States for deliberate self-injurious acts, such as jumping from high places, burns, stabbings, or overdosing on medications.

Suicidal behavior usually occurs when children are clinically depressed. A pattern of impulsivity and risk-taking has been linked to adolescent suicide as well. There may be physiological underpinnings to these behaviors. Researchers are discovering biochemical brain abnormalities in suicides akin to those present in depression. They believe these chemical irregularities heighten impulsivity and aggression, behaviors that are logically necessary for a person to attempt taking his own life. Eating disorders, substance abuse, or emotional problems resulting from sexual abuse are other psychiatric disorders commonly associated with suicide.

Certain personality traits also put children at higher risk for suicide. Children who are perfectionists and black-or-white thinkers often can see no way out of a bad situation other than death. These are the children who might view a bad grade, poor athletic performance, or rejection from a prep school as a humiliation from which they cannot recover. These children tend to consistently use the words "always" and "never" to describe themselves or life. They'll never be good at football, never have a romance, always screw up, always be fat. There is a quality of hopelessness to their speech and behavior.

Teenagers who commit suicide have often had a recent breakup with a girlfriend or boyfriend. A particularly acrimonious divorce or a parental obsession with a child succeeding have also been found to be contributing factors in a child's choice to try to end his life. So, too, is persistent social isolation. If a child doesn't have friends or outside activities, he feels alone, unwanted, somehow unacceptable to his peers, as well as having nothing to think about other than his troubles.

According to the NIMH, reasons for attempting suicide include: to find relief from hopelessness, shame, or illness; to punish loved ones or to change their behavior; to be reunited with a deceased loved one; to become a memorable martyr. The latter is a particularly dangerous temptation for adolescents experiencing their first failed love affair.

If a child begins to romanticize suicide, saying that he wished he "had the guts" to do it or that it would prove his devotion to someone, be sure to discuss the realities of death with him. It's best if you have laid the groundwork before any such crisis, by talking about the finality of death when a pet or a relative dies. Experts speculate that some children who have witnessed many violent deaths dramatized on television may not fully understand that death is permanent.

Take any threat of suicide seriously. It's a myth that those who talk about it don't follow through. Other warning signs that children may be contemplating suicide include: any sudden disinterest in friends, school, or once-favorite activities (see *Depression*); giving away prized possessions; hoarding pills or suddenly obtaining a gun. Young children may be taking extreme risks in their play, or drawing pictures of people crying or disfiguring themselves. (See *Self-Injurious Behavior.*)

The occurrence of one suicide in a school or the media discussing a suicide may create a time of heightened risk for vulnerable children. Communities should avoid romanticizing or overly memorializing children who have taken their own lives, as this can give rise to what experts call a "contagion effect," which could spur others on to choose suicide as an attractive alternative to life.

What to Do

Seek professional help immediately. Look to community crisis and suicide intervention centers, hotlines, and hospitals. Or ask teachers, guidance counselors, and clergy to recommend mental-health professionals. Look for therapists who specialize in treating children.

Remove all potentially lethal objects from the house to protect a child from harm and to show that you do care. Numerous studies suggest that the presence of a gun in a home greatly increases the likelihood of suicide as well as homicide.

Participate in recommended therapy. Even if a child claims he was only trying to shock or to manipulate, that he didn't intend to go through with anything, he needs help learning more effective methods of communicating and coping. So, too, should his parents.

For more information, contact the National Institute of Mental Health's Public Inquiries Branch, 5600 Fishers Lane, Rockville, MD 20857 (301-443-4513); the American Association of Suicidology, 2459 South Ash Street, Denver, CO 80222 (303-692-0985); the American Psychiatric Association, 1400 K Street, NW, Washington, D.C. 20005 (202-682-6000); or the American Suicide Foundation, 1045 Park Avenue, New York, NY 10028 (212-410-1111).

Sulking

(See *Moodiness*, *Irritability*, *Sadness*)

Swearing

By the age of four or five, children have discovered that words can be as useful to them as physical behavior to display aggression or garner attention. They can pick up provocative language just about anywhere: from friends, siblings, family, school, television. There is no way to keep a child from hearing such words, but parents can try to control a child's use of them.

Avoid overreacting to risqué language since parental shock is likely to encourage future use. Say, "We don't use those words around other people. If you want to use them to see what they sound like, you must do so in your room by yourself or outside." Make sure you don't use the language yourself; then, you're justified in adding, "I don't like that kind of language and I don't want to hear it." Offer the child other words that somehow convey the same feeling without the shock or disrespect of an obscenity. (See also *Aggression* and *Attention-Seeking*.)

Talkativeness

It's common for preschoolers to go through an extremely chatty period. In part, they're just "feeling their oats" verbally. Their vocabulary is growing; their enunciation is better so that people understand them more easily; and they can spin tales that fascinate and amuse their parents. It can be a problem, however, if a child rarely or never allows someone else in the conversation, is loud, or constantly interrupts others.

In those instances, you may want to help a child learn some restraint. Children don't like to play with peers who never let them contribute to a game. Teachers don't appreciate students who always dominate the class. (Actually, most children whom parents describe as "talkative" wait their turn in school. Often it's something about the home environment that elicits their chattering.)

Try to set gentle limits on how long a child talks or how many different ways he can ask for the same thing. During dinner, encourage siblings to take turns telling about their day. Say, "Slow down" if a child talks in a torrent that keeps you from understanding what he's trying to describe. Model the conversational style you want him to use. (See also *Loudness, Interrupting, Rudeness and Developing Manners*, and *Making Friends*.)

Talking

(See *Language and Speech* and the Developmental Tasks Appendix)

Tattling

Tattling on a toy-stealing playmate is common in toddlers and pre-schoolers as they learn to negotiate social interaction. It is also common among five- to seven-year-olds because they are at a cognitive stage in which they are very moralistic about right and wrong behavior. They'll quickly bring a transgression to the attention of an adult to garner praise.

After that age, tattling is more unusual. Between the ages of seven and nine, children become much more aware of the fact that there are gray areas to moral dilemmas—that someone may do something wrong for the right reasons. Tattling also makes a child nine years of age or older terribly unpopular with his peers. He'll be viewed as a snitch, and will probably develop some peer difficulties.

On the other hand, tattling remains common among siblings. Parents need to try not to rise to the bait. Follow the practice of teachers: If something happens out of your view, either discipline all concerned or none at all. If you constantly take the report of one sibling over another, you may lay the groundwork for a more serious behavior problem: that of the good-child-versus-bad-child kind, with the resulting self-esteem difficulties.

Tattling does put parents in a bit of a bind. You want children to be honest and to tell you when a sibling has put himself in danger. But you don't want a child to become a habitual chronicler of minor infractions, since his peers and siblings will begin to avoid him. Teach children about safety issues—that those are things you *do* always want to hear about, and swiftly. But let siblings work out minor difficulties and squabbles among themselves. (See also *Sibling Rivalry*.)

Teasing

Children mainly tease younger siblings. It's probably a way to gain attention or power, or it's a weapon against the recipient. Teasing has an underlying aggressive thread to it, and usually those who dish it out can't take it.

If it's occurring in your family, teach the recipient child to ignore the teasing. Talk to the one who's doling it out. Ask him why he does it, what he's trying to achieve. Ask him how he'd feel if someone teased him in a similar fashion. (See *Insensitivity* and *Aggression*.) Then discuss more socially acceptable and kinder alternatives.

It's best to let siblings work it out themselves. But if the teaser persists, consider applying some consequences to his behavior, forewarning him that a punishment will follow. (See "Time-Outs" and Behavior Modification in the Parenting Skills Introduction, and *Sibling Rivalry*.)

Sometimes a child becomes the specific target of the school bully. If he does, you'll probably need to talk to the parents of his assailant or to school personnel directly. Bullies rarely stop harassing their victims on their own volition. (See *Bullying*.)

Teeth-Brushing

Brushing teeth is an essential hygienic practice that children must learn to incorporate into their daily routines. By eighteen months of age, most of a toddler's teeth will have come in and should be cleaned gently by parents on a daily basis. Preschoolers really should be managing to do most of the brushing themselves.

Many young children balk at brushing their teeth, probably because it has to be done and, therefore, presents an excellent opportunity for a power struggle with parents. If it has to do with some kind of fear (a brush once hurt his gums, for instance), be sure to find out what worries your child and reassure him that you'll take care that it won't happen again.

Use polite direction and positive reinforcement to motivate his brushing. Say, "It's time to brush your teeth" not "Would you like to brush your teeth now?" which is likely to bring a negative answer. Try adding some impetus: "When you've brushed your teeth, it'll be time to read a book before bedtime," or when he's done it speedily, try: "Boy, it sure is helpful when people brush their teeth. Now we have time to read *two* books." Remember that going upstairs alone is often intimidating to a young child. Go with a preschooler or ask an older child if he wants you to accompany him.

Perhaps set up a reward system, such as stickers. If a child brushes his teeth without prompting or argument, put a sticker on a chart. After he's filled up a column (usually representing a week), give him the reward he's earned. Remember that time with you in a favorite activity is the best reward of all.

Teeth-Grinding

Teeth-grinding (bruxism) occurs in younger children and usually is transient. It tends to run in families and be more common in boys. No one is completely sure what causes bruxism, although anxiety and stress are suspected to exacerbate this nocturnal behavior. Some children, for instance, grind their teeth during the school year and not during summer vacation.

Talk to your pediatrician, so that he can rule out the possibility of seizures or other medical causes. In the vast majority of cases, bruxism will fade on its own, given some time. Remember that teeth-grinding happens while a child sleeps, so that no manner of nagging will help him stop. If you want to do something tangible, assess a child's stress load and see if there is a way to ease his anxiety or help him cope better. (See *Anxiety*.)

Television-Viewing

Does TV promote aggression, sedentariness, or obesity, and discourage reading and conversation in children? These are hotly debated issues, and the answers to these questions depend heavily on what parents let their children watch and how much time they spend in front of the TV.

Studies have indicated that televised violence can act as a trigger for aggressive behavior in some children. Immediately after watching a violent show, children have been observed to become more aggressive in their play, pushing and hitting objects with toy bats provided by scientists. However, the aggression quickly dissipates in those children who, perhaps by virtue of their nature, are less physically assertive. The influence appears to last longer for those with a history of and predisposition to aggressive play.

Witnessing real, filmed violence on TV news broadcasts may also serve to heighten anxiety and worry in some children. The Gulf War and the Los Angeles riots frightened many young children, who were afraid the violence would spread to their own street. (See also *Fears and Phobias.*)

Children who are temperamentally more prone to anxiety may have been just as tense had they merely read or heard about the fighting. The larger question of watching televised violence is probably one of desensitization. By the time he is a teenager, the average American child may have witnessed a thousand deaths (dramatized and real) being broadcast on TV. Parents need to consider whether or not children really understand the meaning of death, its finality and pain, after passively viewing it on the television screen over and over again.

Other morals and ethics may be influenced by TV as well. Certainly, a preschooler who watches a cartoon character whack another and make off with a bunch of carrots is probably going to think this is a funny and perfectly acceptable act. He has no experience and only fledgling values with which to weigh and judge such behavior in his Saturday-morning idol.

Also, obesity can be aggravated by sitting in front of a television and eating in a kind of mesmerized binge. (See *Obesity.*)

On the other hand, television has a lot to offer, particularly in terms of educational programming. There is strong indication that watching programs such as *Sesame Street, Barney and Friends*, or *Mr. Rogers' Neighborhood* actually improves a young child's school readiness. He learns about colors, shapes, numbers, and vocabulary, and how to follow dramatic plot lines. Documentaries continue to remain an excellent source of education as a child ages. Nature programs and PBS's award-winning series on the Civil War are prime examples.

The trick is for parents to use television to suit their own purposes. It can serve as a stimulus for family discussions about moral issues and problems facing society today, as well as entertainment.

What to Do

Limit but don't totally ban TV. A child who knows nothing about Big Bird, Barney, or Raphael will clearly seem ill informed during his peers' conversations. Monitor TV according to program topic (you may watch this program but not another) rather than simply by number of hours. That promotes the idea that one watches television when there is something worthwhile to see, not just out of habit.

Watch with a child. That familiarizes you with his universe and keeps you in touch with his knowledge of world events.

Then, use the program as a springboard. Help him test the reality and morals portrayed in it. Preschoolers in particular cannot understand the subtleties of a character's motivations. Ask what he thinks about what he just saw, how the characters felt, if the action was justified or not. You're teaching him to question and to think, just as you would be discussing the events portrayed in a book.

It also gives you a chance to impart some of your own values. But be sure to listen to his opinions, to create an environment in which a child can ask anything, voice any idea. You want a dialogue, not a lecture.

Continue this on into teenage years. Many programs provide an excellent, spontaneous opportunity to discuss ticklish issues with adolescents. You can use music videos or TV advertising to talk about sexual aggression and gender stereotypes, and reports of AIDS research to give definitions of unsafe sex. But to be able to do this with an adolescent, it helps to have watched and discussed the dangers portrayed in a movie such as *Bambi* with him when he was six years old.

Be sure to keep an eye on young children during shows you're not certain about yet. If children seem to be getting overexcited or are playing too aggressively as they watch, turn off the program.

Avoid using the television as a baby-sitter. Don't leave it on as background noise, or sit and doze or eat junk food in front of it. Remember that as with most behaviors, especially one as seductive as television-viewing, it's monkey-see-monkey-do.

Temper Tantrums

Little in life is as mortifying as standing in the grocery checkout line with a full cart and a shrieking two-year-old. You are positive you are the worst parent in the world and that everyone in the store thinks so, too. But beleaguered parents need to remember that tantrums are a common, even important part of a toddler's development. Tantrums are about a child's growing autonomy, about his establishing confidence and a sense of self. They also offer parents the opportunity to help children learn constructive ways to express anger and frustration.

Admittedly, that's difficult to remember when faced with a kicking, screaming, out-of-control preverbal child. Tantrums usually begin around eighteen months of age, when a toddler is just starting to separate a bit from parents and wants to express his own opinion. That's hard for him to accomplish when he's wobbly and not particularly dexterous, and has only a very limited vocabulary. Tantrums erupt when a child becomes frustrated or is denied, causing him to lose control emotionally. As such, they are ultimately about achieving independence.

Tantrums come in all forms. Some children just whine and cry, others go rigid and throw themselves to the ground, kicking, screaming, and biting. Tantrums occur more frequently when a child is tired, hungry, or in a place that requires too much self-control or is overstimulating. More often than not, they function as a response *against* parents—something you won't give or can't do, something you choose for them to eat or wear. (See *Oppositional Behavior* and *Attention-Seeking*.)

Parents call this predictable stage the "terrible twos," and usually the frequency and velocity of tantrums diminishes as a child reaches his third birthday. Improved language skills greatly reduce a child's frustration, because he can make himself understood. (See *Hearing* and *Language and Speech*.)

Preschoolers are also beginning to become socialized and are learning what's acceptable to peers. Children don't like to be around unpredictable, temper-ridden playmates. By the time a child is four years old, when he is more sure of himself, who he is, and what is acceptable behavior, full-blown tantrums should be rare occurrences. If they haven't almost disappeared by then or are extremely violent, happen several times each day, or are accompanied by sleep disturbances and other aggressive behavior, consult your pediatrician. (See *Aggression.*)

What to Do

Remain calm. Try not to yell, plead, or ridicule. Don't reward the behavior by giving it too much attention or by immediately giving in to demands in order to quiet a child. Remember that in many ways tantrums are about testing boundaries. If a child sees that tantrums get him nowhere, he'll eventually give them up and find more socially appropriate ways to achieve.

Try to be supportive while you're setting the limit that throwing a fit is not okay. If a tantrum is so physically violent that a toddler is in danger of hurting himself, either hold him (gently and not too tightly) or put him into a playpen, where he's physically safe. Try saying, "I know you're upset, and I love you, but this behavior is not okay. I cannot let you hurt yourself. We'll talk about it when you're calm."

Once he has collected himself, assess his request. If it was reasonable, go ahead and do it or agree to do it later. Make it clear, however, that you're doing so because he's now asking in an appropriate, reasonable voice. Some flexibility is important in showing a child he has a certain amount of control and self-determination.

This approach is appropriate for an eighteen-month-old and has much the same goal as the formal time-outs parents may use to help an older child learn to modify unacceptable behavior. In fact, many experts feel time-outs don't work with younger toddlers because they are much more likely to test you during one, to try to get out of whatever holding environment you've put them in. A child could easily fall out of a chair, for instance. Specific time-outs, then, are much more productive once a child is two and a half or older, because he can understand better what you're saying, and language is beginning to control his behavior. (See "Time-Outs" in the Parenting Skills Introduction.)

Once a preschooler is calm and can listen, explain why his actions earned him a time-out. Make it clear that if he repeats the behavior, he will again receive a time-out. This helps him learn logical, predictable consequences, so that a four-year-old can literally say to himself, "If I do this [kick and scream while Mommy's fixing dinner], I'll get a time-out, because she's told me that's what will happen." He begins to check his own behavior *before* he loses control, to have some degree of impulse control. (See also *Interrupting, Attention-Seeking*, and *Impatience*.)

When he falters, remind him, "Remember what we talked about? I can't stop to play right now, as I'm putting dinner into the oven. I will play in a minute, if you wait quietly." If he persists, go ahead with the consequences you've discussed. Tell him why, perhaps saying, "Time-out: throwing a tantrum while I'm cooking."

Time-outs should last no longer than one minute per year of the child's age. It's very important to remember that time-outs work only when they are applied sparingly and judiciously for *extreme* behavior—merely whining while you're trying to prepare a meal doesn't qualify—and only when done in the context of a generally warm, loving, encouraging environment.

Don't keep reminding or reprimanding a child about a tantrum once it's over. Give him a hug and go about your mutual business, preferably something different from what caused the explosion. With a three- or four-year-old, ask what made him so angry. The reason for his rage may be totally acceptable; it's just the way he exhibited it that wasn't. Tell him that "it's okay to be mad [or disappointed], but it's not okay to hit or scream." Discuss alternatives. (See *Anger*.)

Children will probably throw more tantrums when they are not allowed to make any choices for themselves. Letting a child choose between hot dogs and tuna fish for lunch may actually decrease tantrum frequency because he feels some independence; he'll be less frustrated in general.

On the other hand, not setting any kind of clear, understandable limits or household rules leaves a child feeling unsure of what is expected of him. That's why it's important not to reward temper tantrums. If a tantrum didn't get him what he wanted yesterday but does today, he'll be sure to try it again tomorrow.

Also, it may actually frighten a child if he feels he's defeated you by his behavior. It gives him more power than he really wants, especially between the ages of three and five, when a child engages in magical thinking (believing that what he thinks or wants will come true). A child who completely dominates his parents will become anxious, which in turn can fuel and increase tantrums.

* * *

Prevent tantrums by "childproofing"—making your home user-friendly for children. If you don't want him playing with the china figurines, don't tempt and frustrate him by putting them within his reach. Try not to make too many demands on a child when he's tired and cranky, or when you're in a rush or in a place that makes him anxious. In those pivotal moments, try distracting him ("Look at those birds!") if you see a storm brewing.

Also, tantrums generally occur over the same events: bedtime, dressing, eating. In calm moments, parents should think about whether the requirements that are causing the trouble are really worth it. Does she have to wear a T-shirt under her dress? Can he go to bed fifteen minutes later and still get enough sleep? Plan your response for the next time he throws a fit over the same thing.

For some children, tantrums can be related to their temperament. Those with an inborn sensitivity to bright lights, loud noise, crowds, or certain textures of food or clothes are far more likely to react with a tantrum in overstimulating settings. It's important to know the difference between a manipulative tantrum and one that's thrown out of real discomfort, fatigue, or fear. Try to recognize the signs of a child becoming overexcited or anxious and take her to a quiet place to calm down *before* a full-fledged tantrum erupts. Try not to interrupt a poorly adaptable child's playtime without warning. Set up rituals to help make the transition into new activities: "Let's count to twenty together and *then* let the bathwater out." (See *Temperament* and *Adaptability*.)

It takes self-control and empathy to remember the reason for a child's tantrums and to act in a supportive yet firm fashion. But handled well, tantrums provide opportunities for parents to teach children about emotions as well as build on their relationship. Discipline, after all, should really be about teaching.

Temperament

For decades, scientists and educators have debated which has more importance: nature or nurture. Which has the most profound impact on a child's life: genes or the home environment? For a long time, the environment provided by parents was given all the credit or blame for children's development and outcome. The idea that a child could be *born* a certain way was criticized as letting parents off the hook or as discouraging them from trying to help their child modify or change his behaviors.

But increasingly experts are coming to accept what parents and workers in hospital nurseries have long observed: Some babies just come into the world fussy or calm, squirmy or subdued, outgoing or restrained. Temperament is thought to be a child's natural, inbred style of behavior—his way of responding to the world around him, his characteristic disposition.

However, that's not to say parenting plays no role at all. Values plus methods of communicating and dealing with conflict are things that the home environment clearly creates in children. Other family factors: birth order, number of siblings, and life events such as moves, illnesses, and changes in parents' economic fortunes and jobs all contribute to molding a child's personality as well. "Easy" babies certainly can be made hostile by parental abuse or neglect; "difficult" children can become less volatile with patient guidance and behavior modification.

So, temperament is hardly a manifest destiny. What it probably does represent is the range in which a child can operate. An innately shy child can learn to be more comfortable socially but may remain less apt to run for student-body president or to be the center of a clique. Parents, then, should serve as gentle editors of temperament, helping to shape, modify, or strengthen inborn personality traits that can affect children's development.

Research indicates that the most persistent temperamental styles involve physical activity level, emotionality, and sociability. These characteristics are thought to be physically and genetically based to a significant degree. It is much more likely that an energetic child comes from athletic, active parents; an anxious child from worriers; a shy child from introverted adults, and so forth.

But heredity is not the only determinant. A trait such as creativity is far more complex. So, too, is aggression, since it is a product of more basic characteristics such as activity level and sociability in combination with learned behaviors. But given the right parental modification, it is actually one of the more malleable of temperamental styles.

Another way of looking at children's inborn personality traits is through their sensory sensitivity, which may make some children uncomfortable with loud noise, bright lights, scratchy clothing, or pungent foods. These children may be susceptible to becoming over-stimulated or throwing tantrums that have more to do with feeling overwhelmed or rattled than with manipulating parents.

An important study of temperament in children was done in the 1950s by Drs. Alexander Thomas, Stella Chess, and Herbert Birch, called the New York Longitudinal Study. As they followed 133 children from birth to adulthood, the researchers identified nine temperamental traits:

activity level (rambunctious and unable to sit still or plays quietly?)
distractibility (has strong concentration or is inattentive and easily
    distracted?)
persistence (sticks to a project or demand or gives up easily?)
intensity (easily upset and hard to console or tranquil and quickly
    calmed?)
regularity (predictable in sleep, eating, bowel habits or not?)
sensitivity (easily bothered by textures or crowds or not at all?)
wariness (takes easily to new people, places, or things or is hesitant?)
mood (irritable and whiny or generally cheerful?)
adaptability (adjusts quickly to change or balks at it?)

Most children analyzed along these nine traits can be classified, according to temperament experts, as "easy," "difficult," or "slow to warm." The remainder are described as being somewhere in between the three styles. Children are often easy in one category and harder to deal with in another. How parents deal with a child will have an important effect on his temperament. Calling a child "difficult" should not tag him as a brat—it means *his parents* have difficulty dealing with him; his sudden, intense emotions, persistence, or poor adaptability have a derogatory impact on their ability to relate to him productively.

The beauty in attempting to understand the components of a child's temperament is that it will lower parents' frustration and, at the same time, raise their respect and tolerance for both their child and themselves. After all, trying to manage a child who is prone to anxiety, who is easily startled, or who doesn't just whine but whips herself into a crying frenzy within a matter of seconds is a hard and often lonely endeavor for any parent. Parents who blame themselves for a child's poor behavior and expect change to occur overnight set up a cycle of unproductive control battles that can also damage the child's self-esteem.

What parents need to try to achieve is "goodness of fit," as Thomas and Chess called it, meaning a synchronous way of responding to a child that is appropriate to his inborn personality and promotes more constructive interactions between them.

For example, consider two toddlers and two mothers. One toddler is cautious and shy, the other adventuresome and boisterous. One mother is protective and prone to worry, the other less intrusive and more laissez-faire in her parenting style.

The protective mother may hover too much over the cautious child, making his inborn wariness even more pronounced. She will probably chase and frustrate the curious adventurer, perhaps fueling his defiant and stubborn nature.

The more confident, hands-off mother, on the other hand, might be impatient with the reserved child, exacerbating his anxiety, self-doubt, and clinginess by insisting he try new things before he's warmed up to them. That mother may also fail to monitor the reckless child adequately, so that he risks physical injury with his antics and perhaps never learns about assessing danger.

None of these pairings works very well because the mothers are not adequately adapting their personality styles to match their child's. They need to work out a better "goodness of fit."

What to Do

The view that temperament helps dictate a child's behavior can be controversial. It could be misinterpreted to mean that parents shouldn't bother trying to modify a child's behaviors, because that's "just the way he is." That just doesn't make sense.

Dr. Stanley Turecki's basic, commonsense message in *The Difficult Child*, for instance, is that since parents are the adults, they can adjust themselves to suit a child's innate style better. Accepting a child's temperament and comprehending predictable behavior patterns will produce a better, more empathetic, productive, and happy "fit" between parent and child. It helps a parent recognize warning signs of trouble; what situations are likely to distress a child or place too many demands on her; plus how to smooth the way for that child. It teaches parents when they need to coax, gently challenge, or help contain and develop a child's self-control.

Don't take a physically active, impulsive child to a china shop. Allow yourself some time to remain on the sidelines before leaving when a baby-sitter comes to care for a child who is slow to make transitions. Try not to interrupt her play without warning. (See *Adaptability*.)

It's better to invite one peer, not a group, to your house to play with a shy child. Try introducing an introspective child to arts and crafts, a child who can't sit still to very active sports, thereby channeling their natural proclivities productively and in such a way as to enhance their self-esteem. Avoid labeling your child as shy, loud, or impulsive, since it pigeonholes her and perhaps prevents both you and her from evolving. (See *Self-Esteem*.)

Finally, try to learn to walk a line of moderation that can change from day to day according to your child's cues. Go back to those two toddlers and two mothers.

The protective mother must learn to challenge her cautious toddler subtly, literally to hold his hand, if she must, as the child tests out a new swing. Then, once he is comfortable, that mother needs to recognize his budding assurance, step back, and let him play on his own. With the adventurous toddler, she must let him explore, while teaching him about safety precautions where appropriate.

The more casual or self-assured mother must accept her shy child's reticence, wait for him to show interest, then reassure him (without pressure) that a new situation might be fun. She can take pleasure in her rambunctious child's exuberance but must work to help him modify his impulsivity, recklessness, or aggression.

Good parenting takes constant assessment of who a child is and how he might be evolving emotionally and developmentally. Knowing a child's basic temperamental style and working within that context should help make that awesome job easier.

Recommended reading: *The Difficult Child*, by Stanley Turecki, M.D., with Leslie Tonner (Bantam Books); *Know Your Child*, by Stella Chess, M.D., and Alexander Thomas, M.D. (Basic Books); and *Infants and Mothers* and *Toddlers and Parents*, by T. Berry Brazelton, M.D. (both Delta Books/Dell Publishing).

Threatening

(See *Aggression*, *Bullying*, and *Anger*)

Thumb-Sucking

In the past, thumb-sucking was frowned upon. Now, it is often viewed as a normal, perhaps even desirable behavior in infants. It can mean a baby is capable of finding a way to calm himself. He's actually becoming *more* self-sufficient, resourceful, and independent—not needy and dependent, as our parents might have warned us when we were children.

The need to suck seems instinctive. Ultrasound has shown that many babies actually suck on their fingers in the womb, and upon birth, sucking is necessary for survival. If a baby can't suck, he can't eat, and won't survive without intervention.

Soon, sucking becomes a baby's way of exploring and learning. It evolves into a source of pleasure and comfort. His hand is one of the first things a baby discovers in this world. And certainly a reliance on his thumb has its advantages. Unlike a pacifier, it's always within easy reach.

Most children stop sucking their thumbs as toddlers. For others, particularly shy or "slow to warm" children, it's as soothing to them as their "transitional object," their favorite stuffed animal or blanket. The preference may be partly due to temperament or a tendency to be especially gratified by oral sensations. (See also *Anxiety*, *Temperament*, and *Adaptability*.)

Don't be overly worried about thumb-sucking in preschoolers. By the time they're five years old, most thumb-suckers have given up the practice, except when they're tired, nervous, or trying to drop off to sleep. And there is no long-term physical danger in it until a child's permanent teeth begin to come in, around six years of age.

However, you may want to help speed a child's natural self-weaning, if she seems to suck out of nervousness or does it so much that it isolates her from her peers. (A child sucking her thumb can't easily throw or catch a ball with playmates.)

Remember that times of stress or change can increase or exacerbate a child's thumb-sucking or cause some backsliding in her campaign to stop. Moves, the start of school, and the birth of a sibling may make a child feel insecure and spark more thumb-sucking. (See *Regression*.)

What to Do

The key to changing a habit that's been serving to soothe anxiety is to capitalize on a child's innate desire to become more independent and grown-up. Discuss together when she's most likely to feel nervous and suck her thumb (you'll have to watch for the pattern in a preschooler), and come up with alternative, "big-girl" ways for her to calm herself. (See *Fears and Phobias, Anxiety, Adaptability*, and *School*.)

Be patient, empathetic, and persistent, but nonpunitive. Avoid embarrassing or chiding her in front of people or calling her "a baby" when she has a setback. You're trying to help a child achieve something herself.

First try to minimize the amount of time she sucks her thumb in public. Explain that you're worried she'll be teased by her friends. Perhaps add, "I don't like that. Please don't do it in front of me." Or try to get rid of conditions that may prompt her thumb-sucking: "I notice you tend to suck your thumb most when we watch television. Since I think the two are connected, I'm going to turn it off for a while."

If you manage to limit a child's thumb-sucking to when she's alone or going to sleep in her bed, you're well on your way to having eliminated it entirely.

Be sure to praise her for her improvement when her thumb is *not* in her mouth. Set realistic, obtainable goals, such as: "I want you to go for half an hour without sucking your thumb, then I'll turn the TV back on [or read a book or play basketball with you]." Be sure to grant the reward you promised when she's earned it. The trick is to find something a child values more than thumb-sucking to use as an incentive to give it up. (See *Habits*.)

Tics and Tourette's Syndrome

A tic is an involuntary, repetitive, nonrhythmic movement, usually involving the facial and neck muscles or the eyes. Blinking and eye twitching, mouth grimaces, and neck jerking are most common. Tics may also be vocal, including coughing, throat clearing, or sniffing.

In most cases, tics are what we call "nervous tics," transient in nature, appearing during times of stress or anxiety. It's estimated that as many as one in ten children have them at some point, usually in late childhood right before puberty. Tics are more common in males than females.

In some cases, tics are chronic. Such tics have a genetic basis or may be brought on through insults to the central nervous system (i.e., illnesses or exposure to toxic substances). The most severe type of tic disorder is Tourette's syndrome, which combines multiple motor and vocal tics, often in complex and extreme combinations.

Tourette's syndrome is rare (1 in 2,000 people) and runs in families. The median age of onset, according to the American Psychiatric Association's diagnostic manual, is seven. Children with Tourette's syndrome may blink, twitch, shrug, retrace steps, twirl, or bang their heads. Their vocal tics may include repeating words or sounds, humming, clicking, yelping, or uttering obscenities (coprolalia). These children are at risk for depression as well, since their disorder can make them and their families extremely self-conscious in social situations.

What to Do

Parents can probably help children modify their "nervous tics" by trying to reduce the stress at home or helping children learn ways of coping with their own anxiety. Such commonsense methods should help alleviate the tic, but parents may also want to talk to a pediatrician or child psychiatrist. Children with chronic tics need to have a thorough medical evaluation, since they can be treated with certain medications that can reduce the severity of the symptoms.

For further information, contact the Tourette Syndrome Association, 42-40 Bell Boulevard, Bayside, NY 11361 (1-800-237-0717).

Toilet Training

Toilet training is such a wonderful misnomer. You're not training the toilet and you can't really "train" a child to use the potty. No one can *make* a child relieve himself in the toilet simply by putting him on it, unless he's ready to do so.

Instead, try to view "training" as helping a child master the socially accepted process of recognizing a need to urinate or pass a bowel movement and holding on long enough to do so in a toilet instead of his diapers. It is a mutual, collaborative effort, but it is your child's ultimate accomplishment. It is an important step forward in his growing independence. Perhaps "toilet learning" would be a more apt phrase.

The key is waiting until a child is *ready* to learn. Look for signs of his becoming interested. When he has begun to recognize the connection between feeling the need to urinate or defecate and the end result and is physiologically capable of controlling his bladder and bowels, the time is right. Generally, all these factors don't coincide until roughly around two years of age.

If you try earlier, you may have a few lucky successes, but you run the risk of incurring a lot of accidents and discouraging relapses. Also keep in mind that the birth of a younger sibling may interrupt toilet training, so try to begin either well before or just after the arrival of a new baby.

What to Do

Some general tips:

Get a potty chair or a child seat for the toilet so he won't be afraid of falling in. Even though their usefulness is short-lived, it is probably best to have a child-sized potty, which is far less intimidating than a toilet that reaches to his shoulders.

Remember that the loud noise and swirling motion of flushing a toilet can frighten many toddlers, so avoid doing it while they're standing right there or sitting on the toilet. (With magical thinking, a toddler might believe that if a toilet could suck down his bowel movements, it could do the same to him.) Also, a child may be hurt if you immediately flush down the product he worked so hard to produce for you. Perhaps wait until he's lost interest before disposing of it, or let him be the one to flush the toilet.

302

Use words he can use as well to describe urinating and defecating. It helps him learn the meaning of the terms more easily as well as being able to tell you when he needs to go. Because children learn through imitation, perhaps let a child watch the parent of the same sex take care of business, if you're not embarrassed by it.

Use praise and positive reinforcement. Try not to shame a child for having an accident. Instead, say something like: "Oh well, it's no big deal." Then, clean up the mess without further comment. Also, don't go overboard in your praise. "What a good job you did. You're such a big boy" is sufficient.

Keep a sticker chart. Since a toddler can't count, use a graph that has a clear column in it for his stickers or stars, so that he can watch it fill up with each successful potty trip. As you do with any reward system, be sure to give the child his reward when he's earned it. The best rewards are favorite activities with you. (See the Parenting Skills Introduction.)

Try beginning with bladder training first. Even though it's usually easier to anticipate when a child is going to have a bowel movement (many stand still and grunt), bladder control is often easier for a child to master. For one thing, you have more opportunities within a day (six to eight times a day as opposed to one or two bowel movements).

Also, with children who are prone to constipation, early bowel training runs the risk of exacerbating the problem. Children who become worried about bowel movements and where to pass them can get into a vicious cycle of holding back and then having pain, prompting further withholding. Try not to embarrass or chide a child when he has an accident.

Summer is the best time for training because the most effective thing to do is to take off the diapers. It does set you up for some accidents, but a child wearing a diaper will probably just let it happen in the diaper. He also is less likely to make the sequential connection between feeling full and relieving himself.

Take a child to the potty every hour or so and slowly he'll learn to associate the feeling of a slightly full bladder with the process of using the toilet. (It's probably best to start a little boy sitting down, so that he doesn't have to worry about his aim until he's gotten the idea of what the toilet is for.)

After a period of letting them run around the house naked during

303

training, put children in "big-boy pants." Little girls in particular are very proud of "pretty panties" and are often motivated to stay dry to keep them clean.

When bowel training, put a child on the potty when he's most likely to pass a bowel movement, generally in the morning or after a large meal. Don't distract him with toys while he's sitting there. Let him concentrate on the task. Or read him a child-oriented book about using the potty. (See below for recommendations.)

It is very common for a child to sit on the potty for ten minutes without result and to pass a bowel movement immediately upon getting off and having a diaper put on. That's actually good news. It means he started the process of pushing while sitting on the potty. Don't reprimand him; simply drop the waste into the toilet and say, "That's where it goes. We'll try again tomorrow." Remember, the process must occur at the child's pace.

While a child is learning day-control, leave diapers or pull-ups on him as he sleeps at night or during naptime. Don't take them off until he's been dry *through* the night. Night-wetting remains common in children until the age of five or six and typically will end with physical maturation. (See *Bed-Wetting*.)

Recommended reading for children: *Going to the Potty*, by Fred Rogers of *Mr. Rogers' Neighborhood* (G. P. Putnam's Sons); *Once Upon a Potty*, by Alona Frankel (Barron's Educational Series); *KoKo Bear's New Potty*, by Vicki Lansky, illustrated by Jane Prince (Bantam Books); and *I Want My Potty*, by Tony Ross (a Cranky Nell Book / Kane / Miller Book Publishers).

Tomboyishness

(See *Playing with Dolls*)

Truancy

Children who skip school enough to be called truant generally are poor students, don't like school, and may come from families that don't place a high emphasis on education. A large percentage of these children actually have learning disabilities, so school has become a constant source of frustration and embarrassment. Their truancy typically is sporadic, brief, and unknown to their parents, since they generally don't go home while skipping class. They tend to hang out with other truants.

Don't panic if you discover an otherwise well-motivated student has skipped school once. However, when a pattern of truancy is discovered or suspected, you do need to take the problem seriously. Often, simple intervention early on can make a major difference in a child's life. Left unattended, truancy is usually part of a larger pattern of more en-trenched aggressive or antisocial behavior. (See *Oppositional-Defiant Disorder* and *Conduct Disorder*.) Seek consultation from a qualified school or mental-health professional.

Trustworthiness

(See *Self-Sufficiency*, *Cheating*, *Lying*, and *Stealing*)

U

Unaffectionate

(See *Aloofness*)

Uncooperative

(See *Oppositional Behavior*)

Vomiting

During their first year, many babies vomit or spit up. The muscular reflux entrance of the stomach is not fully developed and doesn't close properly, so sometimes food flows back up into the esophagus and is vomited out. Avoid overfeeding an infant; sit him up and elevate his head after eating to help control this involuntary reaction. Of course, any concerns about vomiting should be promptly brought to your pediatrician's attention.

After infancy, children generally vomit only when sick. Some children, however, are so volatile emotionally and cry so hard that their bodies can react by vomiting. It can become a pattern of behavior if a child learns that getting upset enough to vomit elicits heightened attention. It's hard not to become anxious when a child cries hard enough to vomit, but try to clean up in a neutral, unalarmed manner. Avoid giving a child lots of liquids right before the baby-sitter comes, and don't leave abruptly, to help keep a crying jag from turning into a vomiting incident.

It is less common for a young child to suffer from a rumination disorder that causes vomiting regularly without any clear triggers (such as an event upsetting him enough to vomit). In this case, a baby uses vomiting as a tension releaser, to self-soothe. Initially, he may use his hands to gag himself, or arch his back to stimulate his stomach muscles. If rumination persists, his stomach may come to automatically regurgitate. Children with rumination need immediate professional intervention, since they are at high risk for dehydration, electrolyte imbalance, and malnutrition.

An older, preadolescent child may be experimenting with bulimic behavior. (See *Eating Disorders*.)

Walking

Walking is an important developmental milestone that children may achieve as early as ten months of age or as late as sixteen months. The difference in time can have a variety of perfectly normal, acceptable reasons. Some children are very physically active and courageous, others more cautious. Some children just don't like to take the risk of toddling or falling and literally stand up and walk one day. Also, babies tend to practice one major task at a time, so that if they are babbling and experimenting with sounds or words they may wait to concentrate on walking at a later time.

(If a baby isn't cruising—pulling himself up and walking along the edge of furniture—by the time he's eighteen months old, or there are other significant problems with his walking, you should discuss it with your child's pediatrician.)

With walking comes freedom: freedom to explore, to retrieve something that's all the way across a room, freedom from complete dependence on Mommy and Daddy. It's the real beginning of autonomy and its backlash anxiety—an exciting yet often trying time for parents and children. (See the Developmental Tasks Appendix, *Anxiety*, *Temper Tantrums*, and *Oppositional Behavior*.)

You should have already childproofed your home when your baby began crawling, but it is critical to do a thorough job when walking begins. (See *Accident-Prone*.) A childproofed home allows a toddler to explore in unrestricted delight, a positive way to encourage his growing independence and curiosity, and to lower his frustrations.

Whining

Most parents are probably already familiar with the sound of incessant, high-pitched, nasal whining. It is probably one of the most irritating things in a child's repertoire of behavior. It's meant to be coercive and to capture your attention. But remember that whining can also be the result of anxiety, the language of an unhappy or worried child. Children normally whine when they're tired, hungry, afraid, or frustrated, in addition to when they want attention or are about to throw a full-fledged tantrum.

Don't reward whining by responding to it. Instead, try to react to a child's request before he works himself into a whine, while he's still speaking in a normal tone of voice. Stand your ground if you've decided to deny a request. If he gets a cookie or your undivided attention after ten minutes of whining, he'll continue doing it.

Try saying, "I don't like that tone of voice. I'll talk with you when you use a nice voice." Praise him when he corrects himself. Distraction can also work. Perhaps make a kind of game out of it: "Can you tell me what you want in a whisper or in a deep voice like the Big Bad Wolf's?"

If your child whines constantly, it may very well be part of his personality makeup. (See *Temperament* and *Adaptability*.) But you also might need to examine your schedule, your own attitudes, your relationship, or the limits you set.

Sometimes there's a simple solution, such as his needing a longer nap. Perhaps you yourself are prone to complaining and your child is picking up the behavior. Perhaps you say no more often than you really need to or, conversely, aren't clear and consistent enough about limits and household rules. (If one day he can't have that cookie before dinner but the next day he can, he's going to whine or throw a tantrum to see if today is the day he can push you to give in.) Perhaps you need to spend a little more concentrated time with your child right now, so that he doesn't feel he has to whine to win your attention. Or perhaps he's being forced into social situations for which he's not quite ready. (See also *Temper Tantrums*, *Anxiety*, *Attention-Seeking*, *Interrupting*, *Clinging*, and the Parenting Skills Introduction.)

Wishes to Be Opposite Sex

(See *Gender Identity Disorder*)

Withdrawn

(See *Reaction to Parental Conflict, School, Reaction to Loss, Social Isolation*, and *Depression*)

Worries

(See *Anxiety*)

Developmental Tasks
Appendix

So often when we assess a child's progress, we think only of motor (or bodily) and speech milestones—at what age does he stand, walk, talk, use the potty, ride a bike? These feats are really only the overt behavioral manifestations of what's going on inside a child's mind and body. To really understand a child's behavior, we must also understand what motivates him to try new physical acts; what he feels about himself and the world when he accomplishes them; and how he thinks and processes the new information brought to him through those achievements.

A human child is an intensely complex being trying to achieve many things at once. His psychological, social, and cognitive development interact with, influence, and are dependent on his ability to master those motor and language skills, and vice versa.

Take, for example, a hallmark behavior of a stage generally known as the "terrible twos": the tantrum. Why does a toddler scream like that? There are many reasons (and for a more complete explanation and advice on handling them, see *Temper Tantrums*), but basically they stem from his newfound ability to physically move away from his caregiver during play. He desires autonomy but is anxious about what that independence might bring; he doesn't yet have adequate language skills to express his wants with words; his emotional and social egocentrism and immaturity allow no delay of gratification or sharing of coveted items with playmates; and he lacks cognitive reasoning or dexterity—he can think of no way to achieve his desires other than crying or grabbing for them. The result is a messy, kinetic mix of physical/motor, psychosocial, linguistic, and cognitive reasons.

Each entry in this book tries to describe the interplay of the many factors that are relevant to a given behavior. However, to supply you with an overview of how these different developmental elements coincide with one another during certain ages, a chart collating them is included at the end of this appendix.

Two columns bear further explanation: the Psychosocial Processes and the Cognitive Processes. The psychosocial stages come from the work of Erik Erikson, the cognitive primarily from Jean Piaget.

Erikson, a German-born psychoanalyst who studied under Freud before emigrating to this country, believes that man goes through eight psychosocial stages. At each stage, a person is presented with a different emotional and social challenge or conflict. Achieving that developmental task (or failing to) brings clear psychological benefits (or repercussions) and allows the child to progress and develop further (or become somewhat "stuck" at that stage). It was Erikson who coined the phrase "identity crisis" when describing the fifth, or adolescent, stage: "identity versus role confusion." (If you wish to read Erikson's own description of these stages, they are contained in a chapter titled "Eight Ages of Man" in his book *Childhood and Society*, Norton.)

Piaget was originally a zoologist by training and initially had little interest in the emotional development or social bonding of people. The Swiss scientist was more concerned with studying how a child's thinking changes and grows as he matures. He, too, developed a stage concept, although each level was not as much an evolution as a complete reorganization of the way in which a person thinks about the world around and within him.

Because the two scientists were studying such different things, their stage concepts don't always correlate precisely. But both offer helpful insight into the *whys* of child behavior. Because of this, the two theories are explained together under age brackets, just as the chart is delineated.

Remember when reading the chart that there are completely acceptable and normal variations of achievement. The ages that are noted are *averages*, with exceptions being very common.

The other vital element that parents must take into account is a child's individual temperament, the emotional style he brings with him at birth. Some children, by virtue of their personality, may have more difficulty negotiating these stages than others. (See *Temperament, Shyness, Adaptability*, and *Anxiety*.)

Birth to One and a Half (Infants)

Erikson called the stage that represents a person's introduction to the world "trust versus mistrust." It really has to do with what we are currently calling "the synchronicity" between an infant and his primary caregiver. When a baby cries, does his mother or father respond quickly and accurately? Does that parent correctly access what he is crying about and tend to his needs? (I.e., if they change his diaper when he's really hungry they may not be reading his cues properly, or he's not giving them well.)

If his parents do take care of his needs reasonably quickly and accurately, a baby comes to *trust* them (as "an inner certainty," writes Erikson) and his environment; he believes it to be a predictable, rewarding place. From his perspective, he is accomplishing the meeting of his needs, so he also comes to *trust* that he can positively influence his world.

If his needs go unsatisfied, on the other hand—if he cries for long periods without being answered or reassured—a baby may come to feel that he is a helpless victim in a threatening land. He comes to *mistrust*.

If an infant cannot achieve trust, he is likely to be anxious, tentative, unmotivated to play or learn, perhaps even depressed. He will not move easily or confidently into the next Eriksonian stage, which demands that he begin to separate a bit from his parents.

(See *Crying* and *Anxiety*.)

Piaget believed that children begin learning and developing the capacity to think in infancy, not from instruction but from incidental experiences brought to them through their senses and their physical movements. He called this stage "sensorimotor." It means that a baby first absorbs her world through her hearing, sense of smell, taste, and sight, and then moves (her eyes, head, hands, fingers) in response to those sensations. This correlation of events creates a set of expectations for her about movement and relationships, about how things fit together, how her body has to feel to achieve certain physical acts. She repeats acts again and again to absorb their meaning in what Piaget termed "circular reactions."

A baby discovers, for instance, that her hand can shake a rattle and that the rattle then makes a noise. She learns about size, textures, and spatial relationships by putting that rattle into a bowl, or by stacking blocks. She slowly learns that things exist outside her immediate vision (that they have "object permanence") by playing games such as peekaboo.

To facilitate learning at this stage, then, parents need to provide infants with a stimulating environment, with lots of brightly colored, mobile objects, room for unrestricted exploration, and, most important, plenty of interaction with them. (See *Play* and *Curiosity*.)

One and a Half to Three (Toddlers)

Erikson labeled the second stage of a child's psychosocial development "autonomy versus shame and doubt." Toddlers are now capable of performing many physical acts on their own. They can walk, pull on or off (mainly off) their clothes, open intriguing drawers, feed themselves, perhaps control their bladder and relieve themselves in the toilet. They want to be allowed some independence, some freedom of choice not only because of their new physical skills, but also because of their increasing awareness of the fact that they have a separate existence from Mommy and Daddy.

(When children this age are placed in front of a mirror with a dot of red paint on their nose, they reach up and touch their nose to investigate—at a younger age they might have merely laughed at the funny image—in a tacit statement of: I exist, I am that person reflected in the mirror.)

All this means that a child will begin to test limits, to try to break the symbiotic connection with his parents, to see how far he can get on his own. But it doesn't happen smoothly or without anxiety ("doubt," as Erikson put it) on the part of a child. What is the price of his independence? He doesn't know yet. A toddler's cry of "Let me do it" will often be closely followed by clinging to his Mommy's knees.

This is the age of tantrums because a child's physical capabilities often don't match his desires. His vocabulary is often inadequate for him to make himself understood. He is impatient and easily frustrated. And if he is temperamentally slow to warm, he may be unnerved by situations that require more autonomy on his part.

Erikson wrote: "Muscular maturation sets the stage for experimentation with two simultaneous sets of social modalities: holding on and letting go." As such, it requires a parent to be patient, to have a strong sense of humor or at least an amused tolerance, and to lovingly guide a child "by prohibition and permission," as Erikson puts it. A toddler has little ability to recognize danger, so a parent must watch him carefully. But if his steps toward independence, his *autonomy*, are not allowed, he may develop *doubt*; if they are not applauded, or perhaps ridiculed, he may develop *shame*. "Doubt is the brother of shame," writes Erikson.

It can be a trying time for parents because of a child's propensity for tantrums, but a critical one for his developing a sense of self. Successful negotiation of this tempestuous stage brings a child the beginnings of self-esteem and confidence. Failure to do so may leave him incapable of separating from parents, of trusting his own judgment and innate capabilities, or of befriending his peers. In short, he will be emotionally hobbled and unprepared for the next stage of development.

(See also *Oppositional Behavior, Food Refusal, Temper Tantrums, Compliance, Walking, Self-Esteem, Self-Sufficiency, Risk-Taking*, Separation Anxiety under *Anxiety*, and "Time-Outs" in the Parenting Skills Introduction.)

Piaget's concepts in this and the following age-group (three to five years old) are a little less clear-cut. Basically the ages two to seven years old are lumped together in what he called the "preoperational" stage. Children continue to be largely egocentric in thinking (meaning they perceive and understand the world only through their individual point of view) and to be very reliant on sensorimotor information. They think in an instinctive, almost animalistic fashion. They cannot *reason* or understand logical cause and effect—a cognitive capacity that comes in the next stage, which Piaget labeled "concrete operations."

Three to Five (Preschoolers)

By the time a child is a preschooler, he should have moved away from parents somewhat and into a stage Erikson called "initiative versus guilt." He should be self-motivated, driven almost, to try new things, to climb high slides, to imitate the goings-on of the same-sex parent. Parents will often say of a child this age: "He's such a little person now."

Writes Erikson: "The child is at no time more ready to learn quickly and avidly, to become bigger in the sense of sharing obligation and performance than during this period of his development. He is eager and able to make things cooperatively, to combine with other children for the purpose of constructing and planning, and he is willing to profit from teachers and to emulate ideal prototypes."

According to Erikson: "He is in free possession of a surplus of energy which permits him to forget failures quickly and to approach what seems desirable (even if it also seems uncertain and even dangerous) with undiminished and more accurate direction."

There are two critical things parents must do at this stage. The first is to praise a child's perhaps unorthodox attempts at a task, his "initiative," even if their outcomes are unsatisfactory. (Applaud his unusual block tower, for instance, even if it topples because of "faulty" construction.) Set up a safe environment that facilitates his independent experimentation. (See also *Play* and *Accident-Prone*.) If parents overtly or indirectly criticize a child's attempts, he may fail to build *initiative* and instead develop *guilt*, the fear that he is doing something wrong if he acts without adult direction. (See also *Self-Esteem*.)

The second important thing parents must do for their child is to make sure he has ample opportunities to play with another child his age. He is now ready to share toys and to "play cooperatively" with peers in constructing a castle or a make-believe scenario. Individual friendship is an important prelude to enrollment in nursery school. Otherwise, he may have distinct trouble assimilating himself into a classroom situation. (See *Making Friends*.)

Preschoolers are known for their "magical thinking." It's a wonderful stage in which they believe in fairies, Santa Claus, and the tricks of magicians. The downside is that they begin to develop fears and nightmares. You cannot reason with a child this age and convince her that no monster lurks under her bed. Better to give her some sort of magic power over that monster (a stuffed animal endowed with protective properties); a night-light so that she can actually *see* that there is nothing hiding in the dark; or assurance that if a monster comes, you'll take care of it. (See also *Fears and Phobias* and *Nightmares and Night Terrors*.)

Also be aware that while a child this age may dream she is being chased by a dragon, she might also fantasize and pretend that she is a huge beast capable of squashing someone who angers her. Preschoolers believe what they think or wish can come true. Therefore, if a child is mad at a parent and wishes her injury, and the very next day that parent is in an accident, the preschooler is likely to believe *she* caused the mishap. It will be very scary for her. She doesn't really want that kind of power. That is also why it is important for parents to set consistent limits for a child this age, to prove that they are the authority figures responsible for helping her navigate the world.

Selma Fraiberg, the child expert who expanded on Piaget's thoughts about this stage, sheds more light on the subject in her book *The Magic Years*: "A magic world is an unstable world, at times a spooky world, and as the child gropes his way toward reason and an objective world he must wrestle with the dangerous creatures of his imagination and the real and imagined dangers of the outer world, and periodically we are confronted with his inexplicable fears or baffling behaviors. Many of the problems presented by the child in these early years are, quite simply, disorders created by a primitive mental system that has not yet been subdued and put into its place by rational thought processes."

Six to Eleven (School-Aged Children)

Erikson labeled this stage "industry versus inferiority," and wrote that it represents a child's "entrance into life." He is stepping into a world increasingly of his own making, beyond the boundaries and safety of his home. For the first time, a child receives systematic instruction. School "seems to be a culture all by itself, with its own goals and limits, its achievements and disappointments," writes Erikson.

Much of the emotionality of the previous stage has subsided. Children this age are absorbed in mastering skills. Their self-esteem and self-concept are largely determined by what they feel they can do well.

A school-aged child, then, is typically diligent about practicing skills. He takes pride in them. He may classify himself accordingly, saying that he is a swimmer, a runner, a painter, or someone who likes science projects. He seems to have an almost natural drive to tackle the work involved in hobbies, completing homework, even doing chores.

Writes Erikson: "He now learns to win recognition by producing things. . . . He develops a sense of industry."

To encourage and reinforce this *industry*, parents need to help their child discover what he likes and excels in—interests that may be very different from what they originally envisioned for him. (Professionals call it "individuation.") Parents must also try to help him achieve his

321

goals but in such a way that he is truly accomplishing them himself. Parents who are overly anxious or uninterested in his accomplishments can have a very detrimental impact. (See *Self-Esteem*.)

If a child fails in this developmental stage, he may develop a sense of inadequacy or *inferiority*, which can make him uncertain and unmotivated. He may feel "doomed to mediocrity," as Erikson puts it.

On the other hand, if she succeeds, a ten- or eleven-year-old child will emerge from this developmental stage self-assured and proud of her abilities in one or two areas; capable of maintaining at least one significant friendship; and able to answer affirmatively the question, Do I like myself? She is more apt to step forward to embrace the world and all it offers, rather than wait and merely react to what it hands her.

All this prepares a child for the next stage, in which she must decide "Who am I?"

A child can accomplish much of this psychosocial development, this industry, because of a new cognitive capability (or reorganization of the way in which he thinks), which Piaget called "concrete operations." Without these new intellectual capabilities, a child would be unable to really achieve *mastery* of skills.

The switch from magical to concrete operational thinking seems to occur around seven years of age. Suddenly, a child develops the ability to understand cause and effect, that there are multiple solutions to a problem. He can think through logically the best method to achieve something he wants. And because he can now accept that there are systems for determining outcome, a child is also able to understand the reason for rules and consequences for breaking them.

That kind of facileness in thinking results in many different and new behaviors. For instance, he now will wait until Mommy is off the phone (and more likely to respond favorably) to make a request. He is apt to stop himself before he does something he knows is unacceptable, no longer solely because he fears disapproval but because he knows it to be wrong.

He may begin to make puns because he's recognizing that words can have many meanings and be used in a humorous way. After reading a story he can now talk about its meanings or emotional content in addition to its descriptive details. He also understands "conservation," as Piaget termed it, the fact that different-sized objects can still hold the same quantity. (Before he would have insisted that a tall, thin beaker held more liquid than a short, fat one. Now he understands that the quantity may, in fact, be the same.)

He still needs concrete representations of ideas, however. He can understand an abstract feeling, for instance, as long as he sees an appropriate facial expression to go with it. It is not until the next stage, or "formal operations," that he can understand intangible notions such as truth and justice.

Twelve (Preteens)

Children this age are just beginning to flirt with adolescence. Parents will see glimmers of Erikson's "identity crisis" and Piaget's "formal operations" stages. A precocious eleven- or twelve-year-old will begin to wonder, Who will I be when I grow up? Will I be happy? She may want to debate the concepts of justice and fairness with her parents. These things should occur, however, without the heat and emotion so typical of the teenage years.

As you see your child acting more and more like the adolescent she will soon become, it may be time to consult another book that treats this period more intensively.

The information and milestones included in the following chart were drawn from several sources, the experts at the Children's National Medical Center and from these books: *Developmental Assessment in Clinical Child Psychology: A Handbook*, edited by James H. Johnson and Jacquelin Goldman (Pergamon Press); *Developmental Psychopathology*, by Thomas M. Achenbach (The Ronald Press Company); and *Terminology of Communication Disorders: Speech-Language-Hearing*, by Lucille Nicolosi, Elizabeth Harryman, and Janet Kresheck (Williams & Wilkins).

Developmental Tasks Appendix

Ages	Psycho-social Processes	Cognitive Processes	Developmental Milestones
Birth–1½	Basic Trust vs. Mistrust	Sensorimotor	2 MONTHS: coos; in prone position, pushes up on forearms. 3–4 MONTHS: laughs; beginnings of purposeful object play, such as shaking rattle and reaching for dangling object. 5–6 MONTHS: rolls over, back to stomach. 6–9 MONTHS: sits; begins to understand simple words such as "Bye." 9–12 MONTHS: crawls; says "Mama" or "Dada"; sips from cup with assistance; begins self-feeding; can pick up small object between index finger and thumb; puts one toy inside another and shows beginnings of recognition that objects have permanence even out of sight. 15 MONTHS: stacks two blocks; hugs dolls; attempts simple puzzles; pretends to talk on phone; understands simple one-step directions such as "bring me the ball"; points to major body parts when asked. 18 MONTHS: walks well; uses 10–20 intelligible words, mostly nouns; begins to combine two words, "more juice" or "big dog," and to use phrases: "go bye-bye."

Social Behavior	Common Concern
BIRTH–2 MONTHS: smiles in response to parent's touch or voice.	Feeding and sleeping problems
3–5 MONTHS: smiles spontaneously; reaches toward family members	
	6–18 MONTHS: separation anxiety
9–12 MONTHS: plays peekaboo; hands toy to someone when requested by gesture; makes many different sounds and inflections during babble talk; waves at "bye-bye."	9–18 MONTHS: stranger anxiety
15–18 MONTHS: still needs to know location of primary caregiver while playing; helps pick up toys to put in box. May begin pro-social play with stuffed animal (carry, pat, hug, etc.).	

Developmental Tasks Appendix

Ages	Psycho-social Processes	Cognitive Processes	Developmental Milestones
1½–3	Autonomy vs. Shame and Doubt	Preoperational	20–24 MONTHS: uses up to 50 words; has adjectives such as "good," "bad," "hot"; and verbs such as "go," "see," "want"; may create three-word sentences; can refer to self by name.
			24 MONTHS: can use one object to represent another, such as using a block to represent a car; develops play scenarios with series of objects; makes simple six-to-eight-block constructions; understands two-step directions; can identify objects in pictures.
			27–30 MONTHS: understands size differences and concepts of "just one."
			30 MONTHS: can jump with both feet; uses verb contractions.
			36 MONTHS: rides tricycle; can give own first name; uses personal pronouns; talks when playing by self; can describe the action of a story; begins to ask "why"; engages in short dialogue; counts three objects.

Social *Behavior*	*Common* *Concern*
20–24 MONTHS: begins to imitate peer, but still stays in parallel play (side by side but not together).	Separation difficulties Temper tantrums Oppositional behavior Language delays Bedtime routines
24–36 MONTHS: enjoys "helping" (wiping, cleaning, sweeping); important to develop a special friend; plays best with one other child rather than many.	Appetite changes Toileting
28–30 MONTHS: aware of gender differences; may show preference for a specific playmate; knows the concept of "mine."	
32–36 MONTHS: begins to separate more easily from mother; understands the concept of taking turns; interested in toilet training and dressing self.	

Developmental Tasks Appendix

Ages	Psycho-social Processes	Cognitive Processes	Developmental Milestones
3–5	Initiative vs. Guilt	Preoperational; Magical Thinking	36–48 MONTHS: has 900-to-2,000 word vocabulary; average sentence length: four words. 48 MONTHS: can count four objects correctly; hops on one foot; throws overhand; may cut with scissors. 60 MONTHS: skips; learning to ride bicycle; can name four colors and count ten objects; sentences average six words and include many details: "I rode the yellow tractor at Granddaddy's house"; grammar usually correct; can answer telephone; can use comparative adjectives (big, bigger) and prepositions (to, of, in); tells fantasy stories; asks about the meaning of words.

Social Behavior	*Common Concern*
36—48 MONTHS: begins to enjoy small playgroup; engages in cooperative play with other children; toilet training is complete.	Nightmares Fears of dark, imaginary monsters, animals, and hurting self
48 MONTHS: can play with several children at once: may boss people around; engages in imaginative, fantasy play (knights and dragons or playing house); asks to play with specific playmate.	Bed-wetting and toilet-training regressions Articulation problems: difficulty pronouncing *r, l,* and *th*
60 MONTHS: dresses and undresses by self; fastening, shoes on correct feet; plays games with rules.	Shyness Questions about death and dying

Developmental Tasks Appendix

Ages	Psycho-social Processes	Cognitive Processes	Developmental Milestones
6–12	Industry vs. Inferiority	Concrete Operations	Reading comprehension and math skills increase markedly with adequate instructions. Development of interests, hobbies, and pleasurable skills such as sports, games, and art or music. Ability to hold and defend a personal opinion, attitude, or belief. Gradual and steady increase in intellectual capacity to analyze a technical problem and devise multiple steps toward a correct solution.

Social Behavior	*Common Concern*
Formation of steady, individual friendships.	School problems and phobias
	Peer acceptance and rejection
Identification with one or more social groups based on interests or abilities.	Conduct problems
	Attention-Deficit Hyperactivity Disorder
Achievement of a clearly recognizable and distinct sense of self.	Learning disabilities
	Self-esteem issues
Increased capacity to relate to adults via discussions and conversation. Gradual and steady increase in ability to devise strategies for negotiating difficult or challenging social situations.	Worries about family and world events
	Early or late physical maturation and its effects on the child's behavior

About the Authors

David A. Mrazek, M.D., is the Chairman of Psychiatry at the Children's National Medical Center in Washington, D.C. He earned his undergraduate degree from Cornell University and his medical degree from Wake Forest University, and received postdoctoral training at the University of Cincinnati and the University of Colorado. Formerly on the faculty of the University of London and the University of Colorado, he is currently a Professor of Psychiatry, Behavioral Sciences, and Pediatrics at George Washington University School of Medicine. Dr. Mrazek directs the Division of Psychiatry and Behavioral Sciences, which provides comprehensive mental health services, at Children's Hospital in Washington, D.C., as well as at the four Children's National Medical Center satellite clinics, in Spring Valley in northwest Washington, D.C., Gaithersburg and Laurel, Maryland, and in Fairfax, Virginia. He is a Fellow of the American Psychiatric Association, the Academy of Child and Adolescent Psychiatry, the American Psychological Society, the Royal College of Psychiatrists, and the Royal Society of Medicine. Dr. Mrazek is the father of a teenager, a preteen, and two young children.

William Garrison, Ph.D., is the Chairman of Psychology at the Children's National Medical Center in Washington, D.C. He received his doctoral degree from Cornell University and completed a postdoctoral fellowship at Harvard University. He has been on the faculty of Harvard Medical School, the University of Massachusetts, and Tufts Medical School. He is currently Associate Professor of Psychiatry, Behavioral Sciences, and Pediatric Medicine at George Washington University. Dr. Garrison is the author of numerous research articles on child psychology and early behavior development, as well as textbooks on child temperament and the effects of chronic illness during childhood. He is the father of three young children.

Laura Elliott is a senior writer at *The Washingtonian* magazine, where she frequently writes about family issues. She is also co-author of *Shattered Dreams: The Story of Charlotte Fedders*. Ms. Elliott is the mother of a preschooler.

Books to help you keep your baby happy and healthy

Baby & Child A to Z Medical Handbook
by Miriam Stoppard, M.D., M.R.C.P.
A fully illustrated guide that details more than 150 baby and child ailments.

Checklist for Your New Baby
by Dylan Landis
An indispensable guide to what expectant parents need to have on hand before their baby arrives.

Children's National Medical Center A to Z Guide to Your Child's Behavior
From the leader in treatment of the whole child and family, an essential reference for understanding your child's development.

Complete Guide to Pediatric Symptoms, Illness & Medications
by H. Winter Griffith, M.D.
A comprehensive guide to diagnosing and treating childhood illnesses and disorders.

The First Twelve Months of Life
by the Princeton Center for Infancy and Early Childhood Development
The definitive guide for tracking infant development, newly revised and updated.

The First Twelve Months of Life Companion
by the Princeton Center for Infancy and Early Childhood Development
A record-keeping companion to the classic bestseller *The First Twelve Months of Life*.

Johnson & Johnson From Baby to Toddler
edited by John J. Fisher
The essential month-by-month resource, from the most respected name in baby care today.

The Second Twelve Months of Life
by the Princeton Center for Infancy and Early Childhood Development
Guides parents through the development of their infant to toddlerhood.

These books are available at your bookstore or wherever books are sold, or, for your convenience, we'll send them directly to you. Just call 1-800-631-8571 (press 1 for inquiries and orders), or fill out the coupon on the following page and send it to:

The Putnam Publishing Group
390 Murray Hill Parkway, Dept. B
East Rutherford, NJ 07073

Books to help you keep your baby happy and healthy

		Price U.S.	Canada
_____ Baby & Child A to Z Medical Handbook	399-51765-0	$13.95	$18.50
_____ Checklist for Your New Baby	399-51657-3	5.95	7.75
_____ Children's National Medical Center A to Z Guide to Your Child's Behavior	399-51796-0	14.95	19.50
_____ Complete Guide to Pediatric Symptoms, Illness & Medications	895-86816-4	14.95	19.50
_____ The First Twelve Months of Life	399-51804-5	14.95	19.50
_____ The First Twelve Months of Life Companion	399-51736-7	15.95	19.95
_____ Johnson & Johnson From Baby to Toddler	399-51393-0	9.95	12.95
_____ The Second Twelve Months of Life	399-50776-0	14.95	19.50

Subtotal $_____

Postage & handling* $_____

Sales tax (CA, NJ, NY, PA, Canada) $_____

Total amount due $_____

Payable in U.S. funds (no cash orders accepted). $15.00 minimum for credit card orders.
*Postage & handling: $2.50 for 1 book, 75¢ for each additional book up to a maximum of $6.25.

Enclosed is my   ❑ check   ❑ moneyorder
Please charge my   ❑ Visa   ❑ MasterCard   ❑ American Express

Card # _____ Expiration date _____

Signature as on charge card _____

Name _____

Address _____

City _____ State _____ Zip _____

Please allow six weeks for delivery. Prices subject to change without notice.

Source key #57